FREE TO BELIEVE

Rethinking Freedom of Conscience and Religion in Canada

Free to Believe investigates the protection for freedom of conscience and religion – the first of the "fundamental freedoms" listed in the Canadian Charter of Rights and Freedoms – and its interpretation in the courts. Through an examination of decided cases touching on the most controversial issues of our day, such as abortion, same-sex marriage, and minority religious practices, Mary Anne Waldron explores how the law has developed in the way that it has, the role that freedom of conscience and religion play in our society, and the role it could play in making it a more open, peaceful, and democratic place.

Although the range of cases explored will be of interest to scholars, *Free to Believe* is also written in an accessible style, with legal terms and concepts explained for those who wish to learn accurate, detailed information about the impact of the law on contemporary social policy issues. As such, this book widens the debate about this fundamental freedom and the influence of public opinion on what is often a misrepresented and misunderstood issue.

MARY ANNE WALDRON is a professor in the Faculty of Law at the University of Victoria.

Free to Believe

Rethinking Freedom of Conscience and Religion in Canada

MARY ANNE WALDRON

UNIVERSITY OF TORONTO PRESS
Toronto Buffalo London

© University of Toronto Press 2013
Toronto Buffalo London
www.utppublishing.com
Printed in Canada

ISBN 978-1-4426-4555-4 (cloth)
ISBN 978-1-4426-1384-3 (paper)

Printed on acid-free, 100% post-consumer recycled paper with vegetable-based inks.

Library and Archives Canada Cataloguing in Publication

Waldron, Mary Anne, 1948–
Free to believe: rethinking freedom of conscience and religion in Canada /
Mary Anne Waldron.

Includes bibliographical references and index.
ISBN 978-1-4426-4555-4 (bound). – ISBN 978-1-4426-1384-3 (pbk.)

1. Liberty of conscience – Canada – Cases.   2. Freedom of religion –
Canada – Cases.   I. Title

KE4430.W24 2013   342.7108'52   C2013-901064-5
KF4483.C52W24

This book has been published with the help of a grant from the Canadian
Federation for the Humanities and Social Sciences, through the Awards to
Scholarly Publications Program, using funds provided by the Social Sci-
ences and Humanities Research Council of Canada.

University of Toronto Press acknowledges the financial assistance to its
publishing program of the Canada Council for the Arts and the Ontario
Arts Council.

    Canada Council   Conseil des Arts
for the Arts   du Canada

University of Toronto Press acknowledges the financial support of the
Government of Canada through the Canada Book Fund for its publishing
activities.

Contents

Acknowledgments

The author would like to thank the Centre for Study of Religion in Society at the University of Victoria, its staff, fellows, and associates, and its director, Dr Paul Bramadat, for extending support and assistance during the writing of the manuscript. And special thanks to my dear husband and best friend, Guy, for his unfailing encouragement.

FREE TO BELIEVE

Rethinking Freedom of Conscience
and Religion in Canada

Chapter One

Introduction: How Freedom of Conscience and Religion Are Protected and Why It Matters

1. A Look at Some of Today's Issues

As I am writing this, the newspapers are reporting the efforts of two plaintiffs in legal proceedings to overturn sections of the Criminal Code that make it illegal to assist in a suicide.[1] This matter has already been litigated in Canada. In 1993, in a decision cited as *Rodriguez v. Attorney-General (British Columbia)*,[2] the Supreme Court of Canada declined to hold that there was a legal right to assisted suicide. Nonetheless, the debate has gone on, and it is one on which Canadians, on both sides, have passionate views. And once again, our top Canadian court will likely have an opportunity, whether it takes it or not, to significantly alter Canadian law and public policy.

It may not be immediately apparent, but these new cases, like *Rodriguez* before them, are fundamentally about belief. The point is illustrated by analysis of a column in the *National Post* published August 5, 2011, discussing the new attempt to overturn the assisted suicide ban. The columnist first referred to "objections rooted in religion" to changes in the law. Obviously, this involves the beliefs of some who oppose legalizing assisted suicide and recognizes that beliefs play at least a role in the debate. He also acknowledged other arguments against legalization such as "fears of a slippery slope" and "worries about accidental applications of euthanasia." These concerns he ultimately dismissed with the comment, "How can a humane society compel [Ms Taylor, the plaintiff in one of the cases], to suffer on in agony against her expressed wishes?"

This discussion leads us to what this book is about. The columnist, Mr Matt Gurney, appeared to be pitting reason and compassion against religious belief and fallacious arguments of the slippery slope variety. But what is the origin of the reasons he has expressed in favour of assisted suicide? In fact, while his reasons were not based on religious belief, Mr Gurney was expressing a deeply held belief in personal autonomy which has led him to espouse the rights of people in at least some situations to decide to die. In addition, he has decided that this belief should overcome religious objections or predictions about how the law will be applied. This too indicates a belief system that places the exercise of autonomy at the top of the moral pyramid. In summary, his arguments are reasoned, but the reasoning begins with a system of belief. Of course, there are facts about assisted suicide, not only beliefs. Several countries have legalized it, and their experiences have been reported on and will undoubtedly be argued about in evidence before the court.

But the divide on each side of which these facts will be marshalled and their implications debated is a divide of belief. If we turn to the report of the *Rodriguez* decision, we will see that nine groups were given status by the court as interested parties (although not directly affected by the issue) to present briefs supporting one side or the other. Of those nine groups, two (the Canadian Conference of Catholic Bishops and the Evangelical Fellowship of Canada) were explicitly religious organizations; two were groups with philosophical commitments to promoting life (Pro-Life Society of British Columbia and Pacific Physicians for Life Society); three were organizations protecting the rights of the handicapped; and two were organizations promoting the right to die. All of these organizations, whether religious or not, were there because of their beliefs about the issue of assisted suicide. And those beliefs were underpinned and influenced by a variety of other belief systems, whether religious or secular, about human beings, their value, purpose, and rights.

The court in *Rodriguez* decided against a right to die because, the judges said, the concerns about abuse and the difficulties of designing adequate safeguards were such that the matter was better left to legislation. However, the court was divided, with only five of the nine judges supporting the majority judgment while four would have held that assisted suicide was required by provisions in the Charter of Rights and Freedoms.[3] The judgments did not openly discuss underlying differences in belief. Yet, the key difference between the majority and the minority judgments, just as in Mr Gurney's column I have quoted, was a difference in the weight to be given to a belief in personal autonomy, in the face of other beliefs, that would have made protection of personal autonomy the decisive factor.

Thus, at the bottom of this debate is a morass of conflicting beliefs. And the cases about assisted suicide are by no means the only cases of which this is true. Almost every aspect of public policy in Canada is affected by conflicts in beliefs that lead directly to opposing opinions of how our law should be maintained or changed. More obviously, but just as significantly, conflicts about religious practices and accommodation for them, tolerance of diverse moral standards about sexuality such as the legitimacy of same-sex marriage or polygamy, questions about the value of a gun registry, debate over regulations governing abortion, and many, if not most, other issues of divided opinions on public policy in Canada today are significantly influenced by our varying beliefs.

All this suggests that we need to pay more attention to belief conflicts and their influence on the law and, in particular, to do some serious thinking about how our legal system and we as individuals reflect on, debate, and decide about matters that are heavily, and often exclusively, influenced by conflicts in belief. These include conflicts about religion, of course, but also about secularism and about other commitments of conscience that drive our decision-making processes.

As a major part of this consideration, it is crucially important to consider how our rights to hold and express conflicting beliefs are protected and what limits to that protection there should be. What if columnists such as Mr Gurney were not allowed to express their beliefs in personal autonomy? Most of us would probably not want a society in which such opinions were suppressed. But what if the Canadian Conference of Catholic Bishops or the Evangelical Fellowship of Canada or the Right to Die Society of Canada were not permitted to appear before the court or express views in accordance with their beliefs? Should they have been permitted to intervene in the *Rodriguez* case? Should there be a difference between the rights of the overtly religious organizations and those with other kinds of beliefs? Are there limits to what we can do and say in expressing beliefs that oppose the beliefs of others, particularly if those "others" are a significant majority? Or a minority? Or a particular group with particular historical disadvantages? All these questions need to be answered as our political and judicial processes unfold and as policy choices are made that are driven by beliefs that some hold and others oppose. Many of these questions have been answered by the decisions of the courts.

As I will argue below, without protection for the expression of conflicting beliefs of all kinds, democratic processes cannot function adequately. My contention, as the reader will see, is that we have done an inadequate job in thinking about the role of conflicting beliefs in our system and the necessity of protecting our rights to believe, express those beliefs, and use them to influence public policy while still preserving the democratic right to debate and dissent.

I invite the reader, therefore, to accompany me as we try to "rethink" freedom of conscience and religion in Canada. This is primarily a book about law because, as we will see, it is the task of the courts to decide the extent and meaning of protections for beliefs that we hold. There is a voluminous literature on the topic of freedom of religion (in particular) in Canada's legal system. I will not primarily be engaging with debates that have emerged from this literature, although the reader will from time to time find references to those debates. However, my purpose is to return to the source materials of our courts – their judgments in which they have delineated the protections and the limits to the protections of conflicting beliefs.

The reader does not have to be a lawyer or legally trained to participate in this exercise. In my experience, ordinary citizens are fascinated by the legal process and are quite capable of understanding the courts' judgments, although rarely do people have easy access to those materials. But if we are going to "rethink" where the courts have taken us in dealing with our belief conflicts, it is precisely those materials that we must tackle and must discuss. In this book, I hope to do just that. We will turn now to some basic principles that we will need in our task ahead.

2. Fundamental Freedoms and the Democratic State

There has been a tendency among theorists and lawyers, particularly where the belief system is religious in nature, to treat it as a private exercise, valuable only insofar as it contributes to the well-being of the individual. As one writer put it, "nowadays, religion is treated more as a hobby than as an object of hostility."[4] Another writer has suggested that the usefulness of religion, and the reasons for its constitutional protection, are found in its ability to assist in the emotional well-being of some individuals for whom a reasoned commitment to positive values in life is "intellectually inaccessible or psychologically unendurable."[5] This assessment of a particular subset of belief (religion) as being helpful only for the stupid or the weak (to put the academic language in more blunt terms) to ensure their participation in the liberally defined social good overlooks, of course, what I have described as the pervasive nature of belief, whether religious or not, underlying our policy choices. In this section, I will argue for a much more robust understanding of the role of "faith" of all varieties in the democratic society and its vital contribution to the success of the democratic project.[6]

Freedom of conscience and religion is listed in the Canadian Charter of Rights and Freedoms[7] as the first of the "fundamental freedoms." The other freedoms are freedom of thought, belief, opinion and expression (including freedom of the press and other media of communication), of peaceful assembly, and of association.[8]

In this book, we will investigate the legal meaning in Canada of freedom of conscience and religion with a critical eye to the role that the fundamental freedoms play in a democratic society and with a sceptical eye to the treatment freedom of conscience and religion has received in the courts. As I have said, this is not a book primarily for lawyers. But we will be dealing in detail with the case law which is the material lawyers usually work with. This is also not a book of political theory, although I will reference some of these theories briefly from time to time. The idea on which this book is based is that by starting with the court decisions and reviewing them in detail, we can learn a great deal about how and why our attitudes towards freedom of religion and conscience have developed as they have. I also believe that by analysing the decisions of the courts, we can better understand both the role freedom of conscience and religion now plays in our society and the role it could play in making our society a more peaceful, open, and democratic place to live.

The courts develop the meaning of the laws legislatures write, including the law written in our constitution. When courts issue reasons for a decision interpreting the law, they are often reflecting much that is current in public opinion, yet they may also be shaping popular thinking as their reasons are disseminated in the media and commented upon by journalists and academics and in public debate. Judicial reasons traditionally follow a certain pattern. They usually refer to previous case authorities and develop a chain of argument based upon those past authorities. To decide whether the reasons are good or bad ones, someone reviewing the decision must subject the reasons to a detailed review, looking at the past authorities quoted in the judgment and determining whether the reasons follow a logical route to the conclusion.

As well as conducting this kind of critique, lawyers also look at how the reasons and the decision affect our society, both in practical and theoretical ways. If the courts have misconceived the social problem the law is designed to address or misjudge the practical effect of their decision, their interpretation can hinder the development of our society along the lines the democratically elected representatives have drawn or lines that may be important for the society's survival and well-being. In this book we will explore how courts have interpreted freedom of conscience and religion from all these perspectives.

Before we turn to the case law, however, I suggest we spend a few minutes thinking about the Charter and about what the fundamental freedoms represent. We will take this step by step and, at this stage, we will not add information that we do not absolutely need to begin our examination of the source material. Later, when we have examined some of the cases in detail, we will have the information we need to assess these questions with more sophistication.

Let us start with the simple question of whether there is a difference between a "right" and a "freedom." The Charter suggests that there is by using the two separate words and by setting the "fundamental freedoms" out in a separate section from those sections that follow and are devoted to "rights."[9] Yet it is easy to argue that the distinction is merely a matter of semantics.

If you are free to associate with others, then it would seem to follow logically that you have a right to associate with them. So is not a "freedom" simply another way to talk about "rights"? Like the rights specified in later sections of the Charter, the freedoms are not absolute, but have prescribed limits. And those limits, for both rights and freedoms, are expressed in the same section of the Charter in the same terms.[10] Thus there seems no initial reason why we should analyse the fundamental freedoms differently from the way we analyse rights.

This similarity in theory is also evident in practice, fuelled by the fact that lawsuits, where the courts have the opportunity to interpret and apply the Charter, usually arise when individuals bring forward a fact pattern to the court claiming some specific relief. Whether it is the freedom to practise one's religion by wearing a kirpan at school[11] or the right of a citizen to be free from unreasonable search by the police,[12] the matter becomes one of assertion of personal entitlement against the state's power. "Right" or "freedom" seems to make no difference.

Yet it bears some further consideration whether this is all there is to it. In this book, I will propose that there is indeed another element to the fundamental freedoms that needs to be taken into account. We may explore this in a preliminary way by asking: To what are these listed freedoms "fundamental"? Freedom of association does not seem as central to the ability of citizens to thrive as equality rights. Freedom of expression does not seem as crucial to survival as economic rights, which are not even included in the Charter.[13] Freedom of conscience and religion, as we shall see, is often not popular in the public mind when it is used to defend practices we may think socially destructive.

I suggest, and will further explore in later chapters, that the listed "fundamental" freedoms are fundamental not simply (or even primarily) to our rights as private citizens to live as we please and maximize our well-being, but to the very nature of the democratic process. They go beyond our personal and private rights. To individuals, they may not even be the most prized of their rights, but they are the foundation without which the democratic state cannot function or survive.

It is well beyond the scope of this work to engage in a lengthy discussion of democracy, what it is and how it is defined. There is a large theoretical literature on the nature of democracy, on what justifies it as the best choice of political system, and on the dangers to which democracy is heir. No doubt many difficulties do attach to various forms of democratic government: dangers from extremes of political partisanship that democracies often produce, from the "tyranny of the majority" that can oppress others, and from the many problems inherent in representative democratic government, including apathy and alienation. Various theorists, such as Kant, Rawls, and Habermas (to name only a few), have elucidated substantive theories of democracy that add limiting principles to the simple, procedural "majority rules" concept.[14] And there is no doubt that such limits are worthy of discussion.

The Charter itself, of course, imposes very real limits on the powers of majority governments, and part of what we will be examining in this book is how those limits ought to work. Yet, I suggest, there is a danger in going too far too quickly. Once we adopt a robust theory of democracy, its justifications and its necessary limits, we will approach the law by a well-worn path and may arrive too easily at well-worn conclusions. As we discuss the "raw material" of this book – that is, the judicial decisions – no doubt we will have questions about the processes, the protections, and the limits appropriate to a democracy. If we start from some basic principles and proceed to a detailed examination of the facts, we may find some theory emerging. Not that the purpose of this book is to address the democratic system as a whole; but in considering freedom of conscience and religion, questions about democracy will arise and some outlines of theory may emerge to warrant further thought. I suggest, at this moment, that we begin only with a simple, procedural idea and see where it leads us.

One aspect of democracy (and the one with which I suggest we begin) is indisputable: that the governed have some participation in the way in which they are governed. That participation may be greater or lesser, depending upon the structure of government. The hallmark, however, is some ability to participate. The participation, again to a greater or lesser degree no doubt, must also be a free participation. While communist states frequently have referred to themselves as "democratic people's republics," such elections as are allowed give the citizens no real choice. They may vote for the party's representative or they may stay home. We may debate in the West how free our choices about a whole range of matters in fact are,[15] but much thought is given and much legislative ink spilled on efforts to secure that choice, at least in elections. Limits to advertising and election spending, transparency in election contributions and fundraising – all are justified by the argument of protecting free choice in the electoral system.

Free participation in the political process requires the ability to obtain information, to form opinions, to share those opinions, and to attempt to convince others. This process requires that in a democratic society, citizens are engaged in multiple series of ongoing conversations,[16] whether in direct debate or through third parties such as the media. It is through these many conversations that ideas are shared, opinions formed, governments elected or defeated, and public policy forged. Indeed, a healthy, functioning democracy depends upon these many conversations and the gradual (or sometimes not so gradual) coalescence of opinion to which they may or may not lead.

These conversations enable change in a society to occur. Fifty years ago, few Canadians would have worried about whether women could earn equal pay to men for equivalent work. Many would have considered that for women to work outside the home was unacceptable. Prior to 1918, women in Canada did not even vote.[17] No one contests that the social change in this one area of our culture has been dramatic. While the political and sociological reasons for the reversal are no doubt complex and many, the mechanism by which this revolution was produced was the conception, communication, and discussion of ideas of equality between men and women. In a remarkably short time span, a large majority accepted those ideas. The public conversations produced real and rapid change.

Many of the fundamental freedoms (freedom of speech, for example) obviously protect directly our ability to have these conversations. It may be less clear how freedom of conscience and religion does so. But the information on which we base our opinions is not merely the data stream of facts. For us to make sense of the facts, we must adopt some organizing principle and some method of judging good from bad, right from wrong. All of us have such an organizing system. Otherwise, we would lack the ability to organize data and make decisions about the data's relevance or import. Many of these organizing systems are religious in nature. All religions offer a comprehensive world view that includes some belief about the meaning of events and some teaching as to what is right or wrong.

The Supreme Court of Canada has defined "religion" in a traditional, but somewhat narrow way as requiring faith in a divine being. In a leading case, it defined religion as what a person sincerely believes she must do to connect with the divine.[18] But for purposes of informing and shaping democratic conversations, the usefulness of this definition is limited. Belief systems that are atheistic share many of the characteristics of traditional religion for these purposes. Commentators have criticized the court for its failure to appreciate that secularism can be as comprehensive a belief system as any religious faith in its power to shape our visions of the world.[19]

These non-religious systems also provide organizing principles for the interpretation of events and the determination of what is good and what is bad and thus are also contributors to our social conversations. The emphasis on connection with the divine, although a feature of most religions,[20] is the private aspect of religious belief. In this book, we will concentrate more on the public issues of religion in which it is more similar to any organizing belief system, whether or not a transcendent being is a feature of the system, than the Supreme Court's definition suggests. And it is important to note that the fundamental freedom protected by the Charter extends beyond the protection of religion and also includes conscience, which may be formed through religious commitment, but may also be formed by world view commitments that have no supernatural element to them. Thus, we will often speak more broadly of organizing belief systems, rather than of religious belief in the narrow sense. However, the distinction must be kept in mind, particularly when considering the language used in legislation and in judicial processes.

Some hint of the importance of fundamental freedoms, and particularly the freedom of conscience and religion, was recognized by the Supreme Court of Canada in its decision of 1985 in *R. v. Big M Drug Mart.*[21] After reviewing the English history of laws relating to religion, Dickson J. stated:

> ... an emphasis on individual conscience and individual judgment also lies at the heart of our democratic political tradition. The ability of each citizen to make free and informed decisions is the absolute prerequisite for the legitimacy, acceptability, and efficacy of our system of self-government. It is because of the centrality of the rights associated with freedom of individual conscience both to basic beliefs about human worth and dignity and to a free and democratic political system that American jurisprudence has emphasized the primacy or "firstness" of the First Amendment. It is this same centrality that in my view underlies their designation in the Canadian Charter of Rights and Freedoms as "fundamental." They are the *sine qua non* of the political tradition underlying the Charter.[22]

However, as we shall later see, courts have not generally made much use of this principle in their determinations of how freedom of conscience and religion should be interpreted and applied.

A central problem in interpreting and applying freedom of conscience and religion has been the question of what legitimacy these often-conflicting organizing belief systems have or should have in the influence of public policy. Some theorists have insisted that these belief systems should be kept strictly private and out of public debate.[23] They argue that only reasons accessible to all, whatever their beliefs, should guide our legal system. While such style of argument certainly may be a practical necessity to convince those who do not share the same belief system, it is hard not to conclude that even if the public argument is couched in these terms, the actual process of decision making for the individual will be significantly, often decisively, influenced by his or her belief system. I have already showed how this is so in our brief discussion of the issue of assisted suicide.

If, then, most of the deepest divisions in our society are based upon opposing beliefs which lead to opposite conclusions about what the law and public policy should be, and people's opinions about almost every public issue you can imagine divide along lines of fundamental belief, how does this in practice influence the democratic debate? Those fundamental beliefs may lead to more general reasons which are used in the public forum. But when we come to make up our mind, our beliefs often cause us to favour one set of reasons as weighing more heavily than another.

But all this does not explain why (or whether) the law should protect public expression of belief. It is often the public expression that gives rise to much conflict in our society. Why not simply allow people a private personal commitment and curtail stringently the divisive public expressions of those differences, even though we know that the differing belief systems are leading to differing policy conclusions and support for different legal outcomes? There are several things we could say about this idea. First, most belief systems require some public aspect. Whether a Muslim woman wears a headscarf, a Catholic man attends Mass on Sunday, or a secular humanist insists that the decorated tree in the town square be named the "Holiday Tree," the expression of belief is usually an inherent part of the commitment. We sometimes fail to recognize this if the beliefs we hold are part of our broadly accepted culture and their expression is then unnoticed by most of us.[24] But more importantly, for the purpose of fostering the democratic state, if we acknowledge that these beliefs will, directly or indirectly, influence our public choices, we will do better to become familiar with them in their variety, understand them in their impact, and explore our differences with them than try to pretend they do not exist. Acceptance of public expression of belief is the only way in which this understanding can be achieved.

This issue will be discussed in some detail in later chapters. Indeed, a theme to which I will return is whether it is productive to have conversations when, like an iceberg, the substantial mass of supporting reasons for a position is concealed. In part, those favouring such concealment are motivated by the belief that a conflict in organizing systems (as we have called them), because it may be irreconcilable, must necessarily lead to impasse, conflict, or even violence. That assumption will also be later discussed and challenged. For the moment, we may simply observe that, indeed, it is the very differences among our organizing belief systems that bring new values into the conversation and provide the opportunity for society to strike out in new directions. Without the wellsprings of conscience and religion, new challenges to current thinking would be less likely to arise.

For example, prior to the nineteenth century, slavery was largely accepted as part of the natural order of the world. There may have been limits to its scope or protections for the treatment of slaves in some cultures, but few questioned seriously the economic necessity and, indeed, the natural rightness of the institution. It was the growing emphasis on a religiously based belief in the dignity of every human person that introduced as a serious topic for public discussion the question of whether slavery should be legally prohibited.[25]

For our purposes at this point, it is enough to conclude that the fundamental freedoms, including freedom of conscience and religion, are key contributors to the essential conversations that a democratic state requires. That being so, each time a matter of freedom of conscience or religion is before the courts in some dispute, another party, the public interest, is also in the courtroom. Limits to these freedoms there must obviously be. However, such limits should not be imposed without a realization that there is more at stake than simply the parties' rights. A weakening of any of the fundamental freedoms means a curtailment in the process of democratic conversation, a reduction in the opportunity for social change, and a limitation on citizens' free participation in our society. I will argue later that this understanding of the role and significance of the fundamental freedoms should weigh in the courts' decisions of how far those freedoms can extend. I will also suggest that recognition of this role can be usefully employed in those situations in which rights appear to conflict and in which courts have generally seen their task as balancing the conflicting rights.

With this perspective established, at least as a working thesis, we can turn to some more technical aspects of the problem. To this point, we have been focused on the direct protection of freedom of conscience and religion in the Charter. That is not the only system in Canada by which this freedom is protected, however. At this stage, let us turn to a general overview of how religion and conscience fit into the Canadian legal landscape.

3. The Legal Framework

Many readers will be aware that the Canadian Charter of Rights and Freedoms directly curtails only government action.[26] The protection it extends is primarily a protection from the power of the state. Thus, to take the most straightforward case, the guarantee of freedom of conscience and religion would likely prevent either Federal, provincial, or municipal governments from passing legislation to outlaw the practice of a particular religion.[27] It also, as we shall see, limits the operation not simply of legislative but also of administrative arms of government, such as school boards or the public service.

As well as the guarantee of freedom of conscience and religion, the Charter also contains a protection for citizens from discrimination based upon religion, and upon other prohibited grounds such as race, age, or disability.[28] These equality rights, contained in section 15, also address themselves to the citizen's right to equal benefit and protection of the law. Just as the state may not normally impinge upon one's freedom of religion, so it may not deny the benefit of the law to anyone based upon his or her religion. This right appears to reinforce the guarantee of religious freedom in section 2. That it does not appear to protect belief systems that are not religious will be discussed below in the provincial context.

I have also mentioned several times in the preceding section of this chapter that the rights and freedoms the Charter contains are subject to limits. The limits, expressed in the first section of the Charter, are "such reasonable limits prescribed by law as can be demonstrably justified in a free and democratic society."[29] Substantial jurisprudence (cases decided by the courts) has grown up around the interpretation of these words, as might be expected. We will see how it has applied to our topic in some detail throughout this book. However, we may note that this section of the Charter gives credence to the idea that its aim is not only the protection of individuals but also the protection of a "free" and "democratic" society. Particularly when the limits to freedom and rights are considered, the Charter itself prescribes that consideration of preserving and promoting freedom and democracy should be weighed in the balance. Limits which undermine a free and democratic society ought not to be imposed. I will also suggest that courts have not given this factor the attention which it deserves.

The court or tribunal applies the limiting principles in a two-step process known as the *Oakes* test.[30] The decision-making body will ask itself, first, whether there has been an infringement of the right or freedom alleged. If so, it will proceed to consider whether the infringement constitutes a limit "prescribed by law and demonstrably justified in a free and democratic society." For a claimant of a Charter right or freedom to successfully contest government action, the answer to this first question must be positive and the answer to the second, negative. Determination of whether the infringement (once found) is supportable requires, first, a determination that the state has a pressing interest that should be allowed to override a constitutional right and, second, whether the mechanism the state has chosen to further this pressing interest is proportional to the need. This test will be described in more detail in chapter 2 and we will return to it frequently as we review the jurisprudence.

In the private dealings of one citizen with another, there also exists some protection for conscience and religion, albeit in a much more limited sphere. Every province has legislation which prevents discrimination against persons on the basis of certain specified characteristics when engaging in certain types of transactions.[31] There is also a Federal human rights act addressing similar situations in enterprises that fall within the Federal jurisdiction, such as the broadcasting industry.[32] Typical transactions to which the legislation applies are renting of accommodation, the purchase of property, employment, membership in trade unions, and access to services commonly available to the public. The breadth and scope of the transactions to which the legislation applies vary from province to province.[33] Many statutes also prohibit certain kinds of publications negatively targeting those persons with specified characteristics.[34]

All the provincial statutes prohibit discrimination in these selected areas on the basis of "religion,"[35] "creed,"[36] "religious belief,"[37] or "religious creed."[38] The Federal act lists "religion" as a prohibited ground of discrimination.[39] There is much less commonality, however, in the protection extended to non-religious beliefs. British Columbia, for example, also protects political belief, but only in employment or membership in trade unions. Ontario does not mention any belief other than religious. Saskatchewan's act contains, as well as protection from discrimination, a bill of rights that affirms the right to freedom of conscience and religion. Manitoba protects political belief in all transactions to which the act applies.

This lack of consistency in the treatment of other beliefs that are not religious in nature seems surprising. However, it may in part be explained by the fact that non-religious beliefs are likely to be less easily definable for a class than are religious beliefs. Human rights legislation has been primarily concerned with the fair treatment of identifiable groups,[40] such as visible minorities, women, or persons with disabilities. In addition, discrimination on the basis of what we may call personal opinion rather than membership in an identifiable religious group has, perhaps, been historically less prevalent. Nonetheless, it seems no less offensive to deny an atheist accommodation on the grounds of her atheism than to deny a Catholic accommodation on the grounds of her faith.[41]

The role of provincial and Federal human rights legislation is very different from that of the Charter. In their more limited role, these statutes aim at protecting individuals from exclusion from important parts of social life on the basis of innate qualities such as sex and race or pivotal aspects of one's life such as religion or because of issues that should be irrelevant to the transaction where there is a societal interest in ensuring access to social life such as the existence of an unrelated criminal conviction for a person seeking employment. They do not aim particularly at protecting the democratic process or a free society. Indeed, they restrict the freedom of citizens to make decisions for certain reasons that our society finds repugnant, such as racial prejudice. However, indirectly, these statutes contribute to the same end as the fundamental freedoms of the Charter. They protect individuals with diverse characteristics (including religious faith) from being shut out of such fundamental needs as shelter, employment, or education. This protection permits the greater flourishing of such diversity and the ability of citizens with various perspectives to be heard in the ongoing public conversations of the day.

As the jurisprudence has developed, the provincial legislation has become, in three particular aspects, interwoven with the Charter. The first of these is the obvious application of the Charter to the provincial legislation itself. Human rights codes are government acts subject to the requirements of the Charter. Provisions of these statutes may therefore be challenged on the grounds of violation of Charter rights. Such a challenge was, for example, made to the exception once found in many human rights statutes that protected forced retirement at age sixty-five.[42] The exception was argued to be in violation of the equality rights in the Charter which list age as a protected characteristic. While the Supreme Court of Canada found that, at least in the case of university faculty members, the limit was justifiable,[43] subsequent cases raised the very real question of whether that decision would have survived a later challenge.[44]

The second area of connection is a more subtle one. In an argument that illegal discrimination has occurred under provincial law, it can be a defence to show that in the particular situation, the complainant (and the characteristics protected by law) could not be accommodated without undue hardship. Case law has held, for example, that while an employer had discriminated against an employee whom it fired for absences due to illness, in the particular circumstances where the employee had no reasonable prospect of being able to return to work on a regular basis, the employer was not liable. It would have constituted undue hardship for the employer to have been required to retain the employee any longer.[45] This defence is expressly set out in some provincial legislation[46] but, where it is not, it has been read in by the courts as a limiting factor on the protections of the act.[47]

The test of undue hardship, developed in the context of the provincial laws, has been transferred by the Supreme Court of Canada to play a role also in jurisprudence under the Charter at least in some categories of cases involving religious freedom.[48] How this has occurred and what it may mean for the future are topics that will be analysed in a later chapter. The undue hardship test, however, is stringent. The burden falls heavily upon the party alleging undue hardship as a defence to show that it made serious and sustained efforts taking into account the particular individual to accommodate the complainant. Its application to the exercise of freedom of conscience and religion may mark a departure for Canada from lesser protections of religious freedom available in, for example, the European Union.[49]

A third area in which the Charter is relevant to provincial and Federal human rights statutes is also one that I will give significant attention to in this book. I have earlier commented that human rights statutes limit the freedom of citizens in making decisions in spheres of action that would otherwise be considered private matters. For example, a restaurant owner might prefer not to spend money on wheelchair access to his establishment. However, failing to provide such access would likely be discrimination on the basis of disability in a service commonly available to the public. Or he may prefer to hire only young women to wait on his customers. Again, refusing employment to a young man would clearly discriminate on the basis of sex.

But where freedom is limited by statute, the limitation may in some cases restrict a freedom guaranteed by the Charter. In such a case, the Charter freedom may be raised as a defence to a claim of illegal discrimination under the provincial law. This has happened in several cases where freedom of conscience and religion has been used to defend against claims under provincial human rights acts.[50] These cases deserve careful consideration because they reveal much about how the courts value the "fundamental freedoms" given by the Charter and how they view issues of conscience and religion. Courts often speak of "balancing rights" in these situations, but I will argue that balance is not an accurate description of the process they have used, nor is it a helpful tool to resolve the conflicts between parties' rights and freedoms.

4. Our Divided Culture

Freedoms of conscience and religion are inconvenient. Most of us would be much happier in a world in which our organizing belief system was dominant and we were able to decide matters of law, public policy, and morality as we thought fit. Instead, we live in a society with a plethora of cultures and their belief systems, which vary substantially one from the other and may vary also between generations or on a highly individualized basis. We frequently read in the press of problems caused by the clash of beliefs in our society, whether it is a report of demonstrations pro-Israel (or pro-Palestinian),[51] of prosecution of members of a community in which polygamy is openly practised,[52] or of disapproval of a voter who wishes to vote without showing her face to the election official.[53] Decisions of our courts shock or annoy us, sometimes in their acceptance of manifestations of belief systems that differ from ours, sometimes in their rejection of those that reflect ours.

Escape is promised by some writers who suggest that we can simply dump our superstitions and live on rational premises alone. Unfortunately, their promise proves to be another organizing system of belief (albeit not religious as the Supreme Court uses that term) that competes with the multitude of organizing systems already in play.[54] Schools attempt to teach students about various beliefs and philosophies and garner protests from religious parents who see the program as one of promoting secularism, a belief system which they have rejected.[55]

On top of this, when many of us would much prefer limits to the freedom of conscience and religion, we find the Charter listing it in first place among those fundamental freedoms which we all have and which must be respected in all of us, whether we like it or not. In this book, we will review and discuss many of the controversial, unpleasant, and difficult issues that freedom of conscience and religion present. Are there no better ways to handle the situation than we have yet found? Are there no solutions other than the extremes of political impasse and discord on the one hand and repression on the other?

A difficulty that we will often encounter as we pursue this inquiry arises from the fact that because we all have our own organizing belief systems, we are convinced as a result of those belief systems that certain legal outcomes are right or wrong. In attempting to persuade others of the rightness of our causes, we are often tempted to argue not the direct merits of our case, but a limitation on the freedoms of those who would oppose us. Lawyers, in particular, will often seek victory through procedural manoeuvres, especially if the likelihood of success is greater than it would be by attacking the substantive issue directly. Accepting the legitimacy of limiting our freedoms in an effort to win the end result we desire is very like drilling a hole in the bottom of our own leaky boat in an effort to let out the water. The point about conscience is that while one can (with difficulty) compel outward observance, one cannot compel inward assent. Only the most stringent repressions can even produce uniformity of observance. And such repressions are not only inconsistent with a democratic state but are easily pressed into service by opposing factions against the other side as power shifts.

While we progress through this discussion, we must keep in mind that despite inconvenience and all the difficulties, our belief systems, whether religious or non-religious, are an inescapable, even if often un-articulated and sometimes unacknowledged, influence on the conversations in which our society engages. John Milbank has written:

> Indeed, any sharp separation of reason and faith is dangerous for a politics that is "liberal" in the sense of constitutional. It implies that faith at its core is "non-rational" and beyond the reach of any sort of argument, while also implying that reason cannot really have a say on issues of crucial substantive preference. But in reality, reason and faith are always intertwined in a beneficial way, even if this is hard to formulate theoretically. Reason has to make certain assumptions and trust in the reasonableness of the real – as indeed Kant himself acknowledged. Faith has continuously to think through the coherence of its own intuitions in a process that often modifies those intuitions themselves.[56]

As suggested earlier, a society that cannot hold conversations limits its ability to function as a democracy. The health of those conversations is of vital importance therefore to all of us. Seeking better ways to understand and accommodate freedom of conscience and religion, not restrict it unnecessarily, is a fundamental part of that health.

If our fundamental freedoms are crucial to our democratic system, and thus to our ability to change our society in whichever direction we believe to be right, then we must all, whatever our politics, share a commitment to preserving those freedoms. In the course of the chapters that follow, I will attempt to illustrate this point and, as we consider ways in which we might open our democratic conversations and speak openly about our cherished beliefs and principles, I will suggest that honesty in our discourse about our freedoms is a first requirement for finding a more profitable approach.

To discuss these questions, I will review many of the legal decisions under both Federal and provincial legislation. We will also look at many of the controversies in our recent history surrounding the topic. Finally, we will see whether there is any approach that might provide us with a more sophisticated method of dealing with conflict in belief and with the policy conflicts those beliefs produce than our current practices have discovered. Our current approach, which I suggest has primarily consisted of inconsistent applications, lack of clarity about the issues, and lack of understanding about why our freedoms matter, does not seem to have served us particularly well.

In the next chapter, we will turn to the earliest of the decisions in the Supreme Court of Canada that began to shape our legal understanding of freedom of conscience and religion. From that decision, I suggest, a pattern will emerge that reveals a court system that has never found its way to a principled approach in matters of freedom of conscience and religion. To a degree, this is the fault not of particular judges, but of the method by which our legal system works. Courts are expected to solve the dispute in front of them. As each judgment is rendered, a body of principle is expected to be formed. Eventually, a particular judge articulates those principles and perhaps reforms or reorganizes them. That is how the common law has grown since at least the sixteenth century. It has worked remarkably well for many areas of law, although it has not been without what we would judge as missteps. But it has worked less well for the application of the Charter freedoms where social policy, value systems, and belief systems come directly before the court for adjudication. As we will see, the result has often been the unthinking privileging of some belief systems over others and the imposition of some beliefs on reluctant minorities. For these reasons, the time seems appropriate to stop, reflect, and, as a consequence of that reflection, rethink some of the basic principles that enable our society to govern itself.

Chapter Two

Early Cases: Getting Off on the Wrong Foot

1. Introduction

In this chapter, we will consider the reasoning in and the implications of the first case to consider the Charter right of freedom of conscience and religion.[1] As we will see, the case had particular implications for the issue of expression of belief in the public forum. Because the cases in this chapter are all Charter cases, we will be talking about issues of government facilitation or support of such expression, not purely private exchanges. But I will suggest that as the line of cases progresses, the courts' approach becomes a root from which problematic implications for the private sphere grow. Before undertaking a detailed analysis of the case law, however, it may be helpful to consider the issues in the abstract. What ought we to be aware of as we think about freedom of conscience and religion when groups seek to express their beliefs publicly (with or without government aid) and others claim a right to curtail that expression?

Core to the concept of freedom of conscience and religion is the freedom to adopt and practise the beliefs of one's choice and to refuse to acknowledge as true or practise the beliefs of others.[2] Ideally, these two parts of the freedom complement each other, and this allows citizens maximum freedom to live out their principles. This maximization is likely to promote diversity of viewpoints, engagement of each person, whatever his or her beliefs, with the issues in our society, and conversations out of which democratic decisions acceptable to the broad community can emerge.

But a potential for conflict may seem to arise when members of one belief system display their allegiance publicly, with or without government aid. Others then become observers, at least, and perhaps to a degree (perhaps unwilling) participants in the practice. Has this infringed their freedom to reject the beliefs of others? If not, has any other right to which they, as citizens, are entitled been infringed?

If we must all keep the practice of our beliefs confined to the church, temple, synagogue, mosque, or humanist meeting room of our choice, then we can say with certainty that our freedom of religion and conscience has been infringed. Belief systems may make claims that are binding upon their adherents only[3] but usually assert other claims that they consider universal.[4] Universal claims are made because adherents believe either that those claims are binding upon all, whether recognized or not,[5] or that our society would be better if those claims were accepted by all.[6] To prohibit the expression of those universal claims obviously truncates the adherent's right to live his belief system, paring that right down to the right to express only those claims that affect believers and not others. As well, adherents may also wish, or believe they are required, to give public expression even to those parts of their beliefs binding upon them only. In that case, again, a prohibition against that expression is a violation of the freedom of religion and conscience of those adherents. Prohibiting, for example, Islamic students' gathering in a school or university for prayers certainly limits the religious freedom of those students.

But does this public expression, whether of universal or private claims, necessarily violate any right or freedom of those who do not adhere to the belief system? If we take the position that it does, then a problem arises. The issue becomes one of "your freedom or my freedom"; we cannot both have what we want. Either you are prohibited from speaking in public about or displaying your beliefs or I have my rights to be free from hearing or seeing your beliefs in a public space curtailed.

But we do not have to decide that public expression of belief always violates freedom of conscience and religion (or any other right or freedom) of the onlookers. Indeed, we do not generally consider this to be so. For example, a church standing on the corner with a cross on the steeple is a public declaration of belief. However, no sensible person would suggest that this violates the freedom of conscience and religion of non-Christians. It neither prevents them from adopting and practising their own beliefs nor requires an acknowledgment or acceptance of Christian belief as true. There does not seem to be any other right of the onlooker, either, that has been infringed. It seems apparent, therefore, that we can answer our question more modestly by stating that public expression of one organizing belief system does not necessarily violate the freedom or rights of those who do not accept it. Now we have created some room in which we can move forward to give content to freedom of conscience and religion in public spaces.

Whether or not we are all entirely comfortable with the public expression of difference, I have already argued in the introduction that a healthy democracy that is open to change (as all democracies must be) is gravely weakened and indeed cannot exist without such expression. In keeping with those principles, it seems clear that the resolution we should favour is that which can accommodate the widest range of beliefs and the widest range of conduct, promoting the widest range of opinions in public debate. And it is at least clear that we cannot accept the position that the simple public expression of a particular belief violates the freedom of those who do not share that belief.

We can now attempt to analyse what factors (if any) would make a public expression of an organizing belief system, whether religious or otherwise, unacceptable and liable to be restrained by law. On the other end of the scale from simple public expression (the cross on the church steeple) would be a public expression of belief that compelled agreement of others to that belief (a religious test for public office, for example). This compulsion would violate a core principle of the freedom of conscience and religion of others as we have articulated it.

There might, of course, be factors other than compulsion to accept others' beliefs that would persuade us that expression of belief in public should be constrained. It does not have to be all one way or the other. Would, for example, a sense of exclusion on the part of the onlookers, created by the actions of believers, be a sufficient reason? Would inciting fear or fear of riot? Would dislike or distaste for the display suffice? In thinking about this question, I suggest we can conclude that any factor that is sufficient to curtail the freedom of religion and conscience of one group by limiting or prohibiting their public expression of belief must be something that constitutes a right of the onlooker which the public expression has interfered with, in the same way that compulsion to accept the displayed belief would interfere with others' rights to freedom of conscience and religion.[7]

If, at my behest, the law will stop you from doing something which, otherwise, you would be permitted to do, then the court has acknowledged a right for me. Courts do not give me the right to prevent people carrying on their activities simply because I want to. I must have a claim that the court recognizes and the recognition of this "claim" is another way of expressing that I had a right. This right may be one that we are familiar with and would agree ought to be recognized. But perhaps it is a right that I did not already have based on our previous understanding of legal rights. In that case, a new right has been created, and, in evaluating the wisdom of conferring this new right, we may wish to question whether it contributes to our democratic conversations or stifles them. We can illustrate this by contrasting examples.

If the public expression of belief takes the form of burning down my house, that expression can be curtailed. I have a right to my property and to my safety that is seriously jeopardized by burning down my house. On the other hand, if the public expression of belief constitutes a demonstration in favour of a political candidate, it would not seem that I have a right to prevent that expression because I have no right that seems to be curtailed by the demonstrators' exercise of their freedom of assembly. Yet if I successfully prevent the demonstration from taking place, this will acknowledge that I had some right in this situation that the demonstration would have limited.[8] That right may be a well-understood one. Perhaps there is a city bylaw that gives me the right to progress down this particular street without it being blocked by demonstrators. Or it may not. Perhaps the court thought I should not be required to see something that contradicted my own political beliefs. In that case, I have been given a right to protect myself from seeing things I do not agree with, a right that will have the result of limiting the democratic process.

In the cases under discussion in this chapter, the courts have focused almost exclusively on depicting a variety of situations in which the actions of one group, pursuing its right to express its belief publicly, are said to amount to compulsion for others to accept those beliefs and thus to interfere with their freedom of conscience and religion. The exact scope of a word, of course, will always be a matter for some debate. But courts have often used language about compulsion to convey concerns about some of the other factors we have noted above such as distaste or feelings of exclusion. I suggest that this is unfortunate because it obscures the central question of whether the effect that the public act has on the onlooker constitutes a violation of rights or freedom that our society does, or should, legally recognize. If the activity can be characterized as compulsion to accept the faith of another, then it can be immediately classified as violating the onlooker's freedom of conscience and religion. No more careful analysis need be undertaken.

The question is certainly complicated when the action that is being attacked has been facilitated by government legislation or administrative practice. Government action often has an element of compulsion of some sort embedded in it. The most obvious example is legislation compelling or forbidding some act. Yet this compulsion does not necessarily interfere with some right or freedom which citizens are entitled to maintain against government action. Anti-smoking legislation is valid legislation because citizens have no legal right to smoke or to smoke in particular places. Libertarians may argue that the citizen has a right to be free from government interference even so. However, this is not a right our courts (or most Canadians) are generally prepared to recognize. So the question of whether government facilitation of or aid to religious expression is legally allowable (quite apart from whether we might support that action politically) still depends upon whether that facilitation or aid constrains some right or freedom of others to which they are entitled in our legal system.[9]

Therefore, we should not be prepared automatically to accept that all the factors courts characterize as "compulsion" in matters of belief, even when adopted through some form of governmental action, should be enough to curtail public expression of belief. In other words, we may not be prepared to agree, when we analyse what the so-called compulsion actually consists of, that the onlooker has or should have a right which the public practice of others' beliefs violates. In making this judgment, we must also keep in mind that the more broadly we define "compulsion" with regard to the onlooker's freedom of conscience and religion, the less space we will provide for public declaration of belief and the more limits will be placed on the freedom of those who are otherwise entitled to practise their beliefs in the public eye. At the same time, the broader the definition of compulsion, the more rights are granted the onlookers, rights that may tend to stifle democratic debate rather than facilitate it. In the cases discussed in this chapter, the courts seem unaware of this problem.[10]

2. The Seminal Case

On a day in 1982, employees of Big M Drug Mart in Calgary sold a bicycle lock, and some other small items. Because the sales took place on a Sunday, the corporation was charged with violating a Federal statute, the Lord's Day Act.[11] The corporation defended itself on the ground that the statute was unconstitutional, both as violating the legislative division of powers found in the Constitution Act of 1867 and as limiting Canadians' freedom of conscience and religion protected by the Charter.

The Lord's Day Act prohibited a wide variety of commercial activities from being transacted on a Sunday. Its original purpose, no doubt, had been to protect the Christian Sabbath from incursions of a commercial nature, preserving it for religious observance. It was a public, legislative expression of Christian faith by both government and governed. By 1985, when the case made its way to the Supreme Court of Canada,[12] the Lord's Day Act had lost its viability as an expression of the religious faith of Canadians. It was widely regarded as a nuisance, a bar to the development of economic activity, and even a vehicle for the promotion of bad faith. As an example of this last issue, we may cite its prohibition of sales of real estate on a Sunday. The annals of litigation are littered with vendors or purchasers who signed a contract for the sale of their property on a Sunday and who later, with the rise or fall of the market, predictably argued that their transaction was void as being a violation of the statute.[13] No recorded case suggests that such claim was made out of religious conscience.

But the unpopularity and inconvenience of the statute had not precipitated its repeal. Rather, the statute left up to the provinces the ability to enact exemptions to it, and such exemptions might well, in time, have eaten away its force.[14] However, by the time the prosecution of Big M Drug Mart came before the courts, certainly some Canadians realized that while the religious purpose of the statute was spent, a day of common pause had much to recommend it. The Ontario Law Reform Commission had published a report in 1970 in which it had recommended the benefits of a common day of rest in which families could spend time together.[15] It was particularly important, the report noted, to legislate such a day in the retail sales industry where many of its employees had little protection from the demands of management.

The first question the court had to address was whether the statute was invalid because it was Federal legislation in a sphere of provincial jurisdiction. The Constitution Act, 1867, divided the legislative realm into provincial and federal areas. Neither level of government could significantly encroach on the legislative powers of the other. The division of powers selected seems to us now often arbitrary and certainly vague.

An extensive and arcane jurisprudence emerged from the necessity of the courts' classifying legislation under one of the "heads" of

jurisdiction set out in the Constitution Act. The process of classification involves determining the "matter" dealt with by the statute, based
upon the lists in the Constitution Act. The "matter" (or "pith and substance" of the legislation) in turn depends upon some classification of
the intention of the legislature enacting the law. Of course, the intention
of the legislature must, in part, be a fictional determination. The government of the day enacting a statute no doubt has some purpose in
mind in doing so. However, parliament that passes the legislation may
have many, mixed purposes in the minds of the various legislators. Yet
for purposes of constitutional classification, only one purpose and only
one "matter" flowing from that purpose can be recognized.[16]

Into this pot of malleable, complex categories, a provincial statute[17]
enacted to keep Sunday free from work had fallen in 1902 when the
Judicial Committee of the Privy Council (then the final court of appeal
for Canadian cases) had determined that its "matter" was primarily
that of criminal law.[18] Thus it fell within the jurisdiction of the Federal
government of Canada and was, insofar as the division of powers was
concerned, invalid provincial legislation.

The reasons the court gave for finding the statute a part of the criminal law do not need to be elaborated upon here. It is sufficient to note
that the court traced the origins of Sunday protection legislation back
to very early English legislation compelling Sabbath observance and
punishing, through the criminal law, those who failed to comply. Such
legislation had a long history in England,[19] and it was hardly surprising that the provincial Lord's Day Act was found to be part of this same
initiative.[20]

We may question today whether the Canadian courts in 1985 were
required to make the same characterization of the law as did the Privy
Council eighty-three years before. There was certainly little left in
Canada of the idea that the Christian Sabbath should be protected by
criminal legislation. In *Big M Drug Mart*, in the lower courts, the defendant made the argument that while the original intention of the law
might indeed have been Sabbath protection, the current purpose was
to provide a secular day of common rest. If that was accepted, the court
would have to find that the legislation was no longer legislation with
respect to criminal law (in the federal sphere) but in respect to property and civil rights within the province (the provincial head of jurisdiction). Thus, the Lord's Day Act would have been ruled outside the
powers of the Federal government; it would have been struck down as
void; and the defendant would have been acquitted.

The judge of the provincial court, in which the case was first heard, decided precisely that.[21] He dismissed the numerous cases in the higher courts (including the Privy Council decision referenced above) that had uniformly found the Lord's Day Act to be Sabbath observance legislation and therefore part of the criminal law of the land as no longer binding upon him. Unfortunately, as the Supreme Court of Canada later pointed out, the principle of *stare decisis* (which holds that a lower court must follow the decisions of a higher court, whatever the judge of the lower court may think about them) has no exception for cases in which the lower court judge believed social conditions had changed. Only the Supreme Court of Canada was in the position to overrule the line of authorities that preserved the constitutionality of the Lord's Day Act as criminal law.

The Supreme Court, in fact, gave very little attention to the question of whether the Lord's Day Act was within the jurisdiction of the Federal parliament. This may have been because, in their arguments before the Supreme Court, the parties conceded that the Act was within the legislative competence of the Federal government. In once again affirming its validity under the Federal criminal law power, the Supreme Court remarked that the Act had "been held 'early, regularly and recently' to be in relation to a criminal law matter."[22] However, this determination to characterize the purpose of the Act as Sabbath protection legislation was a crucial step in the court's decision that the Act violated Canadians' freedom of conscience and religion as protected by the Charter.

3. Shifting Purpose and Legislative Effect

Earlier in its judgment, the Supreme Court quoted the Court of Appeal's rejection of the idea that a court might consider that the purpose of a statute had shifted, and it later warned that allowing a change in the "matter" of a statute by having regard to changed social conditions since its enactment would introduce a significant uncertainty into the law. Statutes come before the courts for a pronouncement of their constitutionality. But years later, could the case be reargued because the social conditions had changed? According to the court, this would have been productive of considerable litigation and uncertainty, since a statute declared valid today might sometime in the future become invalid.[23]

There is something to be said for this argument. However, it would seem improbable that statutes whose constitutionality is in doubt based upon a division of powers argument would often be so long-enduring that the complete basis for the legislation would change. It was certainly possible to see the Lord's Day Act as an unusual case. As well, the Supreme Court would later hold that, as far as the Charter was concerned, changing social norms should indeed change judicial interpretations of whether a law was valid or not.

In the decision only four years later in *Andrews v. Law Society of B.C.*,[24] the Supreme Court read into the Charter equality rights the protection of non-Canadian citizens. The court in that case expressed the view that equality rights under the Charter should be interpreted to include "analogous grounds" to those listed in the section. This in effect gave the court a wide discretion to shape the content of the equality rights, as cases arose. This decision led, in turn, to the inclusion by the court of sexual orientation as a protected ground[25] – a decision only made possible by the changing mores of the mid-twentieth century.[26] Since the Charter also affects the validity of a law, it seems surprising that the Supreme Court would be unconcerned about instability in the law as the result of the changing nature of equality rights, but very concerned about them when considering cases on the division of powers.

While this may seem an inconsistency in the court's approach to the problem of legislative stability, the Supreme Court was adopting a traditional formula that the "matter" of the statute for purposes of determining legislative competence pursuant to the division of powers is the original legislative purpose when the statute was passed. That purpose, as articulated by the court, does not change despite changed social conditions.[27] This approach preserves the historic decisions on the division of powers. However, must that dispose of the "matter" or purpose of the statute which will also be relevant in determining whether the statute violates the fundamental freedoms of the Charter?

Here we come to a semantic issue[28] that was of key importance to the Supreme Court's decision. In deciding *R. v. Big M Drug Mart*, the Supreme Court had before it an earlier decision in *Robertson and Rosetanni v. R.*,[29] also by the Supreme Court of Canada, which had covered very similar ground. In that case, the Supreme Court had determined that the Lord's Day Act was valid Federal legislation under the division of powers part of the constitution, and also that it did not violate Canadians' freedom of religion as expressed in the Bill of Rights.[30]

The Bill of Rights, the precursor to the Charter of Rights and Freedoms, stood on a very different legislative ground from the Charter. First, it was a piece of Federal legislation that did not have any special status; it was not part of the constitution of Canada as is the Charter. Second, it was simply declaratory of rights as they existed at the time of its enactment. It did not purport to give Canadians anything new. The Charter clearly includes no such limiting language to constrain the rights it confers. For all these reasons, courts are understandably cautious in directly applying decisions related to the Bill of Rights to Charter cases.

Yet, in considering the question of whether the Lord's Day Act offended the protections for freedom of religion in the Bill of Rights, the Supreme Court had held that the effects of the Lord's Day Act were purely financial and secular for those who did not observe Sunday as a holy day. The statute, the court said, did not interfere with any expression of religion, nor did it require the practice of any religion.[31] Thus, it was held not to violate the provisions of the Bill of Rights ensuring religious freedom.

These findings would seem highly relevant to the Charter case, and the facts that the Bill of Rights did not have constitutional status and that it did not expand Canadians' rights seem quite beside the point. In *Big M Drug Mart*, however, the Supreme Court, twenty-three years later, distinguished *Robertson and Rosetanni* on the grounds that the court in the earlier case had focused only on the effects of the legislation. This, said Dickson J. in *Big M Drug Mart*, arose because the court in *Robertson and Rosetanni*, dealing only with the Bill of Rights, was not concerned with the constitutional status of the Lord's Day Act, but only with its application.[32] By contrast, Dickson J. held that, in a constitutional case under the Charter, a court had to examine the purpose of the law, not necessarily its effects. If the purpose of the law was in violation of the Charter, then the fact that the effects of the law were innocuous was irrelevant. Indeed, effects, he continued to say, could never save legislation with an invalid purpose, although they might defeat legislation with a valid purpose if they interfered with rights or freedoms guaranteed by the Charter.[33]

Let us return now to the question asked above: Because the purpose of the legislation used in determining whether it falls within the legislative competence of the Federal or provincial governments is fixed at the time the legislation is passed, does that require the original purpose of the legislation to be used in determining whether its purpose is valid under the Charter? In other words, could there be a shifting purpose to legislation that, while not changing the legislation's category under the division of powers, could affect the question of whether the legislation offended the Charter and violated guaranteed rights or free-doms? We have already noted that the courts have been open to the idea of changing social times affecting the application of the Charter in other contexts.

However, if we allowed that there could be a changing purpose to the legislation, how would we determine that new purpose? As did the judge at first instance, we would presumably look at the current social conditions and ask ourselves what purpose the legislation now served. In other words, we would be considering the operation or the effect of the legislation in determining its present purpose. When confronted with the argument that the shifting purpose of the legislation should be taken into account in analysing its validity under the Charter, Dick-son J. was immediately wary of the impact of that proposition on his analysis that made the purpose of the legislation central to its validity. "This submission," he said, "is related to the argument that the empha-sis should be on 'effects' rather than on 'purposes.'"[34] Thus, the court rejected the shifting purpose argument also in considering the question of Charter rights and freedoms.

4. Sabbath Observance and Religious Freedom

Turning to the question of whether the Lord's Day Act infringed free-dom of conscience and religion, the Supreme Court had set the stage. The purpose of the legislation was determined on the historical record to be connected with Sabbath observance and no other purpose or ef-fect would be relevant, particularly if the purpose connected to Sab-bath observance was an infringement of the Charter. But even given this constrained environment, the question still remained whether Sab-bath observance legislation offended freedom of conscience and reli-gion. The court held that it did.

As the court reviewed the history of Sabbath observance laws in Eng-land, a progression emerged from laws which were designed to enforce the religious views of the governors to laws that were intended to fa-cilitate the religious practices of the governed. Early laws not only pro-hibited a variety of activities on Sundays, they also imposed mandatory attendance at denominational worship services.[35] By the time the Lord's Day Act was passed, the enforced religious observance provisions were a thing of the past. What the Lord's Day Act did was to require a common day of pause in most work activities on Sunday, the tradi-tional Christian Sabbath, apparently with motives of both protecting the Sunday for religious observance and providing a common day off work for all. As early as Blackstone's *Commentaries*,[36] both the purpose of a common day of rest and the purpose of preserving Sundays for worship had been recognized for Sabbath observance legislation. This was not, however, how the Supreme Court described the purpose of the Lord's Day Act.

The Supreme Court's judgment stated in several places that the purpose of the Act was to "compel Sabbath observance"[37] or to require all to "remember the Sabbath day and keep it holy."[38] If that is so, then the Lord's Day Act was very strangely written indeed. While it did prohibit many commercial activities, it made no attempt to require any particular behaviour on Sundays. Indeed, a person who abstained from working on Sunday but who paraded up and down the public street with signs blaspheming the Christian religion would not have been in violation of the Act. Nonetheless, the court repeatedly referred to the "coercion" of religious practice imposed by the legislation.

The court was being more accurate about the nature of the statute when, later in the judgment in *Big M Drug Mart*, Dickson J. stated, "In my view, the guarantee of freedom of conscience and religion prevents the government from compelling individuals to perform or abstain from performing otherwise harmless acts because of the religious significance of those acts to others."[39] Given the absence of any compulsory acknowledgment of the Christian faith in the Act, this appears to be the only possible basis on which the decision that the Lord's Day Act violated the freedom of religion and conscience clause in the Charter could be justified.

But is that basis adequate? We should note, first, that the activities which the Lord's Day Act prohibited, while "otherwise harmless," were not activities for which there is any constitutional protection. If the government decided that everyone should work only four days per week and be prohibited from working on three, there is no constitutional right that would prevent such legislation from being valid. Second, we must also note that no religion requires work on any particular day. Third, abstaining from work does not, of itself, have any religious significance for those who do not consider Sunday a holy day. A person not working on a Sunday is in no way acknowledging the truth or binding nature of a religion that prohibits work on Sunday. The act of not working is not a religious act in itself. In other words, a person forbidden by law to work on a particular day has not been restricted in the practice of his religious faith or compelled to acknowledge the truth of another faith, nor does it immediately appear that he has been deprived of any right to which he is entitled in our society.

But, of course, all these points are points about the effect of the legislation. Dickson J., to the contrary, insisted that only the purpose of the legislation was relevant to the issue and the purpose was religiously motivated. What are we to make of this distinction? I suggest that it is incoherent to talk of freedom of conscience and religion without talking about the impact of legislation on individuals. Freedom of conscience and religion is inherently a freedom to act in connection to one's conscience or religion or to bring about a state of affairs in one's life relating to one's conscience or religion.[40] If, whatever the purpose of legislation may be, one's acts regarding one's conscience and religion are not affected or one is not in any way hindered from bringing about a particular, chosen state of affairs in one's life with regard to one's conscience and religion, how can we say that the freedom has been violated?

An example may help. Let us suppose that the local First Nation has identified certain trees as having a particular significance for their people, based on their beliefs about their history and religion. One of these trees is on your property. Nonetheless, the legislature includes this tree in a piece of legislation protecting such plants. The result is that you cannot now cut down the tree. The purpose of the statute is to protect the beliefs of a particular group as to their religious and cultural heritage. You have no belief in the tree's significance; but you would have liked to cut it down as it is obstructing your view. Has your freedom of conscience and religion been violated? It seems unlikely that we would suggest that it has. By the tests we have earlier discussed, the legislation, although it now compels you to abstain from cutting down the tree, does not require you to alter your own religious or belief system, or acknowledge as true the belief system of your local First Nation.[41] Yet in *Big M Drug Mart*, the fact that the legislation had the purpose of supporting a particular belief system seemed to be, for Dickson J., sufficient to determine that it contravened the guarantee of freedom of conscience and religion.[42]

I will return to this example later in an effort to further elucidate this and later cases. But for the moment, we need to ask ourselves what right the court's decision protected in this case. If the sole objection to the Lord's Day Act was that, historically, the statute was motivated by a wish to assist one religion to preserve its holy day, although that preservation did not affect the rights of others to practise or disseminate their religion or force them to acknowledge as true the religion of another, then the Act can only be a violation of freedom of religion if those of one belief have the right not to be even indirectly complicit in others' practice of their religions. Yet, if this is the case, the legislation protecting the tree in our example should be invalid.

Dickson J.'s judgment provided a further clue to what he considered to be a contravention of the Charter right to freedom of conscience and religion in a lengthy passage in which he described the offence which legislative recognition of a Christian day of worship gives to those of other faiths. "The theological content of the legislation," he commented, "remains as a subtle and constant reminder to religious minorities within the country of their differences with, and alienation from, the dominant religious culture."[43]

There are two things that should be said about this conclusion. Readers may well have a sense that the promotion of a particular religion is something that the state should not, in general, do. And there are very good legal arguments that, at least, limit the state's right to make such distinctions, which I will discuss below in the context of the decision in *Edwards Books and Art Ltd.*[44] But this was not the basis of the decision in *Big M Drug Mart*. Rather, the court in *Big M Drug Mart* relied primarily upon a misstatement of the purpose of the statute (the "compulsion" of Sabbath observance) and, when it more accurately stated the purpose (prohibiting otherwise harmless acts because of their religious significance to others), completely failed to elucidate how that purpose limited or abrogated the freedom of religion of non-Sunday observers (or any other right to which they were entitled) other than to note that, in the opinion of the court, it would cause them offence.

The second point is that, based upon our earlier discussion, this comes very close to conferring on onlookers a right not to be offended by the practices of others, at least if those practices are sponsored by legislation. Recognition of a right not to be offended is a very dangerous and, indeed, potentially disastrous step for a court to take. I will return to this point later. But to look at a preliminary objection, we could characterize the purpose of the Lord's Day Act as being to prevent offence to Christians. Blackstone's *Commentaries* indeed suggested that this was one of the purposes for the ancient English legislation, which dated from the time of Henry VI. And certainly, when the Canadian act was passed, there were probably many who felt quite offended by the spectacle of business being open on the Christian Sabbath.

By 1985, these persons were no doubt a very small minority of the Canadian public. However, their sensibilities were set aside by the court in an effort to protect the sensibilities of another probably small minority: those who felt religiously offended by being required to cease work on the holy day of another religion. The cycle quickly becomes bizarre. In fact, it places us very near the end of the scale discussed in the introduction to this chapter in which public display of any organizing belief system is considered a violation of the freedom of conscience and religion of those who do not accept that system. I have already argued that this is a concept we cannot adopt if freedom of conscience and religion is to retain much meaning.

In a later chapter, we will examine the difficulties of religious groups using human rights codes in an effort to protect not their freedom to practise or disseminate their religious beliefs, but their religious sensibilities. Suffice it to say at this point that the protection of religious groups from encounters with others who disagree with them limits rather than expands those vital conversations about beliefs, truth, right, wrong, good, and bad that democratic societies must foster if they are to survive.

The effects of the deficiencies of the *Big M Drug Mart* decision were soon enough apparent in the later jurisprudence and some efforts were made to repair the damage. But before we turn to the decision in *Edwards Books and Art Limited*, which tried to explain and, indeed, had some success in confining the problems of *Big M Drug Mart*, it will be instructive to take a brief look at the Sunday closing cases in the United States.

5. The U.S. "Establishment" Clause and Sunday Closings

By the time *Big M Drug Mart* was decided in Canada, the American Supreme Court had reviewed a number of challenges to their Sunday closing legislation. Of course, the American constitutional situation regarding religion is quite different from Canada's. In the United States, the First Amendment to the Constitution[45] contains two principles related to religion. First, the government is prohibited from the establishment of any religion; second, free exercise of religion is guaranteed to citizens. These clauses have very often been seen in conflict with and as limitations to each other, although a range of interpretive relationships between the two has, over the years, been discussed in the literature.[46]

Sunday closing laws in the United States were, as in Canada, the relic of legislation in England compelling Sunday observance. Also as in Canada, the various states had long since dropped any compulsory religious observance, although the language of some of the statutes still retained references to Christian beliefs. The U.S. Supreme Court, however, had no difficulty in characterizing the purpose of the legislation as having become secular in nature to ensure a common day free from work for citizens. The court upheld the laws' validity and considered that they did not offend freedom of religion, notwithstanding the religious language and the fact that the day of closing mandated was the Christian Sabbath.[47]

In the seminal case of *McGowan v. Maryland*,[48] however, although the majority upheld the Sunday closing laws of the State of Maryland, Justice Douglas dissented. He, like our Supreme Court, refused to recognize a shifting purpose for the legislation and tied it firmly to its historic roots of religious compulsion. Having made that decision, he would have found the legislation a violation of the first part of the First Amendment, an illegal encroachment by the state on the prohibition against the establishment of any religion. As he pointed out, "The 'establishment' clause protects citizens also against any law which selects any religious custom, practice, or ritual, puts the force of government behind it and fines, imprisons or otherwise penalizes a person for not observing it."[49]

It also appeared that he would have held the legislation to be a violation of the "free exercise" part of the amendment because it compelled abstaining from a particular act because of the religious views of others. However, this part of his analysis was inextricably bound up with his conviction that the state, because of the "establishment clause," cannot be permitted to legislate a preference for any religion.[50]

Thus the grounds of Justice Douglas's dissent sound remarkably similar to the basis on which Dickson J. decided *Big M Drug Mart*, despite the differences in the two countries' constitutions. American cases were cited to the Canadian court, but the court was well aware of the differences in the U.S. context, particularly the existence of the "establishment" clause in the U.S. constitution. Dickson J. quite correctly, I suggest, recognized that arguments based upon the "establishment" clause could only "further obfuscate an already difficult area of the law."[51] Further, while not necessarily accepting that the Canadian state could favour one religion over another, he did not reject such a possibility, stating only, "The acceptability of legislation or governmental action which could be characterized as state aid for religion or religious activities will have to be determined on a case by case basis."[52] In light of this, it is unfortunate that Dickson J. did not clarify why the purpose of government preference for the Christian religious observance under the Lord's Day Act was a violation of freedom of religion, other than saying that it was.

6. Preferential Religious Treatment and the Canadian Charter

Before leaving this initial foray of our Supreme Court into the interpretation of fundamental freedoms, we will now return to the issue of Sunday closing laws in Canada and a case that explicates more clearly the situation in which preference for one religion can, indeed, be a violation of religious freedom. In response to calls for a legislated common holiday each week, the Ontario government enacted a Sunday closing law, the Retail Business Holidays Act.[53] Predictably, the Act was attacked as a violation of freedom of conscience and religion.[54]

The purpose of the Act was clearly secular, at least according to its proponents. However, the day selected for the common holiday was Sunday. Several arguments were raised to claim it was a violation of freedom of religion. Not surprisingly, one was that the statute, whatever its motivation, required citizens to refrain from work on a day that was of religious significance to others and thus constituted a coercion to conform to the religious doctrines of others. Speaking for the court, Dickson J. (the same judge who had decided *Big M Drug Mart*) rejected this argument, placing an important clarification on the language of the earlier case by saying:

> Religious freedom ... is not necessarily impaired by legislation which requires conduct consistent with the religious beliefs of another person. One is not being compelled to engage in religious practices merely because a statutory obligation coincides with the dictates of a particular religion. I cannot accept, for example, that a legislative prohibition of criminal conduct such as theft and murder is a state-enforced compulsion to conform to religious practices, merely because some religions enjoin their members not to steal or kill. Reasonable citizens do not perceive the legislation as requiring them to pay homage to religious doctrine.[55]

The court then proceeded to emphasize that the decision in *Big M Drug Mart* was confined to the situation in which the motivation of the statute was purely religious in nature. This was no doubt the best that could be done. It did not, of course, explain why religious motivation, where no infringement on the practice of another's religion arose from that motivation, was itself an infringement. However, it certainly did remove one of the more outrageous interpretations of the *Big M Drug Mart* language.

The principal argument for an infringement of freedom of religion in this later case, styled *Edwards Books and Art*, was an argument that had been discussed in the U.S. case law and that would have been highly applicable – although it was barely adverted to – in *Big M Drug Mart*. If Sunday is chosen as a day of compulsory, uniform closing, then those who would have closed another day for religious reasons, but stayed open Sunday, are now obliged to close two days. The observance of their religion would, in any event, have cost them a day's income; now the observance of their religion will cost them two days' income. Thus the designation of a compulsory holiday imposes a financial burden on the practice of any religion that requires a day taken off work if the sacred day does not coincide with the day selected for compulsory closing.

Another burden is indirectly imposed by limiting the days on which a person who observes Saturday as a holy day can access services. Without a compulsory Sunday-closing law, the Saturday observer would have one weekend day in which to carry out necessary shopping and commercial tasks; with the closing law, if the person is to continue to observe the Saturday Sabbath, his or her access to other businesses is now restricted to weekdays on which he or she may be working.[56]

The U.S. courts concluded that the interference was an indirect burden imposed upon members of some religions but that this interference did not make the legislation invalid where it was a necessary incident to accomplish a valid legislative purpose. The Canadian court, in accordance with the structure of our Charter rights, framed the first question as being whether an indirect burden on religious practice could be struck down under the application of the Charter. The court held that it could, provided the burden was not trivial or insubstantial. In this case, the court held that a Sunday-closing law did impose a burden upon persons observing a holy day other than Sunday and that the burden was sufficiently significant to require justification.

At this point, the court had to turn to the limits to rights and freedoms found in the Charter and discussed briefly in chapter 1 of this book. The question was whether the limitation was "imposed by law and demonstrably justifiable in a free and democratic society." We have already noted that the application of this limitation has been analysed as requiring two steps. To uphold the limit, the court must find that there is a legislative objective that is of sufficient importance to justify overriding a constitutional right. Then, in addition, the court must find that the means taken to enact this limit and accomplish the pressing legislative objective are proportional to their ends. This final requirement has been divided into a three-part test: The limits must be rationally connected to the objective; there must be minimal impairment of the right; and the effects "must not so severely trench on individual or group rights that the legislative objective, albeit important, is nevertheless outweighed by the abridgement of rights."[57]

The court decided, without much difficulty, that the objective of providing a common day of rest from work was an important objective. In applying the second part of the process, the proportionality test, the court gave little discussion to any aspect other than the question of whether the interference with religious freedom was minimal. The legislation in question contained an exemption from the Sunday-closing law for small businesses (defined by number of employees and square footage of operation) who might choose to close on another day of the week. Most of the court's discussion on the issue of minimal interference centred on whether this was a reasonable accommodation for religious groups that were non-Sunday observers and whether other mechanisms, such as the possibility of legislating a right to refuse to work on Sunday or an exemption for those whose religion required them to close on another day, would have had better effects at limiting the interference with religious freedom. Ultimately, the court decided that the exemption for small businesses was a reasonable provision and satisfied the minimal interference test. The legislation was therefore upheld.[58]

It is an interesting point that what should have been the best reason to hold that the legislation had minimal impact on religious freedom was never mentioned. Whatever day of the week is chosen for a compulsory holiday, everyone who is required to observe another day of the week free from work is subjected to a burden in the practice of his or her religion that did not exist, absent the legislation. Thus the burden is minimized by selecting the day of the week that the largest number of people would normally have to observe as free from work. That day might well, at the time of the case, have been Sunday, since a majority of Canadian citizens practising their religion would have been Christians of the mainline, Sunday observing, denominations. Whether that is still the case today, when no mainline Christian denomination requires abstention from work on Sunday any longer, is probably now questionable. In the event, of course, compulsory closing laws (on any day of the week) are, in most places, now relics of the past.

Although, in *Edwards Books and Art Ltd.*, the court put some limitations on the language of *Big M Drug Mart*, this decision, too, contained some troubling aspects. In applying the first stage of the test to determine whether the interference with religious freedom was justified, the court found that the objective of creating a common day free from work was sufficiently pressing to justify a possible overriding of a fundamental freedom. The basis of this decision was, first, a sixteen-year-old report of the Ontario Law Reform Commission[59] that urged it was "absolutely essential that the government now attempt to preserve at least one uniform day each week as a pause day, before it is too late."[60] The second basis for the decision was the court's own judgment that the importance of a legislated common pause day was "self-evident."[61]

While these factors might have at least suggested that the legislative objective in regulating days of work was not trivial, they do not necessarily meet the test of "sufficient importance to warrant overriding a constitutional right." In fact, outside of mentioning that this was the standard to be met, the court made no attempt to indicate whether these factors met the test or, indeed, how one would go about deciding if they met it.[62] Given that freedom of conscience and religion is a fundamental freedom and one, it has been argued, crucial to our democratic system, one would expect from the court a more detailed analysis of what is required before an interest is so significant that an important constitutional freedom should be set aside. The court's own assumptions and a rather dated law reform report hardly seem sufficient. Certainly without any attempt to compare the interest in the common day of rest with the interest of those wishing to practise their religion without the additional economic burden of taking extra days from work, it is difficult to find the court's analysis either sufficient or convincing.

This part of the constitutional test is largely undeveloped. Courts have tended to follow very much the pattern of the Supreme Court in *Edwards Books and Art Ltd.*. Again, if we are to develop a reasoned and helpful approach to freedom of religion and conscience, we may suggest that this lack is serious. In later cases, we will pay some attention to this feature, particularly as it is an obvious way in which a court can use its own values and assumptions to determine a crucial part of a case without providing adequate justification for the result.

We can note that the argument for interference with religious freedom in *Edwards Books and Art Ltd.* would have been just as applicable in

Big M Drug Mart. Had the earlier court determined that the Lord's Day Act violated religious freedom because it imposed a burden on persons required to observe as holy a day of the week other than Sunday, the court in that case would also have had to move on to the question of whether the limitation was justified. What then would have been the "substantial and pressing" reason for the legislation? If the court found that the original, historical reasons for enacting the Lord's Day Act were still relevant, then certainly it could have found that a desire to preserve free from work the Sabbath of the majority of Canadians was not a sufficiently pressing legislative objective to justify imposing a burden on others in the practice of their religion. Had the court taken this route, much confusion in the later jurisprudence might have been avoided and a more rational development of how religious freedom is protected in Canada might have played out.[63]

7. *Big M Drug Mart* in Perspective

Big M Drug Mart now seems a quaint piece of Canadian history. As noted above, Sunday closing laws are largely repealed. Most Christian denominations, even those that continue to insist on Sunday worship, no longer require their members to refrain from work on Sundays. And, as we have just illustrated, while Dickson J. did not adopt the simplest or clearest argument to strike down the legislation, the result was the same as if he had. The Lord's Day Act, a statute that had outlived its usefulness and its relevance to Canadian society, was rendered a dead letter.

So we may ask whether the reasoning in *Big M Drug Mart* was really so problematic after all. But the incoherence of the decision, even as limited and refined by *Edwards Books and Art Ltd.*, revealed a lack of clarity of thought and left vulnerable major difficulties in the theory and practice of protecting religious and conscientious freedom. It blurred the differences between U.S. and Canadian law in this area by failing to justify how, in Canada, even without an "establishment" clause, a preference given to one religion could be, without more, a violation of freedom of religion; it suggested that the Canadian multicultural ideal required a right to be free from offence at one's neighbour's religious practices; and it encouraged the idea that citizens' rights to regulate their own religious practices included the right to resent the performance of neutral acts that may have benefited the practice of another's religion.

We may discern two factors that seem to have been operating on the mind of the court in these early cases, although the judgments do not directly discuss them. The first factor is the question of equality before the law. The argument in *Edwards Books and Art* was characterized as an argument about whether the legislation imposed a burden on the practice of religion of non-Sunday observers. But it could as readily be seen to be about whether the law was justified in treating differently the class of non-Sunday observers from the class of Sunday observers when that difference arose from religious commitment or, in effect, as an issue of equality between religious groups. The judgments in *Big M Drug Mart*, although they do not rest on the same legal analysis, also reveal a deep concern with the preferential treatment of one religion over others.[64]

The second factor that seems to have been at play in the attitude of the court was the fact that the favoured religion was the majority religion. The court in *Big M Drug Mart* had a great deal to say about the unthinking dominance of the majority culture.[65] Yet, this fact ought not to matter in considering whether freedom of conscience and religion has been infringed. The purpose of protecting freedom of conscience and religion is not tied to whether the belief protected is that of the minority or of the majority; members of both groups are entitled to their conscientiously held beliefs. The court never explained why rights of those who hold the majority belief should be subordinated to rights of those who hold minority beliefs.

However, this question of majority/minority status does matter in considering whether a person has been unjustly discriminated against by the law. The right to be treated equally without discrimination on the basis of one's personal characteristics, including but not limited to religion, may be very much affected by the minority status of a particular group. Indeed, equality rights tend often to be regarded as the protection of the minority against the tyranny of the majority.[66] The court in *Big M Drug Mart* noted that freedom of conscience and religion "safeguards religious minorities."[67] It also referred to the "appearance of discrimination" given by the Act.[68]

The interplay between freedom of conscience and religion and the equality rights of minorities is a complex topic. I will return to this question in more detail in the next two chapters when I will offer some thoughts about how the fundamental freedom of conscience and religion fits with our social and legal concerns about equality. At this stage, therefore, I simply want to make the observation that while I have severely criticized the courts' approach to freedom of conscience and religion in the above cases on the basis that their judgments cannot really be justified by the reasons given by the courts, I am leaving to one side (for the moment) the broader issue of whether and to what extent equality rights do or ought to affect or limit freedom of conscience and religion.

As we discuss the next cases, we should keep in mind whether these same questions about the influence of ideas of equality, rather than ideas about freedom of conscience and religion, are driving the agenda of the courts. At the end of that discussion, I will suggest that the underlying presence of equality concerns in these cases does not change substantially their negative impact on the quality of cultural interaction in Canada; nor does it justify the limits to expressions of belief in the public arena that the courts' decisions in the name of religious freedom have imposed.

8. The Consequences of *Big M Drug Mart*

Big M Drug Mart has been cited as authority in hundreds of subsequent cases.[69] As the first decision on the freedom of conscience and religion provision of the Charter, it was bound to be influential. In most of the cases, however, the facts were so significantly different that a direct application of the more problematic aspects of the decision was not an issue; rather, the case was cited for one or more general statements of law it contained.[70] But to illustrate some of the problems *Big M Drug Mart* left in the law, we will now turn to three Ontario cases involving public prayer.

The first of these cases involves prayer in the schools. Prayer in the schools has been, and certainly continues to be, a contentious issue. From a time when every Canadian school opened its day with recitation of the Lord's Prayer and a selection read from the Bible, we have now apparently achieved a social consensus that we do not want our public non-denominational schools to sponsor religious exercises.[71] Recent controversy about the acceptability of even student-led Islamic prayer on Fridays in a public school, particularly where the prayers require segregation of female students from male, has demonstrated this social consensus.[72] Whether, when the prayers are allowed rather than promoted by the school, there is a case for seeing this as a necessary accommodation for students is a topic I will address in the next chapter.

However, nothing in my discussion below is intended to suggest that the consensus that we do not want non-denominational schools to engage as a matter of school policy in religious activities is either unreasonable or undesirable. Indeed, in a later chapter, I will argue that there are special issues involved in expressions of belief in schools and that schools, in particular, should adhere to a policy of neutrality on contested matters of belief. But this case begins our consideration of the underlying attitudes of the courts that impelled them to use the hand of the judiciary, rather than leave the problem to normal democratic processes of change, to exclude religious practice in the schools. And I will suggest that these underlying attitudes subsequently gave birth to a broader approach to public displays of belief which, in turn, has established a climate in which freedom of belief can be too readily characterized as illegitimate and curtailed.

The first of these three cases, *Zylberberg v. Sudbury Board of Education*,[73] was decided by the Ontario Court of Appeal in 1988. The case was a challenge to s. 28(1) of a regulation passed pursuant to s. 50 of the Ontario Education Act[74] which provided for public schools to be opened each day by a recitation of the Lord's Prayer or other suitable prayers and readings from Scripture or other suitable readings. The regulation also contained a broad exemption from this practice in the case of parental objection (or the objection of the pupil, if an adult). The exemption permitted any pupil's being excused from the exercise, in which case the school was required to provide supervision for those excused, or any pupil's remaining in the room, but not participating, provided the pupil was not disruptive.[75]

The lower court held that the regulation did not violate the claimant's freedom of conscience and religion.[76] The regulation did not compel observance of a particular religion because of the existence of the exemption clause. The majority of the Court of Appeal disagreed.[77]

Evidence before the court from psychologists was divided on whether the practice of having to seek an exemption from the religious exercises was harmful to students. Psychologists for the school board suggested that children from minority religions benefited by being exposed to the Canadian reality that cultures and religions differed. Psychologists for the claimants suggested that children seeking an exemption would be subject to peer pressure from the majority. The court decided that the question of harm was irrelevant. The question was whether the parents' and pupils' freedom of conscience and religion was violated, which, as set out in *Big M Drug Mart*, was a question of whether the pupils were coerced into following the religious practices of others.[78]

Based on the judges' own opinions, the court held that the exemption did not remove the element of coercion from the situation. Peer pressure would be sufficient to coerce participation in the religious exercises, despite the possibility of an exemption. Moreover, the very existence of the requirement to seek an exemption was coercive because it required some declaration of religious belief (or unbelief), which requirement was itself a violation of freedom of conscience and religion. To support this last proposition, the court cited an American case[79] in which a requirement to declare dissent from a particular belief was analogized to the requirements of a religious test for office.

Having found that the element of coercion rendered the opening exercises a violation of freedom of conscience and religion, the court relied on *Big M Drug Mart* as well to find that the religious purpose of the legislation was itself contrary to the Charter. Therefore it was not necessary to consider whether the limitation on freedom of conscience and religion was justifiable in a free and democratic society. As *Big M Drug Mart* had held, legislation with a purpose directly contrary to the Charter could not be saved by the application of s. 1 of the Charter.

This decision was riddled with illogical conclusions. The majority again divorced the question of the effects of the legislation from its purpose, leaving itself free to find that even if the effects were benign or positive, the purpose of the regulation was, in isolation, illegal – so illegal, in fact, that no consideration could even be given to whether any limit it placed on freedom of religion might be justifiable. The existence of "coercion" was not established by the evidence, but only by the judges' opinions of what happened in the classroom, together with parents' evidence that they were unwilling to apply for an exemption because they were concerned about differentiating their children from the majority.[80]

The most puzzling aspect of the decision, perhaps, was the court's finding that being required to express dissent from the majority religious practice was in itself a violation of freedom of conscience and religion. The analogy drawn from the American case cited is quite inaccurate. It would certainly be a violation of freedom of conscience and religion to require, as a prerequisite for public office or public service, adherence to a particular religious faith. In this case, all that was required was a general statement of dissent from the religious exercises, not a profession of faith, and that statement was required to seek an exemption from general practice, not as a requirement to access a service or privilege normally available to all. A more accurate analogy to the exclusion provisions in the regulation would be to a conscientious objector seeking exclusion in time of war from active combat. The finding of the court, if we apply this analogy, is like requiring the army in the Second World War to excuse all its soldiers from combat so that the pacifists might avoid declaring their conscientious objection to killing in battle.

The fact is that, led on by *Big M Drug Mart*, the court in *Zylberberg* was equating offence caused by the practice of religious exercises in the classroom with compulsion to adopt another's beliefs. In his dissent, Lacourcière J.A.[81] found that the regulation was not a violation of freedom of conscience and religion. The exclusion clause removed the element of coercion and evidence of peer pressure had not been established. He also found that the purpose of the opening exercises was not simply religious, but had an educational purpose of introducing students to moral principles.[82] Indeed, its purpose could not be to compel religious observance when no pupil was required to participate in the exercises.[83]

But although the regulation under the Education Act was drafted in such a way as to include readings and prayers from any religion (and, indeed, the Toronto School Board had instituted a policy of reading excerpts from many religious traditions and some non-religious ones as well), the Sudbury School Board required schools to open with the Lord's Prayer and readings from the Christian Bible. Lacourcière J.A. found that this practice was discriminatory and violated the non-Christian pupils' rights to equality under s. 15 of the Charter.[84] He would have ordered the Sudbury board to cease this practice and avail itself under the legislation of either non-sectarian prayers and readings or prayers and readings drawn from a variety of traditions.

In making this finding, he noted that this relief was not what the complaining parents wanted. As he pointed out, what they wanted was to remove any and all religion from the public schools. This, Lacourcière J.A. held, was not justifiable in Canada in the absence of a clause prohibiting the establishment of religion. Rather, the Canadian multicultural landscape required equal respect for all religions, not public obliteration of the role religion and culture play in Canada's diverse communities.[85]

In framing the issue as one of equality, rather than as one of freedom of conscience and religion, Lacourcière J.A. was confronting openly an

issue which I have already suggested may underlie the courts' treatment of the freedom in this line of cases. In a later chapter, I will return
to the judgment of Lacourcière J.A. and discuss how equality issues
might be interwoven with freedom of conscience and religion to produce a more coherent picture than the courts have yet drawn.

But, on the basis of the majority's confused reasons, the complainants
in *Zylberberg* were successful in removing any religious practice from
the Ontario public schools. And the court had continued in the tradition of *Big M Drug Mart* of conflating coercion with the visible exercise
by others of their religious practices. Even more, the court had added to
the mix the idea that multicultural society requires the relegation of religion to the private spaces of one's mind. Religious freedom – the right
to declare openly and practise without interference one's belief – had
become the right to remain silent and the right to impose that silence
on others.[86]

School prayer is a touchy subject, as I have noted, and school boards
may be pardoned if they greeted the result in *Zylberberg* with a sigh
of relief. Whatever alternative the school boards had devised would
undoubtedly have caused some parents to complain. Thus, a simple
finding that exclusive use of Christian prayers and readings was discriminatory would not have solved their problem. Indeed, although the
Toronto School Board's practice had apparently not met with any serious objection, efforts of schools to teach a variety of religious traditions
have been objected to, particularly where the material implies equality
among the religions.[87] But whatever the practicalities of a varied religious menu in school may be, one may reasonably think that it should
have been left up to the political process to solve.[88] The decision of the
majority of the Ontario Court of Appeal removed the possibility of any
use of religious material and thus stifled the expression of belief.

The successful effort to purge religious practice from public schools
was soon broadened into a general assault on the display of religious
belief in public settings. In *Freitag v. Penetanguishene,*[89] the Ontario
Court of Appeal tackled a town council whose mayor opened council
meetings by an invitation to all to stand and say the Lord's Prayer. Mr
Freitag found the practice offensive and, after making various unsuccessful political efforts to have it discontinued, sued the town for violation of his freedom of conscience and religion.

In this case, we were not dealing with a child who might conceivably
(although the evidence for this was wholly lacking in *Zylberberg*) be
pressured into giving up his or her own beliefs in the face of majority

practice. Rather, Mr Freitag stated that the practice made him feel uncomfortable. Nor were we dealing, as in *Big M Drug Mart* and in *Zylberberg*, with legislation mandating certain practices. Rather, it was a custom of the mayor of the community and apparently an expression of his own faith. But again, the court, with little evidence before it, concluded that the purpose of the practice was to "impose a Christian moral tone"[90] upon the meeting. Such imposition was a violation of freedom of conscience and religion. The purpose of the mayor's action was illegal.

The divorce of purpose and effect again permitted the court to ignore the fact that Mr Freitag was in no way coerced into a religious practice he did not believe. The evidence showed that he, and a councillor who was also not a Christian, remained seated through the exercise. No suggestion was made, as in *Zylberberg*, that any process of exemption was required or that, as in *Big M Drug Mart*, any penalty was levied. Indeed, the recitation had no practical effect at all on Mr Freitag's practice or non-practice of religion. It simply offended him.

The final decision in this trilogy, which, I suggest, illumines the problems with the whole, was the 2004 decision in *Allen v. The Corporation of the County of Renfrew*.[91] Although only a decision of the Ontario Superior Court, it considered the decisions both in *Zylberberg* and in *Freitag* and attempted to distinguish them. Mr Allen was a humanist. The County of Renfrew opened council meetings with a prayer which had been, for almost a hundred years, the Lord's Prayer, but which, after the Court of Appeal decision in *Freitag*, was revised to be generic in its terms. It called upon "Almighty God," recognized God as the source of blessings and benefits of Canadian society, and asked for wisdom and assistance for councillors in their deliberations. To this, Mr Allen objected.

The court considered that the purpose of the prayer was neither to impose any particular religious tone on the meeting nor to compel religious observance, as contrasted with the situation in *Freitag*.[92] It is difficult to understand the reasoning behind the distinctions the court found. It was true that the prayer was found not to be specifically Christian in nature. It was, however, clearly theistic. Why was it less objectionable to impose a theistic tone on a meeting than to impose a Christian tone? Why also did the recitation of a Christian prayer compel religious observance, but the recitation of a theistic prayer not? The circumstances seem the same.

It is certainly true that more people would likely be happy with the generally theistic prayer, which they might interpret individually as compatible with their own religious beliefs. However, if it is a mere question of numbers, certainly in *Freitag* the majority of citizens and councillors were likely Christian, at least by nominal adherence. If numbers did not matter there, why did they matter here? Again, one suspects that the court was being influenced by the perceived preferential treatment of the Christian faith which, at least as far as cultural heritage goes, was the background of the majority. If so, however, the court is again silent about how or why this factor should limit expressions of belief in the public arena.

The reasoning of the majority judges in *Big M Drug Mart, Zylberberg v. The Sudbury Board of Education,* and *Freitag v. Penetanguishene* made these questions very difficult to answer within the framework of a logical analysis of freedom of conscience and religion. If any government acknowledgment of a particular belief, even if not coupled with any effort to compel others to acknowledge the belief as true, constitutes coercion, then the theistic prayer of Renfrew County seemed as much at fault as the others. And the result of the case, in permitting expression of a theistic belief but not more sectarian expressions, leaves all but the most generic expression of belief out of the public eye. Those forbidden the expression of their belief have had their freedom of religion and conscience limited and our society has been deprived of the opportunity to engage with the religious cultures of others.[93]

I spoke earlier of factors that may not seem to us to constitute coercion, but that still might be candidates for factors that should limit the public expression of belief. An important insight into the cases discussed in this chapter was contributed by Professor Richard Moon,[94] who, in dealing with this line of decisions, suggested that these cases stand for the proposition that "It is wrong to exclude an individual in this way [by publicly displaying religious practices to which this individual does not adhere] because he has the right to be treated equally or with equal respect in the public realm or to be treated as a full member of the political community regardless of his religious beliefs." Professor Moon also acknowledged, however, that the exclusion of religious practice which these cases support then appears to religious adherents as "limits on their ability to live their lives according to their deeply held religious values and beliefs."[95]

I have already suggested difficulty with the idea of a right not to be offended by the practice of others and illustrated that the acknowledgment of such a right leads to very much the same impasse as Professor Moon suggested. Is there merit, however, to the proposition that, in situations related to the political process, there should be a right to feel included? I say "feel included" rather than "be included" because there was nothing in any of the cases discussed that constituted any legal barrier to participation in the political process; rather, the exclusion consisted in the sense that the citizen was reminded of the beliefs of the majority or made to feel uncomfortable in the council chamber or singled out before her peers in school as different.

Certainly, we must acknowledge that it is highly desirable that every citizen feel included in our society. In pursuit of this goal, school boards, town councils, and other government bodies, confronted with the varying belief systems of their constituents, might well find it both prudent (from the perspective of their members' own re-election prospects) and respectful of difference to use generic prayers that would reflect the beliefs of as many as possible, or even to avoid public display of belief in the absence of any personal conviction that such avoidance is contrary to conscience.

But to establish a right to feel such inclusion is a very different matter. For one thing, the kind of inclusion we are speaking of here is subjective, and subjective feelings can vary substantially across the population. Evidence in *Freitag* established that one town councillor who was not Christian felt no exclusion by hearing the Lord's Prayer recited at council meetings. If any single individual's sense of exclusion violates his rights, then adopting a right to feel included, in fact, allows even one person's discomfort to limit the constitutionally guaranteed freedoms of others. This, in turn, limits the range and quality of conversations in our society because it gives the individual ultimate power to shut such conversations down.[96]

Professor Moon's comments also implied that the real concern of the courts in these cases was a concern for equality rights. This again raises the question, which I have for the time being deferred, of how equality rights may interact with freedom of conscience and religion. It also raises problematic issues in the definition and application of legal rights to equality in this context. I have earlier said that recognition by the court of a right to curtail expression of belief requires that the court recognize or create a right in the claimant with which the expression of belief interferes; I also raised the question of whether we would agree that all such rights recognized or created by the courts are facilitative of democratic processes and whether, therefore, the legal process should recognize those rights. This analysis applies to rights the courts classify as "equality" every bit as much as to rights classified as rights

to be free from "coercion." We must ask what the content of the proposed "equality" right is. If that right consists in protecting the citizen's
sense of emotional well-being, how much room is left for the expression of difference and the discussion of issues with which he may not
feel comfortable?

Let us return to the matter of the protected tree. Prior to the legislation being passed, as the property owner, you had a right to cut down
trees on your property. This right is not constitutionally guaranteed and
it is well within our legal tradition to limit the private rights of property
owners to manage their property as they wish. Would your feelings
that the legislation preferred a belief system which you do not share be
grounds for striking down the legislation as a violation of your freedom
of conscience and religion? If so, has the public pool of belief systems
from which we can generate conversations about differing perspectives
and opinions that shape public policy been diminished or enriched? It
seems quite clear that it has been diminished.[97]

This negative effect of this diminishment, I suggest, provides both a
reasonable and a fair response generally to those who are offended by
or feel excluded by beliefs demonstrated by others that differ from their
own and wish therefore to curtail that expression. There appears to be
no reason why government support for the expression of belief, provided such support does not actually coerce the acceptance by others
of those beliefs or impose non-trivial burdens on the practice of others
of their own beliefs, should be struck down by the courts. Even where
some form of government action is involved, we should be cautious
about granting or recognizing rights of claimants on which the right to
curtail expression of belief may be founded. Where the right, whether
characterized as freedom of conscience and religion, equality, or freedom from coercion, in effect reduces the range of interaction between
belief systems, we should view critically the acceptance by the courts of
the legitimacy of that right.

Government processes should be more open to democratic conversations rather than less. Indeed, why should we not conclude that part of
the function of government ought to be to promote the understanding
that difference in belief can be expressed and debated without loss of
inclusion in the political process? *Big M Drug Mart* and the cases that
followed it have produced just the opposite effect and have taken us
down a road of judicially sanctioned silence and resentment. That they
may have done so out of a vague and unreflective concern for minority rights simply compounds the problem. As we shall see, it forestalls

a clear understanding of the role of majority and minority in a complex, pluralistic society while arousing some of Canadians' less attractive qualities.

In the next chapter, I will turn to expression of belief in the private sphere as an element of minority culture. In these cases, the courts have usually had little difficulty giving a generous interpretation to the rights protecting such expression. This broad recognition seems consistent with the courts' views of the Charter as a defence for minorities against majority action that the cases discussed above also reveal. However, their protection of these expressions has generated significant controversy in Canadian culture. Those persons and communities who object to the visible signs of belief in minority cultures also can claim consistency with the courts' willingness in *Big M Drug Mart*, *Zylberberg*, *Freitag*, and *Allen* to suppress expressions of belief that make onlookers uncomfortable and tolerate expressions only when they can be reduced to bland generalities.

In addition, there are some recent signs that the courts are beginning to pay attention to some Canadians' discomfort with minorities in our society who have counter-cultural beliefs and to draw back from the generous protection that has previously been recognized for them. If that is indeed the trend, then Canada may find itself with a much-weakened protection for freedom of conscience and religion and, perhaps, a much-weakened protection for democracy itself.

Chapter Three

Culture Wars: Majority versus Minority Values

1. Introduction

On January 29, 2007, an article in the *Globe and Mail* pushed a small Quebec town into the national spotlight. The headline read: "Rural Quebec town bans stoning women."[1] Hérouxville Town Council had adopted a set of norms to be given to potential immigrants. The norms were to "ensure that people who come here want to live like us," a spokesperson told Montreal's *La Presse* newspaper.[2] The council seemed to believe it was responding to what a later report would call an "accommodation crisis."[3] Immigrants to the province were seen as receiving unfair concessions that allowed them to set aside the cultural values of Quebec society.

It would be comforting to think that the Hérouxville controversy represented an isolated backwater in Canadian society. Yet the *Globe and Mail* article, when posted on line, received 193 comments, of which a large number were sympathetic to the town's concerns. Established to investigate the state of affairs that would produce such a response, the Bouchard/Taylor Commission later heard many "shocking comments"[4] during its public forums and produced a report that, in tone, appeared dedicated to soothing a widespread and extreme distrust of all difference, but especially difference based upon religious belief.

In case we should consider that these kinds of disputes were confined only to Quebec, we can go back a few years and find a public outcry in Ontario on the question of whether Sharia law could be used in private arbitrations of family law matters in Ontario.[5] Provincial arbitration statutes confer on citizens engaged in disputes the right to decide by agreement the basis on which their dispute will be settled and to achieve in the private forum of arbitration a solution that will then be enforced by the courts.[6] This mechanism can certainly be used to settle disputes on religious principles that do not reflect the general law of the land. Despite receiving a report which recommended, with safeguards,[7] the continuation of this approach in family law matters, the Ontario government amended the Ontario Arbitration Act to remove the right of citizens to determine by agreement the principles that would govern a decision about their own family disputes.

More recently, public pressure to prosecute members of a polygamous Mormon community in British Columbia caused charges to be laid under the Criminal Code section which prohibits polygamous or conjugal-like relationships with more than one person at a time.[8] The accused indicated that their defence would be based upon their rights to religious freedom.[9] Public concerns about the practices of the community have largely been about whether the "plural marriage" doctrines of the sect are undermining equality rights of women in the community and supporting forced marriages with under-age girls.[10] After the criminal prosecutions were dismissed on procedural grounds, the government of British Columbia referred the question of the constitutionality of the anti-polygamy provision of the Criminal Code to the B.C. Supreme Court, which, as we will see in more detail later, declared the prohibition constitutional, despite its infringement of religious freedom.[11]

In each of these situations, an individual or group is claiming a right based upon religious belief to an exemption from some rule, practice, or law that is a broadly accepted feature of Canadian life. The cases to which the citizens of Hérouxville (and many of those appearing before the Bouchard/Taylor Commission) objected were generally accommodations granted as a result of a court, tribunal, business, or agency limiting the application of an administrative rule in face of an objection based upon the complainant's beliefs. In most cases, the belief in question was a minority religious faith. In the case of the Ontario Arbitration Act controversy, a segment of Islamic believers had acknowledged the intent to use the then-current legal regime of arbitration to express religious convictions about the family that were at odds with the rules of family law enshrined in Canadian statutes and Canadian opinion about what is fair in the case of marital breakup. In the case of prosecution for polygamy and the subsequent reference to the courts, the defendants and opponents of the law claimed the invalidity of a law originally based upon a Judeo-Christian concept of matrimony that, among other things, limited the constitutionally guaranteed freedom of religion of a variety of religious groups.

Readers may take exception to my grouping these three incidents of controversial claims together. The cases to which the Bouchard/Taylor Commission heard such objections largely dealt with specific situations in which an individual claimed a relatively innocuous exemption from some practice because of his or her faith: a Muslim woman claiming the right to have a female driving examiner assigned for her driving test; a Sikh boy claiming the right to wear a kirpan to school while complying with stringent protections against its use; a community of Hasidic Jews expressing concerns about the dress of home health care workers intervening in the community.[12] Many of these cases can be seen, as the Bouchard/Taylor Commission later justified them, to be applications of equality rights.[13] Later in this chapter, I will discuss several of these cases in detail. The last two examples, however – the application of Sharia law in Ontario and the practice of polygamy – have the potential for undermining equality rights; in particular, equality rights of women.

Yet we should consider carefully the basis of our willingness to differentiate the three examples. In all three cases, the problem is that the guarantee of freedom of conscience and religion is seen as a challenge to the majority values of the culture. In what we may call the "accommodation cases," while the judges and administrative agencies may have considered that the challenge could be fitted within the academic understanding of equality rights, a significant segment of the population disagreed. The public concern was that the accommodations granted treated the majority voice unequally and threatened the dominance of its values.

In the Ontario case, the government, responding to cries of outrage at the potential imposition of a foreign legal system widely believed to discriminate against women, used its legislative powers to foreclose the challenge. In the British Columbia case, dismissal of the charges on technical grounds before the issues were ever tried caused the government to adopt an alternative strategy to attempt to settle the issue.[14] As we will see, when that case was heard before the B.C. Supreme Court on a reference,[15] the court spent over a thousand paragraphs analysing extensive evidence on the origins and purpose of the polygamy ban and on its effects, particularly on women and children.

The underlying question is: When and under what circumstances should the rights to freedom of conscience and religion be limited to protect the value system of the majority? The reader will recall two fundamental principles enunciated in the first two chapters that will be relevant in exploring this question. The first is that efforts to curtail freedom of conscience and religion for the purpose of excluding alternative visions from the democratic debate should be resisted. While limiting these voices may appear to preserve our social structure, this is misleading. The effect is more likely to tend to totalitarianism and the defeat of the very values those limits sought to protect. The second is that when a court recognizes a right on the part of a person or of the state to limit freedom of conscience and religion, the court also recognizes or creates some right with which the exercise of freedom of conscience and religion is seen to interfere. In deciding whether that right should be recognized, we must again exercise caution in protecting the diversity of democratic conversations. That said, there are certainly rights in the state to protect itself – its values; perhaps its very existence. The issue is when the exercise of that protection is self-defeating and when it is, indeed, a desirable step.

With these ideas in mind, we will consider, first, the seemingly simpler "accommodation cases" of the sort with which the Bouchard/Taylor Commission was so concerned. In doing so, I will comment further on the connections to equality rights these cases display and which aspects were so stressed by the Commission's report. We will then look at a decision of the English House of Lords[16] that might be considered a transitional case in which both personal rights and social values were discussed. After that, we may be in a better position to address the fundamental question I have raised above and see if we can elucidate some ideas about where the limits to freedom of conscience and religion should be drawn. We will then consider these ideas in the context of the Ontario dispute over Sharia and the British Columbia reference on polygamy.

2. The "Accommodation" Cases

Under provincial and Federal law, as we have already seen, some protection is extended to the practice of religion (not necessarily to other belief systems) by virtue of provincial and Federal human rights acts that prohibit discrimination in certain kinds of transactions on the basis of personal characteristics (such as race, religion, or sexual orientation). These rules apply to private transactions (between citizens) as well as to acts of government.[17]

Where a transaction governed by these statutes is undertaken by private citizens and the effect of some aspect of the transaction is held to be discriminatory on the basis of a prohibited ground, an exception is often made to accommodate the protected personal characteristics of the individual. For example, a change in work schedule requires everyone to take a turn working on Saturdays. The employee, a devout Orthodox Jew, objects. The employer will be required to grant the employee accommodation in applying the schedule to her unless to do so would result in undue hardship for the employer. "Undue hardship" is a stringent test which requires the employer (in this case) to treat the employee's situation individually and to try to work out a way in which the employee's religious commitments can be met without causing substantial and serious harm to the business.

These cases are, as noted, based upon the principle that our society will not allow discrimination against individuals on the basis of listed characteristics when those individuals are engaged in certain socially important transactions such as having access to employment, being treated fairly as an employee, finding housing, or seeking membership in a trade union. As the Bouchard/Taylor Commission pointed out, the underlying principle is a particular understanding of equality rights.[18] A rule may appear to treat everyone equally (e.g., the work schedule applies to all employees), but because of the personal characteristics of the individual, it impacts her differently. In our example, because of her religion, she alone among the employees is required by the schedule to disobey the precepts of her faith. This is discriminatory, just as much as if the rule was aimed at Orthodox Jews. If the rule stands without amelioration, the effect will be that Orthodox Jews cannot work for this employer. Accommodation is needed to bring about real equality in rights to employment between the complainant and the other employees. Commentators generally refer to this as the application of principles of "substantive equality."

These cases of discrimination are well understood by the courts and the pattern of the decision has been worked out by the Supreme Court of Canada in a number of high-profile cases.[19] The court looks to see if the rule or practice impacts the complainant differently from others because of some personal characteristic listed in the statute. If so, then the respondent must show that the rule was adopted for a proper purpose, in good faith, and that its enforcement is reasonably necessary in this case because the complainant cannot be accommodated without imposing undue hardship on the respondent.[20] We will address these cases directly in later chapters.

Certain cases in which the claim is not prohibited discrimination but a violation of freedom of religion and conscience share many of the characteristics of the discrimination cases. They are situations in which adhering to a general rule, established by law, requires the complainant to violate his or her sincerely held beliefs. In those cases, courts have often followed the pattern of the discrimination cases in allowing some accommodation for the complainant. In many situations, the lines are blurred between what is an issue of discrimination and what is a claim for freedom of conscience or religion. The major difference between these and the discrimination cases (such as our employment example above) is often simply that in private transactions, the Charter does not directly apply. Thus the provincial Human Rights Code, and a claim of prohibited discrimination, is the only available recourse. In some cases under the Charter, both unjust discrimination (based upon s. 15 equality rights) and protection of fundamental freedoms are argued. Thus, it is reasonable that the courts apply similar considerations to cases of both kinds. How far the willingness to recognize these parallels extends, however, is still in dispute. In the next chapter, I will address the limits. Here, we will look at cases of minority religious practices that seem to engage concepts similar to human rights cases.

We will start our review of these decisions with the well-known decision of the Supreme Court of Canada in *Syndicat Northcrest v. Amselem*.[21] As I discuss several of these cases, we will note, first, that the court has provided generous rights to individuals to express their religious commitments where the expression can be seen as an issue of discrimination and the right to be treated, in substance, equally with others. The decisions, however, have not been unanimous and strong minority judgments have often disagreed with the majority position. In addition, recent developments suggest that the Supreme Court will take a different approach where the alleged violation of freedom of conscience and religion is imposed by statute or regulation rather than through private transactions or state action that is merely administrative.

Second, we will see the limits to freedom of religion and conscience that courts have considered legitimate in these cases and will contrast them with the opinions of the dissenting judgments in the cases in an effort to pursue our question about what rights our society wishes (or should wish) to recognize as sufficient to serve as these limits. We will then turn to consider some of the findings of the Bouchard/Taylor Commission report and their relevance to the question of how the clash between values of the minority and majority can be analysed.

3. Limits to Freedom of Religion in *Amselem*

Mr Amselem, along with other Jewish owners in an upscale condominium development, sought to celebrate the Jewish festival of Succot by building on their balconies a succah or shelter in which they were required to take meals and, if reasonably possible, sleep, during the days of the festival. The condominium development had a set of rules governing the use of balconies which Mr Amselem and the other owners had signed when they purchased their units. The rules made clear that balconies were part of the common property of all, although they were given over to the exclusive use of the owner of the unit to which they were joined. However, they were not to be obstructed (as they might be needed to assist exit in the case of emergency), and they were not to be enclosed or built upon. The prohibition against building might be thought ambiguous as one section of the rules seemed to outlaw it completely, while another seemed to allow some changes with the consent of the condominium board.

After unsuccessful efforts to obtain consent of the board to build their succahs, the plaintiffs took legal action, claiming that the guarantee of freedom of religion under the Quebec Charter of Human Rights and Freedoms[22] was abridged by the refusal. Unlike most other provincial statutes addressing human rights,[23] the Quebec Charter contains a guarantee of freedom of conscience and of freedom of religion in terms very similar to those of the Canadian Charter of Rights and Freedoms. However, unlike the Canadian Charter, the Quebec legislation governs private transactions between citizens; it fulfils, in this regard, the role of the human rights codes in other provinces. Like the statutes of the other provinces, the Quebec law also contains a provision prohibiting certain kinds of discrimination. The guaranteed freedoms, like those under the Canadian Charter, have limits, but, as we will see, those limits are couched in rather different terms and invite, potentially, a different analysis from the type conducted under the Canadian constitution.

Mr Amselem and his co-plaintiffs brought their action under the provision guaranteeing religious freedom. Nonetheless, the claim bore many resemblances to a claim of discrimination. Orthodox Jews who believed that they were required to have a personal succah would, in effect, be prevented by the refusal of the condominium board from acquiring property in the building, as they could not do so without sacrificing this conviction. Under the B.C. Human Rights Code,[24] for example, the claim could be viewed as a claim of discrimination in conditions relating to the purchase of property. Had the claim been brought in most other provinces, it would have been made pursuant to the human rights legislation in that province.

Because of the similarity of the Canadian and Quebec Charters in the conferral of freedom of religion, the majority of the court treated the claim in the same way it would have treated a claim under the Canadian constitution, although the Canadian Charter would not have applied to the private contract between the plaintiffs and the defendant condominium organization. Thus, much of what the majority said in its judgment would also apply to how it would have handled a similar case under the Canadian Charter.[25]

The first important point that the court made was to address what the plaintiffs had to prove to engage the protection for religious freedom. At trial,[26] the judge had heard conflicting expert testimony as to the requirement of having a personal succah in which to celebrate the festival. The condominium board had offered the plaintiffs a communal succah to be erected on the condominium grounds. As well, in past years, some of the plaintiffs had spent the festival with friends or relatives and resided in their shelters. One expert witness testified that these practices met the requirements of the faith. However, there was no doubt that the proposed accommodations were not ideal. The communal succah would have required a degree of cohabitation that might not have been acceptable to all; as well, the restrictions on certain days of the festival on using elevators would have meant inconvenience or, for the elderly, hardship in obtaining food. Another expert witness testified that this could undermine or negate the joyous nature of the festival, rendering its celebration inadequate.

The trial judge found persuasive the evidence that a personal succah was not a requirement of the faith, however convenient or desirable the plaintiffs might have found it. Mr Amselem had testified to his belief that to celebrate the festival properly, he required a personal succah. Even so, the trial judge found that there was inadequate connection with the precepts of Orthodox Judaism to engage the protections of freedom of religion. The majority of the Supreme Court of Canada disagreed. In a ruling that will undoubtedly have far-reaching effects, the Supreme Court decided that it was the sincere nature of the individual's belief, provided that belief has a nexus with religion (defined as what is required to connect that person to the divine), that counts. Whether its experts believe that the requirement is part of the recognized faith was not relevant.[27]

Three judges dissented on this point.[28] They would have decided that the plaintiff must establish a sincere belief in a precept of his or her religion. The test of whether there was a particular religious precept in the plaintiff's faith was an objective test and, the dissenting judges stated, necessary in determining whether the plaintiff's belief was protected by freedom of religion guarantees. While the minority judgment was alive to the issue that views within religious communities about the nature of the precepts of their faith may differ and that it was not necessary that the plaintiff adhere to a majority position, the dissenting judges were obviously concerned about opening the door to protection of religious freedom too wide. They would have held that Mr Amselem could not claim the protection of guarantees of freedom of religion for his belief because he could not show that a personal succah was a precept required by Orthodox Judaism.

Having decided that Mr Amselem's belief that he needed a separate succah was sincere and part of his personal faith, the majority also found that the actions of the condominium organization violated his guaranteed freedom of religion. At that point, it was necessary for the court to turn to the limits on religious freedom under the Quebec Charter. As I have already noted, these limits are not the same as those under the Canadian constitution. As well as the guaranteed freedoms,[29] the Quebec Charter contains a guarantee of peaceful enjoyment and free disposition of property,[30] to the extent allowed by law and a guarantee of personal security.[31] As a general limit to the rights and freedoms, section 9.1 states:

> In exercising his fundamental freedoms and rights, a person shall maintain a proper regard for democratic values, public order and the general well-being of the citizens of Quebec.
>
> In this respect, the scope of the freedoms and rights, and limits to their exercise, may be fixed by law.

I have made the point in the last chapter that property rights are not guaranteed under the Canadian Charter (and can therefore be limited by legislation without constitutional challenge), although, of course, they are legally protected rights against the incursions of other persons.

It was primarily the other co-owners' right to peaceful enjoyment of property, granted by the Quebec Charter, to which the majority gave attention as a potential limit to Mr Amselem's freedom of religion.

While acknowledging that the other residents of the development would suffer some infringement of their rights to enjoy their property by reason of the construction of a succah on various balconies, interfering with the aesthetics of the development, the court found this interference, for nine days each year, to be trivial.[32] The concern for safety and security, although not trivial, could be met by constructing the succah such that it did not block access to any emergency exit. The general limit of section 9.1 was not discussed separately from these recognized rights of others. Because they were infringed only to a minimal degree, the majority appeared to have thought that no balancing was needed.

The final point in the majority judgment was a determination of whether the plaintiffs could be said to have waived their rights under the Quebec Charter by agreeing to the rules governing the development. For a variety of reasons, the majority held that they had not waived their rights. The rules were somewhat ambiguous and waiver of a fundamental freedom (if it could be done at all) would have required evidence of a clear intention to waive. The court concluded that this was not established..

The judgment of a minority of the court, as well as taking a more restrictive view of the application of freedom of religion than did the majority, looked closely at the limits to the freedom imposed by section 9.1. They made the point that in applying the Quebec Charter to private transactions, the limit did not have to be one imposed by law; the second clause of the section applied to government restrictions. Rather, the first clause raised the question of determining whether the plaintiffs had exercised their rights in a manner showing "proper regard for democratic values, public order and the general well-being" of others.[33]

At first glance, section 9.1 appears to give the courts carte blanche to apply a general system of "values" to limit the freedoms conferred by the Charter. There are two points that should be noted about this idea. First, as we have already said, if a court limits one person's freedom at the behest of another, the reason for this limitation becomes, if it was not before, a right conferred upon the defendant. Thus, it is impossible to escape the creation or acknowledgment of legal rights once a limitation on a freedom is imposed.

Second, as we look at the minority's judgment, it becomes clear that it is only well-understood legal rights of the defendants that the minority was taking into account in this case. The minority approach would require the identification of rights that might need to be balanced with the right to freedom of religion. It found those rights in the section 6 rights to peaceful enjoyment of property, in a section of the Civil Code permitting property developments of this type to set rules relating to co-ownership, in the rights under the Charter to security of person, and in the contractual limits to which the plaintiffs had agreed. Because Mr Amselem's freedom of religion could not be exercised in the way he insisted upon in harmony with these rights of others, the minority would have held that restraint upon his freedom was justified.

The majority in this case, I suggest, applied a concept very similar to the concept of accommodation in the discrimination cases, the basic structure of which I have outlined above. While they acknowledged at least two rights of the defendants (the property right and the right to security of the person) that might be constrained by the exercise of the plaintiffs' freedom of religion, they found the impairment to be minimal. In other words, it was not that difficult for the defendants to accommodate the freedom of the plaintiff; they were not significantly injured by that adjustment.

The minority, too, fell back upon a concept of reasonable accommodation, although approached from a different perspective. The minority judgment found that the rights of the other co-owners and Mr Amselem's rights were in conflict and that an effort had to be made to find a solution that would allow them all to exercise their rights in harmony with each other. Because the condominium board had proposed a communal succah, the minority agreed with the trial judge and the Court of Appeal that this "accommodation" was a reasonable way of recognizing the rights claimed by both parties.

Of course, we must consider this finding in light of the minority position that Mr Amselem had not established that his right to religious freedom protected his belief that he should have a separate succah. This, indeed, is the key difference in the majority and minority judgments. The finding of the majority that personal beliefs, even if not part of the objectively determined precepts of one's religion, were entitled to the protection of freedom of religion is precisely what put the parties' rights in this case on a collision course. If there is no protection under the Charter for building a personal succah, then all parties' rights can indeed be harmonized because the offer of the condominium board would allow Mr Amselem a succah in which to celebrate the festival. This is all he was entitled to by the guarantee of religious freedom. The other co-owners' rights to enjoyment of property, security of the person, and contractual enforcement were also protected by this solution.

The expansion of the protection of freedom of religion found in the *Amselem* decision appears to be reasonable. The idea that one must prove a recognized tenet of one's faith to claim the protection of religious freedom has the attraction of lessening the range of private opinion to which the protection extends. Mr Amselem would not have come within its scope, as we have seen. However, we must remember that the guarantee of religious freedom also stands beside a guarantee of conscience. Conscience is exercised on a highly individual basis. How could one require some generally accepted principle to which a claimant would have to show adherence before finding that the individual's freedom of conscience was protected? It would be almost a contradiction in terms.[34] And if freedom of conscience can protect individualized beliefs, what justification can we give for differentiating religious freedom by requiring adherence to some general precept?

However, it must be noted that the willingness to protect individual beliefs will make more common conflicts between freedom of religion (and freedom of conscience) and other rights. As the contrast between the majority and minority judgments makes clear, the accommodation of religious freedom is more difficult and will bring into question infringement of others' rights to some degree more frequently if a purely subjective test for the requirements of a belief protected by the Charter guarantee is adopted. When such conflict occurs, the tendency of the court to employ the concepts of accommodation, based upon discrimination cases, will mean that a plaintiff's rights will be protected unless a substantial hardship is created for others. In this sort of case, therefore, we can expect generous latitude to be given by the courts to minority expressions of belief.

4. Further Cases

The familiar pattern of recognizing an interference with religious freedom, defined broadly, and considering the justifiable limits to be found in competing rights was also followed in *Multani v. Commission scholaire Marguerite-Bourgeoys*,[35] a 2006 decision of the Supreme Court of Canada. Again, the question came down to whether freedom of religion could be accommodated without substantial harm to the rights of others. In this case, Gurbaj Singh Multani was a baptized Sikh who, in accordance with the tenets of his faith, believed he was required to wear a metal kirpan (a form of dagger) at all times. The school board had adopted a rule, pursuant to its powers under statute, which prohibited students from carrying any weapons. Mr Multani, after efforts to reach some form of agreement with the school board exempting him from the rule failed, attended a private school at which he was allowed, subject to safeguards, to wear his kirpan. The school board had proposed that Mr Multani would be allowed to wear a kirpan made out of something other than metal or a small token representing the kirpan. Neither of these compromises was acceptable to Mr Multani's beliefs.

In following the earlier decision in *Amselem*, the court held that Mr Multani's freedom of religion was infringed by the application of the rule. He sincerely believed that he was required to wear a metal kirpan, not one made of another substance or a small token. Perhaps the most important aspect of the decision was the court's repudiation of any internal limits on the freedom of conscience and religion. The defendants had argued that the scope of the freedom could be limited by the court without any reference to s. 1. Such a premise could open the door to broad considerations that could create a wide range of poorly identified factors limiting the right. The court determined instead that while the freedom was certainly not absolute, its limits had to be found in an analysis of the provisions of s. 1; that is, the limits had to be imposed by law and justifiable in a free and democratic society.[36] In keeping with *Amselem*, this finding strengthened the scope of freedom of conscience and religion and provided clearer definition of how limits should be identified.

The court found, in conducting the analysis under s. 1, that the school board was legally entitled to make rules for the safety of students under the statute and that safety of students was a pressing concern. However, the rule failed that part of the proportionality test that requires the rule to effect minimal impairment of the claimant's rights. Only reasonable safety could be assured in schools. With reasonable provisions for storing the kirpan in a wooden sheath sewn inside the clothes and for verification that these conditions were kept, Mr Multani's freedom of religion could be accommodated.[37] The court in this case also explicitly linked the test for minimal impairment to the test for accommodation in cases of discrimination and determined that the standards were similar.[38]

Several other cases can also be fitted within the structure of the *Multani* and *Amselem* decisions. In *Grant v. Canada (Attorney General)*,[39] the Federal Court approved the right of Mounties to wear religiously mandated turbans as part of their uniform. In *Gabriel v. Directeur de l'état civil*,[40] a Quebec Superior Court allowed an appeal of Ms Gabriel from the directeur's decision to refuse her application to change her surname to the last name of her husband. Quebec civil law provided that husbands and wives retained their own surnames upon marriage; Ms Gabriel believed that her Christian faith required her to have the surname of her husband.

In these last two cases, in which the complainants were successful, no right of any particular individual was in conflict with the claim of the complainants. And this is the typical difference between what I have called the "accommodation" cases under the freedom of conscience and religion section of the Charter and the discrimination cases under provincial law. Cases under the Charter normally do not pit rights of individuals against each other because the Charter normally does not directly apply to private transactions. Rather, the interests of the public enshrined in statute, regulation, or administrative decision, which were described in *Grant* as the appearance of independence of public officials in religious matters and in *Gabriel* as the promotion of equality between men and women, were held not to justify the violation of religious freedom of the complainant. In all cases, the state could provide an exception to the normal rule without seriously damaging its legitimate legislative objective. The public legal regime could reasonably accommodate the private claim.

In contrast, in *Bruker v Marcovitz*,[41] a private claim to the exercise of religious freedom was denied by the courts. The decision is interesting and merits some analysis. Ms Bruker and Mr Marcovitz had been married and divorced under Canadian law. The parties were Jewish and, as part of their divorce settlement, it had been agreed that the husband would appear before the rabbinical court and provide his former wife with a religious divorce decree or *get*. Without the *get*, Ms Bruker would not be considered by her religion free to remarry, whatever her status under Canadian civil law. Under Jewish law, it was only the husband who could provide the *get*; the wife had no ability to obtain it on her own or to compel her husband to provide it. Despite his agreement at the time of the divorce settlement, Mr Marcovitz persistently, over fifteen years, refused to provide the *get* to his former wife. Ms Bruker eventually sued Mr Marcovitz for damages under the agreement. Mr Marcovitz's defence, among other grounds, was that the Quebec Charter provided him with a guarantee of religious freedom which would be infringed by requiring him to pay damages for failing to perform what was a religious act.

We can see immediately that the structure of this case was not quite the same as that of what I have called the "accommodation" cases, because it dealt with rights of one individual against another. Nevertheless, it still fitted the overall pattern. Mr Marcovitz was asking to be absolved from the performance of a contract because of his religious beliefs. When private citizens enter into a contract, they are effectively making a law for themselves which the courts will enforce. The case illustrated where a court will impose a limit to religious freedom when a claim is made by a member of a minority culture and it raised some further questions about the nature of those limits.

Abella J., speaking for the majority of the Supreme Court of Canada, questioned whether freedom of religion was at issue at all. Mr Marcovitz's testimony suggested that his refusal to provide the *get*, although permitted in his religion, was not motivated by religious principle, but by simple anger at his ex-wife's conduct. Based upon *Amselem*, she questioned whether Mr Marcovitz had a sincere belief that he was required to refuse the *get* for religious reasons.[42] In this, I suggest that she was probably correct and the defence might have failed there.

However, Abella J. proceeded to consider whether, if the requirement to provide damages was indeed a violation of Mr Marcovitz's freedom of religion, the infringement was justified under the Quebec Charter. We have looked at section 9.1 earlier in this chapter. Abella J. turned to the task of balancing required by that section. She found that the agreement between Ms Bruker and Mr Marcovitz was a legally enforceable contract that was consistent with public policy.[43] Balanced against his right to religious freedom was his legally enforceable and voluntarily assumed obligation under the contract to exercise his religious conscience in a particular way. The contractual entitlement certainly can be legitimately characterized as a right conferred upon Ms Bruker; indeed, it was a right freely and voluntarily conferred upon her by Mr Marcovitz and there seems no reason why, therefore, it should not be sufficient to limit his now-asserted claim to untrammelled religious freedom.

The court made this point when Abella J. stated, in looking at the application of section 9.1, that

> ... he freely entered into a valid and binding contractual obligation and now seeks to have it set aside based upon *ex post facto* religious compunctions. In my view, it is this attempt to resile from his binding promise, not the enforcement of the obligation, that offends public order.[44]

As occurs from time to time, the court's evident outrage at Mr Marcovitz's behaviour led Abella J. to go considerably further than this in determining Mr Marcovitz's liability to pay damages. At the commencement of her judgment, she had opined that

> Not all differences are compatible with Canada's fundamental values, and accordingly, not all barriers to their expression are arbitrary. Determining when a right based on difference must yield to a more pressing public interest is a complex, nuanced, fact-specific exercise that defies bright-line application.[45]

Her confidence in performing this task was supported by her further opinion that "Mediating these highly personal claims to religious rights with the wider public interest is a task that has been assigned to the courts by the legislatures across the country."[46] In support of this proposition, Abella J. referred to human rights statutes and to the Charter.

Turning to these precepts later in her judgment, Abella J. weighed in the balance against Mr Marcovitz's claim to freedom of religion also "the right of Canadians to determine for themselves when their marriage has irretrievably broken down"[47] and the "disparate impact on women"[48] that flowed from the requirement of the husband's power to withhold the *get*. As well as the contractual obligation, she referred to "the public interest in protecting equality rights"[49] and "the dignity of Jewish women in their independent ability to divorce and remarry."[50]

The contrast between this case and the cases that we have looked at earlier is instructive. The court added broad statements of public policy and vague references to a "wider public interest" to the relatively simple considerations of identifiable countervailing rights conferred by law and concepts of accommodation. Of course, this was a case under the Quebec Charter and I have already observed how section 9.1 seems to open the door to such analysis. One would think that the Canadian Charter would be less subject to these vague public policy considerations, especially since the court's decision that rights to freedom of conscience and religion are not to be internally limited, but may only be limited by s. 1. And s. 1, as we know, requires those limits to be "imposed by law." In the next chapter, we will examine whether that is indeed the case.

We can consider, however, the declaration that courts have been given a mission to protect not simply the rights of individuals before them but also the values of a society. To the extent that the courts adopt this mission in the absence of a clear legislative limit, freedom of con-science and religion, and indeed all of the fundamental freedoms, are at risk.[51] If the purpose of the fundamental freedoms is to promote demo-cratic debate, then a limit imposed upon them by the legislature may hinder their exercise and arguably be anti-democratic in nature, but it is not an irretrievable repression of the democratic conversations in which our society must engage. For one thing, courts are there to intervene, as they have found themselves able to do in the accommodation cases, when a fundamental freedom is unnecessarily curtailed. But more gen-erally, statutes can be changed by legislative vote and the purpose of the democratic process is to give citizens the opportunity to elect rep-resentatives willing to carry out their wishes. If, however, a limitation is imposed by the courts under the constitution, the opportunity to de-bate the limitation is very slight. And unless the legislature uses the "notwithstanding" clause to override the decision, it is bound by the interpretation of the courts.[52] The democratic process is curtailed and the rights of the citizens to participate in those decisions are thwarted.[53]

I have already called into question the assumption that the Canadian Charter envisages quite such a broad mission for the courts, although we shall see that Abella J. is not alone in her embrace of the temptation. There is no doubt, particularly in determining whether limits imposed by law can be justified in a free and democratic society, that the courts have a role in considering societal values. However, that step comes only after a limit "imposed by law" has been identified. And the set of values to be considered is limited to the values the legislature intended to enshrine in the legislation. The ability of the legislature to impose these selected values is further limited by the criteria of protection of a "free" and "democratic" society as mandated by s. 1 of the Charter. The courts are not simply invited to define what values they believe Cana-dians wish to protect.[54]

In a later chapter, I will make a similar argument about human rights codes. At this stage, it is enough to say that both the Canadian Charter and most human rights codes appear to confer on citizens broad rights that may be limited only by other legal rules, whether statutory, com-mon law, or constitutional, not by vague value commitments that may exist in the minds of the judges but not necessarily in previously rec-ognized legal rights. As well, the opinion of judges may not reflect the settled consensus of a majority of the public. The ability of the courts to create new legal rights that cut down the fundamental freedoms, and the power of the courts to set their judgments beyond the ordinary legislative processes, mean that their ability to limit the society's democratic conversations is an ever-present risk. Broad statements such as those of Abella J. in *Bruker*, made despite the fact that the case could be justified easily on more traditional grounds, should be a cause of concern.

Yet the idea that we protect our society by putting beyond the reach of debate and change the values that we hold dear is a seductive one. We will now turn to the public debate surrounding the accommodation cases in freedom of conscience and religion and to the conclusions of the Bouchard/Taylor Commission.

5. Accommodation under Attack

I opened this chapter with references to the controversy that arose in Quebec related to the accommodation of minorities in their expressions of culture and, particularly, their expressions of religious beliefs. This phenomenon can be seen as part of a rethinking in the press and public opinion, as well as in the scholarly community, of the multiculturalism to which Canadian society has committed itself.[55] The Bouchard/Taylor Commission organized an extensive investigation into Quebecers' complaints. They undertook 13 research projects, organized 31 focus groups, held 59 meetings with experts and representatives of organizations, held 31 days of public hearings at which 800 people participated, received 900 briefs, over six months operated a website that received over 400,000 visits, held 22 evening citizens' forums that were broadcast live, and on each of those evenings heard an average of 40 people. The figures are impressive.

The conclusions of the Report[56] are disappointing. The first tack of the report was to blame media coverage (which they asserted had often inaccurately reported the facts of controversial cases) for much of the angst. Cases that, when reported more fully, seem reasonable were (the Commission concluded) often reported in such as way as to inflame concern. Thus the Commission characterized the concerns as a "crisis in perception," which they attempted to dispel by reviewing some high-profile cases in more detail than was given in the press.[57]

Yet although the major concerns with accommodations appeared to have arisen from accommodations for religious reasons,[58] the Report contained no defence of freedom of religion and conscience as an institution essential to our democratic state. Rather, the Commission justified the accommodations on the basis of equality rights and justified the existence of equality rights on the basis that they encourage, rather than discourage, harmonization with Quebec culture.[59] In the previous sections of this chapter, I have noted how some of the cases in which religious freedom is accommodated bear both structural and substantive connections to cases of equality rights or charges of illegal discrimination under provincial law. I have also suggested that these are the cases in which courts are most comfortable with recognizing rights to religious freedom. Our examination of the *Bruker* case suggested a potential problem where rights to religious freedom may appear to be opposed to equality rights.

Yet freedom of conscience and religion is an independent right granted by both the Quebec and the Canadian Charters. Its sole justification, therefore, cannot simply be that it facilitates equality among citizens, or there would have been no need for a separate section protecting it. In suggesting, however great the similarities between the structure of equality (or illegal discrimination) cases and some cases protecting freedom of conscience and religion, that equality is the only value in play, the Commission has lost an opportunity to increase respect for the democratic framework on which rights such as equality rest. Instead, it appeared to meet the objections of Quebecers that accommodations for minority religions are "unfair" by explaining notions of substantive equality rather than by explaining the need to keep our society open to democratic change.[60] Perhaps this was because it is precisely fears of that possibility of change that fuelled the controversy in the first place.

Of course, a number of the cases reviewed by the Commission were, in fact, cases where the claim was one of illegal discrimination on the basis of religion;[61] some were cases in which the claim was advanced under the Canadian or Quebec Charter[62] as a case of protection for freedom of conscience and religion. The report did not differentiate which was which. Yet although the Commission did not acknowledge it, those presenting in its forums and public hearings recognized that whether or not the case was one of accommodations granted as a result of an illegal discrimination claim or as a result of an alleged violation of religious freedom, protection of freedom of conscience and religion stands on a different theoretical basis from other types of accommodation cases.

Presenters urged the continuation of protection against unjust discrimination on the basis of gender or disability, for example, but were not equally favourable to protection of conscience and religion.[63] Here, I suggest we take a moment to consider the perceived differences between the kinds of accommodation for disability, gender, or ethnicity, for instance, and those for religion and conscience and relate these differences to my argument in chapter 1 that freedom of conscience and religion has a key purpose in the democratic state.

One does not choose one's gender, ethnic history, or physical or mental limitations. To a large degree, in our society, one does choose one's religion. That is not to say that our culture, upbringing, and social milieu do not influence, and to some extent constrain, our religious beliefs. But our society is often described as if it were a society of religious and conscientious nomads. Quebec society, prior to the 1960s, was overwhelmingly Catholic; now, it is overwhelmingly secular. This change occurred, not because of some magic formula, but as a result of numerous, personal decisions to stop practising the Catholic faith. Mainline Protestant churches have suffered great declines in adherents; some evangelical churches have grown. People do change their beliefs. Even if this change is not perhaps always easy or predictable, it is a common phenomenon about which we frequently read.[64]

In protecting freedom of conscience and religion, therefore, whether through the guaranteed fundamental freedom or through provincial human rights legislation that prohibits discrimination, we often believe that we are engaged on a different, and less worthy, project than when protecting those characteristics about which we can do little. We can have sympathy with those, for example, who are born with or acquire a mental illness; those who hold a religion we dislike are seen to have freely acquiesced in or embraced something with which we disagree or which we may even despise. This somewhat simplistic view, however, has to also take account of the fact that religious and conscientious belief is a core source of identity in all societies for at least a large proportion of the population.[65] The fact that one can, and sometimes does, change one's beliefs is in tension with the central importance of our belief systems in our lives and, once we are committed to a belief, the strength with which we hold it and the lengths to which we will go to live by it. Thus, we often occupy an ambivalent and internally contradictory approach to protection of belief systems. If it is our belief system, we recognize its central importance to our personalities and insist it must be protected; if it is a belief system with which we disagree, especially if we disagree passionately, we are inclined to dismiss the strength of the beliefs as something freely chosen that a rational, sensible, or decent person would change.

Yet this very human but fundamentally inconsistent attitude is inimical to a democratic society. Protection of my beliefs but not yours can only be achieved by repression, because the strength of our beliefs will not give way to anything less. But the possibility will remain open that the repressed will take control. To defend against that possibility, more repression is required. If the possibility becomes a reality, the same approach can then be expected to be employed in the furtherance of the new regime, probably with less opportunity for those with opposing beliefs to effect change. It is the dual characteristic of belief, to be both possible to change yet virtually impossible to command, together with the wide range of beliefs in our society[66] that makes these dangerous spirals foreseeable. To avoid our political system becoming a revolving door of repressive actions that ultimately lead to the door being sealed closed, and democracy extinguished, we must instead aim for a method of understanding and protecting diverse beliefs that preserves the possibility of change in our society, but also ensures that when change occurs further change is not stifled.

In other words, protection of freedom of conscience and religion is fundamental to the continuance of a truly democratic state. As I argued in chapter 1, its existence is fundamental to the free exchange of ideas a democracy demands; I would now also suggest that it is essential in a society of plural beliefs as a protection for democracy's very existence. It is not simply a matter of allowing individuals to achieve a high degree of self-realization; nor is it simply about my comfort in seeing my values accepted. It is about the importance of freedom to believe as central for the ability of our society both to live out and to maintain its character as democratic. The Bouchard/Taylor report could have met the objections to religious accommodation and the attitudes from which those objections sprang directly. By attempting to treat religious accommodation as simply another species of equality right, it failed to convince.

To meet the objections before it, the Commission emphasized the ability of the courts and agencies to refuse requests that contravene fundamental values of Quebec society. In this section of the report particularly, although the issue is pervasive throughout, the authors opined that "Adjustment requests that infringe gender equality would have little chance of being granted since equality is a basic value in our society."[67] They cited examples where, even there, exceptions would have to be made, and among the exceptions they listed "A woman requests for religious reasons that a female driving examiner conducts her driving test as she fears reprisals from her spouse if a male examiner is assigned."[68]

This example revealed some further difficulties with the approach of the Commission. Gender equality is certainly a basiç value in Canadian society and most Canadian men and women are not averse to asserting their claims to it. However, should our laws or administrative practices force gender equality upon those who have, at least apparently, voluntarily agreed to forgo it? Why should a deeply religious Muslim woman not be permitted a female driving examiner because she believes it would be offensive to have a male examiner? The suggestion that some concept of commitment to general equality rights rather than to the equality rights of a specific woman in a specific situation should serve to limit freedom of religion appears problematic. Later in this chapter, I will discuss in more detail the question of apparent voluntary relinquishment of rights in the name of religious belief. At this point, however, we should consider carefully the question of whether this hypothetical Muslim woman should be made to have a male driving examiner unless she can bring forward a personal safety concern (a concern, I should note, that is acceptable in liberal Canadian opinion) to justify it.

The report suggested that while a hierarchy of rights should be resisted, the Quebec Charter should adopt an interpretive clause that "The rights and freedoms enunciated in this Charter are equally guaranteed to women and men."[69] This appears, as the commissioners noted, only to restate the current situation. It does not, I suggest, provide the courts a mandate to impose equality rights (or other rights) on anyone who does not wish to avail herself or himself of them; nor does it therefore give the courts a mandate to restrict religious freedom claims on the basis that the society cannot permit an accommodation that restricts rights of the claimant that the claimant has not chosen to enforce.

The wearing of religious symbols was another area that the report failed to analyse adequately. While it rejected the significant limits imposed in France[70] and proposed by some in the Commission's hearings, it did suggest that the principle of state neutrality among religions requires some self-restraint. The authors agreed with the proposition that it would be reasonable to require those who occupy positions which "by their very nature embody the State and its essential neutrality"[71] to forgo the wearing of religious symbols. These positions include judges, Crown prosecutors, and police officers. The authors seemed to ignore the fact that most Christians, who, at least as a precept of their faith, are not required to wear religious symbols, could obey this rule with a clear conscience, and, of course, it would work well for atheists or agnostics. However, it would exclude from these positions such persons as Sikhs whose religion requires certain external signs. This seems indefensible. Where a new understanding of neutrality was required, the report simply recycled the old prejudices and the old fears.

This oversight seems to support the view that the Commission was narrowly focused only on equality rights as interpreted in Canada as being primarily a protection for the minority against the tyranny of the majority and that it failed to consider the unique situation of protection for religion and conscience. The Commission seemed to focus on the removal or concealment of religious symbols belonging to the historical majority, although that majority is now a thing of the past. Their approval of minority religious accommodation suggested that they assumed accommodation would be made for a Sikh appointed to the judiciary, but they recommended the removal of a crucifix from the National Assembly chamber and the eschewing of public prayer at council meetings.[72]

I have earlier suggested that freedom of conscience and religion is not there simply to protect minority rights, although it certainly does accomplish a great deal in this regard. The freedom, however, extends to all. And the difficulties with efforts to meld equality rights and freedom of conscience and religion into one conceptual unit are illustrated, not only by the concerns I have pointed out, but also, perhaps most clearly, by the problems the Commission was formed to address. When protections for freedom of conscience and religion are seen simply as a vehicle to advance equality for certain minority groups and as having no relevance to others' practices, there seems to be an inevitable rise in fear that minority beliefs will affect the rights of the majority. This leads to a distrust of freedom of conscience and religion and to calls for its restriction.

A reading of the decision in *Grant v. Canada*,[73] referred to above, might have assisted the Commission. In that case, a court held that there was no evidence that interacting with a police officer wearing a turban infringed anyone's religious freedom or gave rise to a reasonable apprehension of bias. This seems correct. When a citizen comes before a judge or a police officer, or any other member of the public service, she is entitled to assume that she will be treated fairly before the law without regard to her religious or conscientious commitments. She will know, however, if she thinks about it for a minute, that the official she is confronting likely has personal opinions about matters of belief that may not mirror hers, whether she is a Muslim, a dedicated atheist, a devout Christian, or an indifferent agnostic. The wearing of an external symbol of commitment to a specific belief system does not declare a greater inability to apply the rules fairly than a private commitment of which no evidence is displayed. Perpetuating the idea that it does brings the apparatus of justice into disrepute and leads to unacceptable and unjustifiable discrimination against certain belief systems that require display of religious symbols and against individuals who feel motivated to make such a display as a personal gesture.

There are many other observations that we could make about the Bouchard/Taylor report. Although it adopted a justificatory and apologetic tone, it did make a plea for greater cross-cultural tolerance. It did recognize the particular difficulty of a French minority culture in the sea of Anglo–North American life and the temptations that such minority status produces to preserve the culture by rejecting an open attitude to difference. However, on the whole, the report seems to have been a wasted opportunity.

I will now turn to a British judgment that provides some further insights into the problem of limits to religious freedom based upon majority cultural and ethical commitments.

6. *Begum (by her litigation friend Rahman) v. Governors of Denbigh High School*

This decision of the House of Lords[74] has striking parallels with the decision of our Supreme Court in *Multani*. It falls into the classic pattern of what I have called "accommodation" cases in the exercise of freedom of religion. Ms Begum, a young woman of fourteen when the issue arose, attended Denbigh High School. The school had adopted a uniform which included several variations. One was designed to protect the modesty of Muslim girls and it had been approved by local Muslim authorities as a reasonable choice. After attending the school for two years, Ms Begum returned after the summer break dressed not in the shalwar kimeez permitted by the school, but in the more restrictive jilbab, a long, shapeless dress that extended to the ankles. The school rejected her choice of dress and refused her admittance until she returned dressed in the school uniform.

The school asserted numerous reasons for its policy on prohibiting the jilbab. It had the legal authority to adopt a uniform for the school and its governors had decided that a uniform was desirable as a sign of cohesion among the students. The permitted Muslim dress was broadly acceptable to most Muslims, while the jilbab was thought to represent an extreme Islamic group. Permitting some students to wear it would, it was feared, differentiate those students from others and might lead to pressure on other Muslim girls to adopt the more rigorous dress standard it represented.

It seems arguable, based upon *Multani*, that a Canadian court would have required the school to permit an exception or to adjust its uniform requirements to permit the jilbab. It was accepted by the court that Ms Begum had a sincere belief that her religion required the wearing of the jilbab in public. While the positive reasons for adopting a school uniform are reasonable, they might well not be considered as pressing as the safety concerns of the school board in *Multani*. Still, the differentiating feature of *Begum* is the question of gender equality. Certainly in Western eyes, the adoption of the jilbab indicates a degree of inequality between men and women that would be repugnant.

The majority of the court found that under the European Convention on Human Rights, Ms Begum's freedom of religion had not been violated.[75] This result is based upon a quite different approach in Europe to freedom of religion from what we have adopted in Canadian law. While our Supreme Court has rejected internal limits to the freedom, European courts have seen the matter differently. For example, employees whose workplace demands adherence to a general rule that would put them at a disadvantage because of to their religion have been denied accommodation on the basis that their religious freedom was not infringed; they had the freedom to leave that particular employment.[76] A woman refused a graduation certificate from a university because she would not abandon the Islamic headscarf for her picture, which the university required, was also refused an exception from the rule; she had accepted the secular nature of the university upon enrolment.[77] Both these situations are cases in which Canadian institutions would likely have made routine adjustments to accommodate the complainant.[78]

The majority of the House of Lords similarly found that Ms Begum's religious freedom was not infringed. She had attended the school wearing the uniform and had known when she sought admittance that the school required a uniform. As well, there were other schools available to which she could have gone at which her dress preferences would have been permissible. This last point captures nicely the differences from the Canadian approach. Mr Multani was, at the time the Supreme Court heard his case, attending a private school. That an alternative was available did not affect the court's judgment at all. State restrictions on the ability to display one's religious beliefs under the European Convention are tolerated to a much greater degree than our courts have accepted.

One of the House of Lords' judges, Baroness Hale of Richmond,[79] took a different approach. She would have found that Ms Begum's religious freedom was restricted by the school's approach. Under the European Convention, if religious freedom has been constrained, the court must pass on to determine whether the limit is justifiable. That, in turn, depends upon whether it is necessary in a democratic society for a permissible purpose, "that is, it must be directed to a legitimate purpose and must be proportionate in scope and effect."[80] One can see that the limits under the Canadian Charter have some similarities.

Baroness Hale gave a thoughtful treatment to the compromise that the school had implemented in adopting a uniform code that recognized religious diversity but did not adopt the more extreme dress. She acknowledged that adult women who choose to live with practices our broader society considers discriminatory must have those choices respected. However, against that backdrop, she also painted the commitment to gender equality that British society had made. In her view, there was a question about the legitimate role of the school in supporting a minor child who would have to make decisions about her culture and the degree to which she would accept or distance herself from it. Baroness Hale's view was that the school had adopted a solution that recognized the religion of the young women in their care, but that preserved some space between these young women and the full acceptance of aspects of their religion of which British society would generally disapprove.[81]

Canadian cases have taken a similar approach when dealing with minors who wish to refuse blood transfusions in life-threatening situations for religious reasons.[82] Provincial statutes provide for the state to assume guardianship of minors whose parents refuse to supply them with necessaries, including life-preserving medical care.[83] Under these statutes, children's aid authorities have acted to take guardianship of children and require them to submit to transfusions contrary to their parents' objections and to their own. The limits to religious freedom imposed by the child welfare statutes have, in these cases, been characterized as limits imposed by law and justified in a free and democratic society. The courts in such cases have acknowledged the right of an adult to make the choice to refuse a transfusion, but have considered that we often cannot be assured that the child is making a free and informed choice.[84]

This approach is not without its critics. Some commentators would deny the autonomy of any person who chooses to submit to what those theorists would consider a discriminatory practice or to refuse life-saving treatment for religious reasons.[85] Others question why the autonomy that the law allows to adults should be potentially denied to a mature minor who has clearly expressed his or her choice, particularly when the age of the minor would allow him or her to make other, significant decisions such as consenting to medical treatment or engaging in sexual activity. Questions have been raised about potential gender bias in a case involving a young woman and whether, had the minor been a male, the same considerations would have been present.[86]

Nonetheless, the decision of Baroness Hale and the Canadian blood transfusion cases illustrate a reasonable role for using our society's broadly accepted values to shape the accommodation cases and, perhaps, the general limits on freedom of religion and conscience. In these cases, the limit was one imposed through a properly created legal rule. In *Begum*, the school had the authority under statute to determine the question of school uniforms. In the Canadian blood transfusion cases, the provincial statute enables the state to require medical treatment of a minor despite objections from the child or the parents. These limits were considered justifiable because of concerns about the ability of the child to exercise a free and informed consent to a religious requirement that stood outside the accepted values of the society.

Before we leave this question, we will turn back to *Bruker v. Marcovitz* for a moment and contrast some of the reasoning of Abella J. in that judgment with the principles I have just discussed. The minority judgment in that case found that the contract Mr Marcovitz and Ms Bruker had made by which Mr Marcovitz was required to give his ex-wife the *get* was unenforceable under the Quebec Civil Code. The reasons for this do not need elaboration since they depend upon a distinction between how the civilian law of Quebec and the common law of Canada determine which promises are legally enforceable and which are not. The minority would then have refused to award Ms Bruker damages.[87] However, although Abella J. found the contract to be enforceable, many of her comments (which we looked at earlier in this chapter) suggested that she might still have found infringement of Mr Marcovitz's freedom of religion justified under the Quebec Charter based upon public interest in equality and the dignity of women.

Apart from the contract, Ms Bruker could point to no legal rule compelling her husband to give her a religious divorce. The other factors Abella J. identified to be weighed against Mr Marcovitz's claim that his religious convictions permitted him to refuse the *get* were such matters as the Canadian civil law that allows broad access to divorce and the societal commitment to gender equality under which divorce is equally available at the behest of a man or a woman. However, the only reason that these rights of Canadian women were denied Ms Bruker was her commitment to Orthodox Judaism. Had she not continued to adhere to that faith – under which she had no right to the *get* without her husband's consent – she would have suffered no discrimination and no limit in her rights under Canadian law.[88] The fact that in this regard Orthodox Judaism stands against our accepted societal norms does not provide any reason for limiting Mr Marcovitz's freedom of religion by requiring him, in the absence of a law (including private law arising from his own contract) to the contrary, to provide the *get* or pay damages. If Ms Bruker was unwilling to abide any longer by the tenets of her faith, freedom of religion would have ensured her ability to remarry under Canadian civil law and live as she chose.

Without the contractual obligation, the role of the state should have been only to hold open the door through which Ms Bruker could exit and take up the same legal rights as any other Canadian citizen. This result is consistent with the disposition of the case favoured by the minority. Respect for religious difference under the Charter should have ensured that she had a free choice to do – or not to do – just that. It is this open door to accept or reject the practices of a particular belief system that freedom of religion and conscience requires the state (and the courts) to protect. In protecting that open door, the court may properly employ the values of our society, such as gender equality, on which there is a broad consensus. Limits to protect this open door are essential to a free society; limits which are unconnected to this open door may be, and likely are, undemocratic because they restrict the autonomy of the individual to make free choices as well as cutting down the society's options.

In the cases of minors wishing to accept inevitable death rather than submit to medical treatment that is opposed to their religious belief, we can see illustrated the idea of this open door. Death is certainly a final choice; if there is any doubt about the minor's capacity to make that choice freely and fairly, respect for the minor's freedom of conscience and religion appears to support the state's refusal to allow an irrevocable choice to be made at this time. The case of *Begum*, involving a school uniform, is less compelling. While Baroness Hale justified her decision by suggesting that socialization to the more rigorous practices of some branches of Islam is a choice that a minor ought to be protected from, one can reasonably question whether that choice is sufficiently irrevocable to justify a limit on the exercise of the minor's conscience. Similarly, where the treatment is only modestly to prolong life, there should be more questions about requiring the mature minor to submit to treatment.

We may also reflect on another aspect of the conflation of equality and freedom of religion that appeared in the Bouchard/Taylor report and in the cases discussed in the last chapter. If the legal system is tasked with preserving an open door of entry to and exit from belief systems for all Canadians, then the belief systems of as many, varied groups as possible need to be available and respected as alternative choices. These include the beliefs of the majority.[89] The focus of equality primarily on minority rights leads, I have suggested, to repression of majority culture and resentment by those in the majority of the very diversity it is meant to protect. Equality rights do not serve, in the same way as freedom of conscience and religion, the democratic processes. Their role is to protect particular claimed rights for individuals, not to open the understanding of the society to the possibilities of difference within the state.

7. Of Sharia and Polygyny

In the last chapter and in the earlier sections of this one, I have argued that limits to freedom of religion and conscience imposed by the courts ought to be imposed in very limited circumstances. These exist solely where a legally recognized right of another person or a valid legislative objective is substantially interfered with by the acts of a person claiming the Charter protection for her freedom and where the exercise of the freedom cannot be accommodated reasonably. I have suggested that courts have tended to conflate equality rights with protection of freedom of conscience and religion and that, while this has led to desirable protection of freedom of conscience and religion for minorities, it has also had unfortunate social effects on the broader community. I have also argued that because courts are generators of legal rights as well as protectors of them, they should exercise caution in recognizing what in effect become new rights that curtail expressions of belief. This picture further implies that courts have little business acting upon their own vague ideas of society's values or interfering with individual autonomy on the basis of some "sense" of Canadians' moral commitments.

The underlying purpose of these proposed principles is to keep open the democratic conversations to which all groups in society are entitled to contribute. Yet this is not to say that a society cannot or should not adopt specific decisions on moral matters, even when those exclude the moral or religious beliefs of some. It has been said that the purpose of an open mind is so that, at some point in the future, it can become closed upon some matter. The purpose of open democratic conversations is so that the society can, after the broadest discussion possible, make decisions enshrined in law that embody the beliefs of the majority or, in our political structure, of the majority of their representatives. The courts then play their role to make sure that these decisions are limited to the extent possible in their negative impacts on those who disagree on the basis of conscience and religion. They also have a role to play in keeping the democratic conversations about the decision open; legislation that is passed can also be repealed and a democratic political process must preserve that possibility.

Two recent controversies illustrated a number of interesting points about the role of the legislative process in matters of freedom of conscience and religion. The first, a broad-ranging debate on the use of Sharia law in Ontario to resolve matters of family breakup and inheritance, resulted in legislation modifying the previous rules on private arbitration. The second, a prosecution of two men from the community of Bountiful in British Columbia, where men believe themselves mandated by their religion to marry more than one woman (polygyny),[90] posed a challenge to the validity of a Federal statute that makes polygamy a criminal offence.[91] As has already been noted, this prosecution was ultimately dismissed and the section of the Criminal Code was later referred to the British Columbia Supreme Court for a ruling on its constitutionality. We will look in some detail at these events. In doing so, I will attempt to suggest how the debate on freedom of conscience and religion has been affected by them.

In 2003, a retired lawyer in Ontario announced the formation of the Islamic Institute of Civil Justice.[92] The Institute, incorporated under Ontario law, would provide private arbitration services to those who wished to have their disputes settled in accordance with Sharia law. Public uproar was immediate. Well-known Canadian women such as Margaret Atwood spoke out against the project.[93] Women's groups such as the National Association of Women and the Law (NAWL) and the Legal Education and Action Fund (LEAF) mobilized;[94] some Islamic groups also voiced opposition. An international campaign was mounted to keep Sharia law out of Canada.[95]

What often seemed to be overlooked in the controversy was that the Islamic Institute of Civil Justice was doing nothing new under Canadian law. Provincial arbitration acts commonly allow people to settle a wide variety of their legal disputes through the auspices of a privately appointed arbitrator rather than through the much more expensive and time-consuming litigation processes. Of course, not all disputes can be settled this way; criminal cases, for example, are subject to the jurisdiction of the state exclusively when it comes to imposing a punishment. Yet arbitration has been a well-recognized alternative, along with negotiation and mediation, to the public civil justice system.

A feature of arbitration, along with its speed and lower cost, is also the ability of the parties to decide the basis on which their private dispute will be resolved; nothing requires them to accept the general principles of the law that would, in court, govern their disputes. No one is required under our legal system to enforce her legal entitlements; she is free, if she chooses, to give up some or all of them in return for some other good, such as a cheaper or shorter process, or intangibles that may not have value to anyone else.

What distinguishes arbitration as a means of settling disputes, as opposed to mediation or negotiated settlements, is that once an agreement is made to submit the matter to arbitration, the parties generally must abide by the arbitrator's decision. In both mediation and negotiation, a legally enforceable agreement is not achieved until the parties all agree to the terms of the settlement of the dispute. In arbitration, the parties must live with the arbitrator's decision, which can be registered with the civil courts and enforced through their machinery. Arbitration statutes do give some supervision to the courts over the process, however.[96] Even more, where the subject of the arbitration is a family law matter, there have always been certain limits to the enforceability of the arbitration award. For example, a decision as to custody of children is always subject to the rights of a court to intervene in the best interests of the child.[97]

However, prior to the announcement of the Islamic Institute of Civil Justice, the public seems to have been unaware of the availability of arbitration and the use of the process to avoid the law of general application in favour of religious rules for settling family disputes. With the announcement came public expression of a wide range of concerns for the equality rights of women and children, particularly in the Muslim community, when family disputes were settled, not under the family law of Ontario, but under religious law. Islam – although not Islam exclusively, but also some branches of Judaism and Christianity – holds views on the role of women and the right way to handle family disputes that do not accord with the beliefs of other larger segments of our society. It is the views of these latter groups that have been primarily expressed in family law legislation and it was the clash of these beliefs with those of religious groups that soon generated pressure on the legislature to prohibit religiously based arbitration in family law matters. A review of what happened in this clash of cultures can illumine for us the role of the legislative, as opposed to the judicial, process in curtailing freedom of conscience and religion in the name of majority opinion.

Marion Boyd, a former Ontario attorney-general, was requested by the government to investigate the situation and produce a report. She did so and, in the course of her report, surveyed the state of the law regarding arbitration and the degree to which the courts could intervene in arbitration processes. She also received briefs from a wide variety of organizations both in favour of and opposed to permitting religiously based arbitration of family law disputes. Her conclusion was a recommendation to strengthen protections for those intending to enter arbitration under rules that differ from the societal norm by attempting to ensure that the consent of the parties was genuine and free. She did not recommend prohibiting religiously based arbitrations, but rather improving safeguards such as requiring independent legal advice, full information about the spouses' financial position, training of arbitrators, a mandatory inquiry in each case into the possibility of spousal violence, and publishing of arbitral decisions.[98]

The Ontario government did not accept the recommendations of the Boyd report. Rather, they amended the Arbitration Act[99] to require that in any arbitration of family law matters, the arbitrator must apply the rules of Ontario and Canadian civil statutory law. This continues to permit arbitration for family law disputes as a quicker and cheaper means of resolving the dispute, but it removed the ability of the parties to select their own principles to govern the arbitration. It is not overtly directed towards religiously based arbitrations, but it is clear that its effect will be primarily felt within religious communities whose views of marriage and divorce do not reflect Canadian norms.

Among the briefs received, those opposing the status quo included briefs from LEAF, NAWL, and the Canadian Council of Muslim Women, who argued that permitting religiously based arbitrations was a violation of a number of Charter rights, including women's rights to equality.[100] This is an interesting argument, because, consistent with some of the remarks in the judgment in *Bruker*, discussed above, it supposes that Charter rights would be applied to limit religious freedom in the absence of any individual before the court who wished to assert them; indeed, apply to individuals even if they have refused to exercise them. Arbitration, to be initiated at all, requires the consent of the parties, who must also agree to the application of any rules that are not part of the normal Canadian law. This certainly indicates, at the time the decision to submit to arbitration is made at least, a refusal to exercise one's normal rights under Canadian law.

Ms Boyd disagreed that the existence of religiously based arbitration was a violation of Charter rights, although for reasons that did not precisely meet the issue of whether a court could use general Canadian values to limit Charter rights. She argued, instead, that the Charter does not apply to private arbitrations. Although the Charter requires the government to ensure that the legal system does not violate equality rights, she concluded that "if the participants choose not to follow that law, but instead to make private arrangements, the government is not required to interfere."[101] This conclusion gave effect to the idea of autonomy in making personal choices, including, if one wished to do so, giving up the enforcement of legal rights for religious beliefs.

The debate, from Ms Boyd's perspective, then turned on the issue of whether women who agree to religiously based arbitrations could be said to be acting with free consent. I have already mentioned that it is easy to question the autonomy of people who make choices that we would not make, such as to die rather than accept a blood transfusion, to give up matrimonial rights on divorce that we think fair, or to wear dress that covers them completely in the name of religious modesty. However, groups presenting briefs to Ms Boyd gave numerous examples of their own experiences in which they had been coerced into decisions they did not want. The difficulties of domestic violence were also raised and the problem of knowing whether, in a culture in which women are subordinated to men in the home and may have little realistic alternative, consent has been freely given. For these reasons, Ms Boyd's recommendations, as I have already said, were primarily directed towards protecting autonomy and ensuring free consent.[102]

Government took a different approach. Negative public reaction to what was often billed in the press as the introduction of an oppressive legal code into Canadian law may have generated simply too much political risk for the government to adopt Ms Boyd's nuanced approach. Yet I suggest that there is a justification for the solution the government of Ontario chose that seems compatible with our foregoing discussion about freedom of conscience and religion. I suggested earlier that the freedom of conscience and religion, which must be available to all, must protect the "open door" by which one can make choices based upon religion or conscience, but also, at least within certain limits, unmake them as well. Once an act based upon conscience or religious beliefs takes some step that intersects with the Canadian legal system, this door may close. For example, in *Bruker*, we saw that once Mr Marcovitz had validly contracted to take an action that had a religious character, his choice could not be revoked without paying damages for breach of contract.

We are quite familiar with this concept in a number of situations that are more common to our Western culture than Sharia law. Suppose a woman decides to enter a traditional Roman Catholic religious order of enclosed nuns. While you might consider her choice irrational, it is unlikely that you would consider that she was acting so far out of the norm that she was not an independent agent. Although the rule of her order would significantly limit her otherwise-available legal rights, such as the rights to marry or own property, it would be within her power to give those rights up. However, it would also be within her power to decide, at a later date, to leave the convent, with or without the approval of her superiors. Canadian law would not enforce her choice beyond her continuing consent. Indeed, if by contract she had given any property to the order, it is possible, although by no means certain, that a court would set that contract aside, should she change her mind.[103] This ability to change one's mind is no doubt partly what gives credence to the notion in our society that a woman making this choice is acting with free consent; she too knows that her choice is not irrevocable and that there are other options.

Despite the Ontario amendments to the Arbitration Act, parties can still agree, upon marriage breakup, to apply whatever principles they wish to an agreement governing their marital dissolution, even if those principles are based upon religious law. Although some submissions to Ms Boyd had suggested that the courts ought to be required to decide all matters connected with separation or divorce,[104] this is clearly impractical and would be a great hardship on couples who want to agree without the cost, delay, and acrimony of court proceedings, even if they might do better before the court. Foreclosing this option constitutes a serious incursion into free choice that it would be hard to justify. As well, family law legislation brings such agreements under the court's jurisdiction if circumstances change.[105] But, making this kind of agreement does, in many cases, close the open door that allows us to rethink our choices.

But agreements to arbitrate close the door more quickly. As I have already discussed, once a valid agreement to arbitrate has been made, parties will be legally required, except in unusual cases, to live with the process and with the result. In fact, the award of the arbitrator effectively becomes a judgment of the court. Refusing to permit arbitration of family law disputes gives the parties more control over the solution and more time before committing themselves to an agreement that will likely be legally enforceable. While it is arguable that the Ontario government's response indicates a lack of respect for the autonomy of, primarily, Muslim women, it is also arguable that, seen in this light, the solution was reasonable and preserves a significant degree of religious freedom.

However, to the extent that it removes a right otherwise available and affects, to a disproportionate degree, persons of religious faith, the provision could be challenged under the Charter guarantee of freedom of conscience and religion. If such a challenge occurred, the courts would approach the question much differently than if they were asked to adopt the arguments of groups like LEAF and NAWL that the Canadian commitment to equality as evidenced by s. 15 of the Charter should have limited the availability of the right to arbitration on religious grounds. I have already argued that compelling autonomous adults to accept equality in light of their religious conscience is an indefensible violation of religious freedom.

Yet, while the amendments to the Arbitration Act do limit religious freedom, the court can employ concepts of broadly held Canadian values in determining whether the limit imposed by the legislature is justifiable in a free and democratic society. Here the court would review the government's decision that equality of women is best protected by preventing arbitrations on religious principles and determine whether protecting that equality could justify the legislation. The courts could also take note that the legislation preserved religious choice in keeping open to a greater degree the ability to change one's mind, while still allowing (if they choose) parties ultimately to arrange their affairs in accordance with their religion through agreement.

The polygamy question has received now a preliminary treatment in the court in *Reference Re: Section 293 of the Criminal Code of Canada*,[106] which asked the British Columbia Supreme Court to give an opinion on the constitutionality of the criminal prohibition. The court had no difficulty in finding that the prohibition did limit the religious freedom of some groups of citizens – in particular, fundamentalist Mormons and Muslims. However, it took a different approach to the problem from that I have suggested above.

Of course, the first problem that the court had to confront was the question of the historical origins of the prohibition against polygamy. If the prohibition was originally enacted to enshrine in the law a Judeo-Christian concept of marriage and coerce others to abide by that conception, then, as we saw in *Big M Drug Mart* in the last chapter, it would seem that those origins would be constitutionally fatal. However, Bauman C.J.B.C.S.C. accepted extensive evidence before him that the prohibition did not originate with Judeo-Christian beliefs, but rather with much earlier Greco-Roman culture. Jews and then Christians adopted what was the moral and legal position of the wider society. Further, although the Canadian Criminal Code provision was apparently enacted in response to Mormon immigration, the court accepted that there was no religious motivation for it; rather, the legislation was in response to a long-standing norm of monogamy and the harms long associated with polygamous unions.[107] This enabled the court to avoid an immediate conclusion that the prohibition was unconstitutional and to proceed to an analysis under s. 1.

In conducting this analysis, Bauman C.J.B.C.S.C. reviewed in hundreds of paragraphs evidence that polygamy was historically prohibited by law, not because of religious beliefs, but because of harms it created against children, women, and men. He extensively reviewed the approaches to polygamy taken in other countries as well as in Canada and its relationship to Islam, Mormonism, Aboriginal practices, and Wicca. Then, beginning at paragraph 485 and continuing to paragraph 793, he discussed the evidence indicating that polygamy did indeed create a range of harms extending from higher rates of teen births, lower educational achievements, exclusion of young men from the community, and the isolation of women. Some evidence was presented to the court by experts suggesting that the actual life experience of women and children in polygamous communities in North America was less negative than assumed by state authorities. In light of the mass of received evidence, the court ultimately dismissed these views as "sincere, but frankly somewhat naïve."[108]

At the end of this lengthy review, the court concluded that the restriction of religious freedom was justified. The *Oakes* test was met because "there is a reasoned apprehension that polygamy is inevitably associated with sundry harms and that these harms are not simply isolated to criminal adherents ... but inhere in the institution itself."[109] And further, "there is no such thing as so-called 'good polygamy.'"[110] Based on extensive expert testimony about both historical and modern polygamy, review of the research literature, and testimony of those living or having lived in polygamous communities, the court concluded that "the salutary effects [of the legislation] ... far outweigh the deleterious."[111]

Extensive reliance on social science evidence in the case to show the anticipated harms of polygamy or, more specifically, polygyny (marriage between one man and multiple women) can be criticized. It is well beyond the scope of this book to review the evidence in detail and it is certainly beyond the expertise of the author to critique it in depth. However, even a brief review reveals considerable weakness in the evidence presented. Much of it was of a highly speculative nature. The harms associated with polygyny were largely extrapolated from studies of areas in which it is practised extensively. These areas also have other problems such as poverty, war, traditions of women's subservience, and many other issues that could certainly distinguish them from Canada. The conclusion that polygamy was the root of the evils identified was based more on unproven theories than on fact. The further evidence as to a negative effect in Canada was largely based upon an assumption of a non-trivial increase in polygyny here if the limit in the Criminal Code were struck down. Experts admitted that their assumptions were speculative but that the practice could spread based upon rapidity of social change and human tendencies to serial monogamy.[112] There appears to be no factual evidence to support this conclusion.

In addition, a number of the perceived harms of polygyny were extrapolated from the harms of serial monogamy. One expert, for example, dealt with the great increase in risk to children where a mother has remarried and a stepfather is in the house. As well, patterns of male jealousy and violence in serial monogamy situations were discussed as illustrating that serial monogamy produced problems as well. A second expert, however, speculated that these harms would be magnified in polygynous relationships.[113]

The approach of Bauman C.J.B.C.S.C. illustrates some interesting points about how the court viewed limits to religious freedom. First, we should note that the problem presented here is, unlike many of those we discussed earlier in this chapter, not a problem that can be solved by allowing some form of accommodation for religious belief. Because the section in question is a part of the criminal law of Canada, it is not possible for certain persons to be exempted from it while it continues to apply to others. As we noted in *Big M Drug Mart*, a provision of criminal law must either be valid for all or invalid for all; basic concepts of justice require that exceptions cannot be made for parts of the population when the consequences are to deprive a person of liberty or impose a fine and criminal record. Thus, the stakes are higher in such a case in that upholding the prohibition means that no one, not even those with religious beliefs that support polygamy, can maintain the practice without being in violation of the law.

While I have suggested elsewhere that the legislature is within its rights to legislate in accordance with majority moral or ethical standards, the case for supporting such legislation is stronger where limited, principled exceptions can be made for legitimate religious practice. This can enable dominance of the majority view and support for it, but protect the rights of minorities. When we are discussing criminalization of a practice, this ability to protect the beliefs of both majority and minority is absent. For this reason, one would think that government should be held to a higher standard of showing that their legislation is needed, in its strict form, to support our liberal, democratic society.

Professor Berger has suggested that criminalizing polygamy "exposes both the stubbornly moral inflection of our criminal law and certain limits of our tolerance for deep religious difference."[114] The judgment of the court appears to try to avoid this conclusion by its lengthy analysis of the social science literature and of expert testimony. Yet, I would suggest, in the end, the decision was based primarily on moral grounds and those grounds gave very little weight to the effect on minority religious belief. The social science evidence seems to have been, at best, largely theoretical opinion which was speculative and based upon conditions in radically different societies from that of Canada. A great many of the harms identified, especially to children, could also be attributed to our well-accepted practice of divorce and remarriage or to the many subcultures in North America in which fathers are generally absent and mothers have no stable relationships with sexual partners. We do not make laws to criminalize unmarried cohabitation, eliminate divorce, or stigmatize unwed parents, despite the social difficulties, arguably not unlike those potentially identified with polygyny, these practices cause. We would consider it a violation of the personal autonomy of adults to do so.

The personal autonomy of women in polygynous relationships was treated dismissively by the court. Chief Justice Bauman acknowledged evidence before him of women in the Bountiful community who expressed their happiness with their living arrangements. And he seems to have ignored the reality that the legal system already preserves an exit for women (or men) who, having entered a plural marriage, wish later to depart. Much of the criticism about the Bountiful communities has come from ex-members.[115] Canadian law will not require anyone to continue in a marriage once his or her consent to that continuation has been withdrawn. These exit strategies were not available to a couple who agreed to a religiously based arbitration of their marital breakup. Furthermore, laws already exist to prohibit under-age marriages and forced cohabitation. Child abuse and child sexual exploitation are also criminalized. Yet the Chief Justice gave short consideration to the arguments before him that the criminal prohibition was unnecessarily broad,[116] relying on the (as noted) apparently inadequate evidence that decriminalization would subject Canadian society as a whole (not simply those who choose to enter polygamous marriages) to a range of serious harms.

In fact, the only evidence as to the result of polygamy in Canada was evidence about the conditions prevailing in the Fundamentalist Mormon community of Bountiful. There were certainly allegations and testimony (contradicted by other testimony) that women and children in Bountiful are subjected to coercive pressure and that forced, under-age marriages have occurred. But the court ignored arguments that measures less than criminalization of polygamy could be employed to curtail abuse. As has been the case with concerns about forced marriage in other countries, establishment of social support systems, including a "help line" and support for those who want to flee from pressure exerted upon them, have proved quite successful.[117] There is no reason to think that these tactics would not also prove successful here.

The effect which this judgment will have on the law is debatable. Because it was a reference, the opinion is not technically binding in future decisions. In addition, the court making the decision was the British Columbia Supreme Court. Thus, it has limited effect. Even in British Columbia, there is an appeal court that could disagree with the opinion and later overrule it;[118] further, the Supreme Court of Canada is the only court whose rulings have national effect. No doubt the decision will be persuasive, at least in British Columbia. However, if prosecutions are brought under the section, a court will still have to consider the constitutionality of the prohibition. There is no guarantee that convictions under the section, if appealed to the Supreme Court of Canada, will be upheld. The higher court could still choose to take its own approach. It seems probable that the question of whether the government can criminalize polygamy, thus limiting the religious freedom of certain minority groups, will not be finally resolved for many years to come.

8. Conclusions

I have argued that courts' willingness to grant accommodation to minority religious faiths largely flows from the tendency of the courts to see these cases as another species of equality rights. As long as that is the situation, courts are comfortable with the legal principles and with a generous protection of minority practices. Where doubts are raised about whether freedom of conscience and religion is compatible with equality, courts, the Bouchard/Taylor inquiry, and the public have seemed much less certain about the preservation of the fundamental freedom. I have suggested that this arises in part from a failure to acknowledge the obvious difference between cases protecting religious and conscientious freedom and cases protecting differences that are less obviously chosen. This in turn has led to institutional failure to explain and defend the purpose of the fundamental freedoms and to hostility towards the exercise of this freedom and towards courts and agencies that accommodate differences in conscience and religion.

I have also argued for a significant difference between the role of the courts in limiting the exercise of religion and conscience and the role of the legislature. I have accepted, within limits, the legislature's rights to impose moral choices upon the populace. In discussing the polygamy reference, I have suggested that more caution should be exercised in criminalizing a practice than in simply legislating limits on the practice, because under criminal law no provision can be made for minority rights. We will further explore the extent of protection which minorities can expect in these situations in the next chapter.

In contrast, I have argued that when a court is not engaged in the process of supervising government action and minimizing its impact on freedom of conscience and religion, it should not employ its own conceptions of Canadian values to impose limits to this freedom. Courts have not been entirely consistent, in the cases we have examined, in recognizing this difference. While they have stated in some cases that freedom of conscience and religion can only be limited by s. 1 of the Charter and not by limitations created independently of legislative action, they have also given some indications that they see themselves as balancing Charter values against Charter rights in less well-defined ways.

This role has been urged upon courts by arguments from equality-seeking groups, as we noted in reviewing the arguments of LEAF and NAWL in Ontario regarding family law arbitrations.[119] Calling on the court to protect Canadian values without legislative action undermines citizens' rights to autonomy. It imposes on others what the judge assumes to be the majority will without even the legitimizing assent of our democratically elected representatives. It creates, in effect, a new right in the majority to control the choices of the minority in matters of their belief. Although the court may see itself as the guardian of Canadian values in such a case, its actions run counter to the preservation of robust democratic debate and to respect for individual choices. In the next chapter, we will see more clearly how confusion about this distinction has shaped the jurisprudence dealing with freedom of conscience and religion in the political sphere.

In introducing the role of the legislature, I have moved our discussion into the realm of political choice. What then is the role of belief systems in political debate and political action? Election campaigns, political argument, and media coverage all seem to suggest that Canadians are nervous about the mix of religion and politics. Yet if belief commitments mean anything, they must influence one's political life. To require belief systems to be kept out of politics seems, first, to be impossible[120] and, second, to commit our nation's governance to the care of hypocrites who will have no difficulty acting contrary to their fundamental beliefs. Excluding belief or certain kinds of belief from political action clearly restricts citizens' rights to freedom of conscience and religion.

Yet courts, I suggest, like the general public, have not thought through the implications of the intersection of belief and political life that even a weak commitment to freedom of conscience and religion makes inevitable. Judges are much less comfortable with allowing freedom of conscience and religion to impinge on the public sphere than they are in granting personal and limited exemptions from administrative rules. When belief systems try to shape those general rules, the judiciary is much less likely to tolerate difference. In the next chapter, we will turn to these intriguing issues.

Chapter Four

When Religion and Politics Intertwine

1. Introduction

Certain ideas about equality are popular with Canadians. We have seen this illustrated, in the last chapter, in the Bouchard/Taylor report,[1] which found that the gravest concern with accommodation for religious belief was with its impact on gender equality. A survey of Canadians published by *Maclean's* magazine in 2009[2] found very much the same things. Yet while many average Canadians view religious accommodation as a threat to equality and evidence of preferential treatment of minority groups, such accommodation is justified by the courts, tribunals, and theorists as an application of equality rights.[3]

I have suggested that this difference between the country's citizens and its judges and bureaucrats arises, in part, because the project in which we are engaged when protecting difference based upon belief is in fact different from the project in which we are engaged when protecting difference based upon less mutable grounds. This is not to say that it is less important; rather that its justification must be based upon different grounds. But courts have been unwilling to acknowledge this fact or to seek the reasons for protecting differing belief systems in our fundamental political structure rather than in notions of equality alone. As a justification for freedom of religion, "equality" alone is unconvincing, particularly when the freedom threatens majority values. This has meant that the judicial treatment of religious difference has often encouraged attitudes of resentment which are then expressed by the majority against minority groups.[4]

This disagreement between attitudes of the citizenry and of the courts reveals a crucial problem with equality rights. It is never enough to speak about them generally. We must also supply answers to these questions: Equality for whom, equality with whom, equality for what, and equality how? The answers to these questions may be hotly debated, usually on the basis of our fundamental belief systems. Thus a pronouncement from the judiciary, or in private argument, that "it's a matter of equality" settles the debate about what should be done in a particular case only for those who are already convinced of the justice of the outcome. Belief cannot be separated from decisions about equality, however we might wish it. These are political questions and they will not be solved without engaging the fundamental beliefs of a majority of citizens.

John Rawls, recognizing the conflicts in belief systems and the difficulties these may pose to political decision making, attempted to separate belief systems (comprehensive doctrines) from the political decision by interposing a family of acceptable fundamental principles to which public debate must confine itself in the political process. These principles, he argued, can be accepted by all "reasonable comprehensive doctrines."[5] His efforts have been criticized on a variety of bases, including the criticism that people cannot honestly exclude their belief structures from their political arguments.[6] His derivation of the fundamental principles, in addition, suffered from numerous flaws.

His mechanism of the "original position" in which actors choose these fundamental principles without knowing anything about their own social position or beliefs (behind a "veil of ignorance") forces particular choices that fit with a politically liberal agenda.[7] In his hypothetical system, one would be insane to choose anything other than a particular view of equality as a fundamental value. Yet that choice is made, not because the actor thinks it right or good or moral, but because, as the game is structured, it is the best compromise to protect his own interests against potentially devastating loss. For persons who hold a set of beliefs upon which their moral, ethical, and political choices are made (in other words, all human beings), principles derived in such a fashion cannot be convincing, unless, that is, the set of beliefs which they hold would in fact produce those principles without the intervention of any "veil of ignorance."[8] In that case, the system can be conveniently used to rationalize the a priori choice.[9]

Other theorists have provided more transactional descriptions of how political decisions are made, and how our society can retain stability, even given the conflicting nature of our beliefs.[10] In general, observation suggests that politics is more about ends than about reasons.

Reasons may differ, but a consensus may develop on the outcome, in which case the political act is relatively obvious. Reasons given by differing interest groups will appeal to some or many, based upon their fit with the hearers' own beliefs. Ultimately, in many cases, some agreement on the action to be taken will emerge. But this is less because of some structured debate of public reason than because of a significant overlap in opinion as to the result.

So, for example, you may favour an increase in social welfare payments because Catholic social teaching has concern for the poor; I favour the increase as well, but because crime is high and I believe that a better social welfare system will reduce property crimes; our friend, George, is a communist and believes that higher welfare rates are a step towards income redistribution. We all agree on the result. Similarly, opposition groups will be divided in their reasoning as well, but united on a particular result.

Belief based in conscience or religion is an inherent component of political choice and cannot, in our modern Canadian system, be removed from it. Of course, certain beliefs could be excluded from political participation. The most obvious of these would pertain to the self-preservation of the state. A belief that I should overthrow our government by force is a likely candidate for exclusion from the political arena and, indeed, our Criminal Code does just that.[11] Short of that, however, we need to be careful, if we wish to preserve our democratic system, just how quickly we are prepared to exclude unpopular beliefs. Protections for freedom of conscience and religion under the Charter, along with freedom of expression, are designed to provide just that care.

It may be useful at this point to add again to the argument that has been made earlier about the importance of freedom of conscience and religion to democracy. Many of Canadians' cherished rights are quite compatible with a totalitarian state. Equality, in particular, is easier to achieve if freedom is limited. For example, suppose parliament enacted legislation that no person could earn more or less than $40,000 per year. Certainly, this legislation treats everyone equally. It would probably contribute as well to substantive economic equality in the country. Yet whatever you think of the idea of absolute economic equality, it is clear that this legislation would drastically reduce personal freedom and would require substantial state intervention and surveillance of elements of life that today we consider private.

Protection of our right to speak about, act upon, and argue for our beliefs, whether arising from religious faith or not, is, I have suggested, necessary to allow us to debate and ultimately to define the kind of society, including the kind of equality, we want. A right to express the belief that human dignity[12] is best protected by a considerable degree of economic freedom, even if this produces a measure of financial inequality (although our belief systems may well limit the degree of financial inequality we would agree to), allows us to challenge any government that would impose this hypothetical legislation upon the country. It would further allow and legitimate, if such legislation were enacted, an ongoing debate about whether it was effective, just, or desirable in accordance with the principles of a wide variety of belief systems and whether the law should therefore be changed. No political choice is ever final in a democracy.

In this chapter, we will first examine decisions of the courts in which groups with opposing moral beliefs are struggling to have their viewpoints enshrined in legal policy through litigation. We will see that, unlike the accommodation cases in the last chapter, the courts are much less clear on how to resolve these issues. I will argue that an important democratic role for our courts is to recognize the need to protect some public spaces as neutral in the face of moral conflict and to hold an even hand between opposing beliefs until some consensus in social policy is reached. Without an understanding of this role for both the public and the judiciary, courts' decisions are all too easily characterized simply as the expression of the judges' own moral commitments.

We will then turn to look at the situation in which sufficient consensus exists that the government through legislation has made a policy choice that adversely affects certain religious groups. We have already encountered several such cases, but in this chapter we will give a more detailed analysis of the court's role in those circumstances. Particularly, we will look at a decision which seems at this time to signal a change in the legal understanding of how much care governments must take to tailor their legislation and regulations to respect citizens' rights.

2. Courts and "Incommensurate" Value Systems

The first case we will look at illustrates a number of crucial problems in the field. Mr Chamberlain was a kindergarten teacher in the Surrey School District. He requested approval from the school board for three books in which children were depicted living with same-sex parents. The board was asked to approve the books under statutory authority to approve supplementary materials for use in the schools. The approval would not have meant that the books were required reading, but it did mean that they were "recommended" for use and could be used in the classroom. Without approval as supplementary materials, they could be available in the library, but not used in class. Mr Chamberlain was gay and was an activist with Gay and Lesbian Educators. A significant number of parents from a variety of religious backgrounds objected to the board's approving the books. Tempers flared and school board meetings became highly contentious. The board, in the face of the parental disapproval, refused to approve the books as supplementary materials for the K–1 classes in the Surrey School District, although it was willing to have them listed as "library resources" available for students to read. Mr Chamberlain joined with other activists to challenge the board's decision in the courts.[13]

In cases like this one, we are not dealing simply with two groups who have, after a period of discussion and thought, come to opposite conclusions about a matter. Rather, each side, acting on its own beliefs, has taken those beliefs to their logical conclusions. But the underlying beliefs, which are often unarticulated, are fundamentally opposed. They are what scholars studying moral conflict have termed "incommensurate."[14] The reasoning, the language, and the conclusions drawn by the two sides are significantly different. Indeed, those of one side may be almost incomprehensible to those of the other.[15] To the religious parents who opposed approval of the books, there was no inconsistency in condemning homosexual relations as immoral and treating persons with different sexual orientation respectfully and without discrimination. To activist segments of the gay community, disapproval of homosexual relations was in itself discriminatory; the action cannot be separated from discrimination against the person. This alone is a conflict in fundamental understandings of personhood, sexuality, and the nature of the world.

It has been noted that where such incommensurate moral systems clash, civility is often an early casualty.[16] The nature of the conflict leads to communication between the groups that is inspired more by frustration than by reason and results more frequently in anger than in resolution. Compromise becomes not only impossible but unthinkable and the issues themselves frequently cannot be discussed in any way that can contribute to a solution. This may be illustrated by the comments in the Court of Appeal[17] that the opponents appeared to have very little at stake in the case. No one was suggesting that the books had to be used in the classroom, nor was anyone arguing that they should be banned.

Courts are ill equipped to deal with this kind of conflict. First, every judge who hears the case will bring to it her or his own belief system, which may favour one or the other of the positions. Despite genuine efforts to judge the parties impartially, the judge will hear the language of the argument and use the language of the judgment informed by one or other of the underlying belief structures. This will make the decision at least rationally impenetrable to the losing side and, in some cases, may lead them to suspect overt bias on the judge's part. Second, judges are accustomed to disposing of a matter with a win to one side and a loss to the other, based on legal conclusions about who is "right" and who is "wrong." Conflicts of the type we are discussing here are not solved by such binary thinking and even the legal question of right and wrong (as opposed to the more difficult moral or ethical question) is generally less clear and more complex than courts are used to handling.

Judges often lose the opportunity to maximize gain for both sides or to minimize harm because they are focused on legal arguments that lead to the win or loss rather than legal arguments that look for outcomes that will enable the belief systems to carry on together most easily. Rather than accepting the reasoning in the courts' decisions in this area at its face value, we should look, I suggest, for broader principles that can achieve this result. In a deeply conflicted society, little is gained by judicial pronouncements that can be written off as a "win" for one side of the controversy or the other. What we need to find are ideas that will, without imposing a moral relativism on our society, promote honest debate and peaceful co-existence.

In considering the decision in *Chamberlain v. Surrey School District No. 36*,[18] and indeed most of the cases in this chapter, we should keep in mind that a judicial decision will not resolve the incommensurate value differences between the parties. It is incapable of doing so. Indeed, it may be beyond anyone's power to achieve such resolution. Solutions to the immediate conflict, therefore, must be sought with that fact in mind.

3. The Arguments in *Chamberlain*

Freedom of conscience and religion, indeed the Charter itself, did not figure directly in the decision of the majority of the Supreme Court of Canada in *Chamberlain*. Rather, the case was argued on the basis of whether the school board had properly exercised its authority under statute and regulation in its decision whether to approve the contested books for use or not. The issues of religion and conscience lurked in the words of the statute, however. The School Act[19] required that schools in the province be operated upon "strictly secular and non-sectarian principles" and that "the highest morality must be inculcated but no religious dogma or creed is to be taught in a school."[20]

The first argument made by the plaintiffs was that this section of the School Act prohibited the board from making any decision that was based upon religious principles. Since many (although not all) of the objecting parents were motivated by religious beliefs and indeed some school board trustees may also have had similar beliefs, the decision was argued to lie outside the mandate of the statute and therefore lie outside the powers of the board. This argument obviously goes directly to the issue discussed in the opening segment of this chapter: What scope should our society give to persons who argue their points from principles that they hold as part of their organizing belief systems rather than from arguments accessible to all citizens, whether fellow believers or not?

The B.C. Court of Appeal[21] focused on this feature of the case, primarily because the trial judge[22] had declared the school board's resolution invalid on this ground. She held that objections to the books were religiously motivated and that, because of the requirement that schools be strictly secular, these objections could not influence the board. The Court of Appeal judgment provided a well-reasoned analysis of why excluding moral decisions based upon religious belief would not only be contrary to the Charter, but indeed highly impractical. McLachlin C.J., writing for the majority of the Supreme Court of Canada, agreed. She also dismissed the argument that the school board had to ignore positions based upon religious reasons because of the use of the term "secular" in the statute. "Religion," she said, "is an integral part of people's lives and cannot be left at the board room door."[23] Moreover, she recognized that school boards were required to take into account the opinions and views of local parents, who would often be religiously motivated. Rather, she held that the term "secular" did not exclude religious considerations, but excluded considerations that took into account the values and beliefs of only one segment of the community.[24] In this proposition, both the majority and dissenting judges of the court concurred.

Thus the existence of some religious motivations did not automatically take the decision out of the statutory mandate of the board. However, the court found that this did not dispose of the main question.

The law governing administrative actions of bodies like school boards or other agencies is replete with arguments over what standard of review is appropriate for a court to exercise when asked to overturn an administrative decision. In some cases, a court will decide that the body should have a considerable degree of independence. In that case, the court will not interfere with the decision unless it is shown to be an unreasonable one. In other cases, the court will express less faith in the independence of the body and its expertise in the area in which it is making a decision. Then, the court will review the body's decision on the stricter basis of whether or not the decision was legally correct.[25] Obviously, a finding that the standard of review is "reasonableness" gives the body more scope for discretion than a finding that the standard is "correctness." In this case, the Supreme Court judges all agreed that it was only the reasonableness of the board's decision that was subject to review.[26]

What then were the arguments about the reasonableness of the decision? The proponents of the books' approval cited the curriculum of the province, which required the discussion in all K–1 classrooms of children's families. They argued that same-sex parented families should not be excluded. As well, since the statute required the "highest morality," that morality surely included tolerance. Those opposing the approval of the books were labelled intolerant and accused of wishing to force a religious agenda on the schools.[27]

The school board, whose decision had sided with the opposing parents, argued that it was not necessary to use these books to allow children to discuss their own families in a tolerant environment. They made the point that parents have the right to teach their moral and religious principles to their children and that children in the K–1 grades had no need to be exposed to questions of sexual morality that were beyond their age-appropriate understanding.[28] They did not deny that the objections of many of the parents were based on religious beliefs that condemned homosexual relationships as immoral. In addition, however, parents had made the point that it was confusing to children to be taught one thing at home and another at school, particularly at this young age.[29]

The majority judgment of the court declared the school board's position to be unreasonable because it had, in the court's view, violated the requirements of the School Act and its own policies that it include all parents' views in its deliberations. It rather failed to take account of the needs of children in same-sex parented homes and preferred the position of a group whose views "denied the equal validity of the lawful lifestyles of some in the school community."[30] McLachlin C.J., writing for the majority, dismissed the concerns of parents about confusing messages between home and school, noting that "cognitive dissonance" was a part of life and exposure to differing views and beliefs did not require children to abandon their own beliefs, but only to treat others with equal respect. Exposure to different beliefs was necessary if tolerance was to be taught.[31]

4. What Is "Reasonable"?

The majority judgment was a good example of the court's failure to understand the incommensurate beliefs underlying the conflict before it and handle the conflict in a constructive way. In the dissenting judgment, Gonthier J. noted that the proposed books presented same-sex families in a positive light; indeed, one of the books clearly presented same-sex parents as morally equivalent to heterosexual parents.[32] While the objecting parents might very easily have acknowledged that same-sex parents love their children and are following their own moral beliefs, they would also make a difference between the kindness, lovingness, or understanding of the same-sex parents and the morality of their relationship. The complainants, on the other hand, would have considered that the kindness, lovingness, and understanding of the parents justified the relationship as moral. That was the message of the books and it is that message to which the parents were opposed. McLachlin C.J. did not confront this distinction at all. Rather, she used the term "tolerance" to suggest approval of the same-sex relationship and appeared to be unaware that "tolerance" could be given (and, indeed, in the dissenting judgment, was given) a more limited meaning of acceptance of the family structure and the positive qualities of the family's life without approval of the relationship of the parents.

We have, therefore, in the judgments themselves, an illustration of how those engaged in these deep moral conflicts use language and hear arguments in very different ways. That was exactly how the debates before the school board had gone.[33] The school trustees had, understandably, decided that to leave the matter alone made more sense than to attempt to force the controversial books onto an angry group of voters. The majority judgment of the Supreme Court simply overturned that decision without considering the court's role in holding an even hand between belief systems. While the court stated that the school board could not exclude the views of one set of parents in preference to others, its decision had precisely that effect with regard to the competing moral view of the objecting parents.

The court sent the decision back to the board for reconsideration. Technically, this did not reverse the board's position and, had the board then considered what the majority held were the correct factors for its deliberations, it could, in theory, could have come to the same conclusion as it had before. However, the Chief Justice's explanation of why the decision was unreasonable left the board very little scope to make that decision. She made it clear that the board's objections to the books were based on factors that they were not permitted to consider, that the provincial curriculum required discussion of same-sex parented families, and that the board was not entitled to ignore these families in their deliberations. Since refusing to approve the books as supplementary resources was equated by the court to favouring only one group of parents at the expense of the other, it is difficult to see how the board could fail to approve the books for these purposes.

Let us consider, for a moment, the reasonableness of the school board's decision, apart from the particular issues of moral conflict in which the court itself became enmeshed and about which we can all too easily become partisan. Suppose A holds belief system X and B holds belief system Y. X and Y are incommensurate; they cannot both be true in several important respects. At the point of irreconcilable difference, A wishes to act in a way that will present A's beliefs alone, leaving B's beliefs excluded. Is it reasonable to permit A to behave in this fashion? There are three additional possible solutions to this problem that could be proposed as reasonable choices: B is also allowed to act in a way that presents B's belief system in contrast to A's on the disputed point; those who follow B's belief system are excused from participating in the expression of A's belief system; or A is not allowed to act out of A's belief system and all action related to the subject is excluded from both A and B.

Any one of these solutions could be reasonable in differing circumstances. Where A is allowed to act alone, one would expect a consideration of whether A's audience had a choice to reject A's message or not. Allowing A to act without reference to B might be perfectly reasonable in a situation in which the hearers can be expected to exercise independent thought or even to refuse to hear the message at all. But if the circumstances are such that the freedom to analyse and reject A's position is constrained, such as where the audience is captive or unable, for various reasons, to make an informed judgment, this choice seems the least reasonable of the four. Yet this is exactly the choice that McLachlin C.J. found to be the only reasonable one in the *Chamberlain* case.

Looked at in this light, the case makes an interesting contrast with the cases discussed in chapter 2. Where public prayer was an issue in the schools, the courts decided that the only choice that did not offend the freedom of conscience and religion of others was the exclusion of all demonstrations of faith.[34] I suggested that this solution was not one that the court should have imposed, but that had the school board decided simply to omit demonstrations of faith from the classroom, it would certainly have been following a rational and politically prudent course of action.[35] The inconsistency between the court's views in the earlier case and the opinions of the Supreme Court in *Chamberlain* suggests a lack of understanding by the Supreme Court of the legitimacy of moral conflict in a democratic society and the role of democratic institutions in managing that conflict. The school board's solution – which gave neither side the rights to propagandize the children – seems to be a reasonable political solution. The failure of the Supreme Court to recognize this is puzzling and leaves open the temptation to dismiss the judgment as simply reflecting the majority's own unarticulated and unacknowledged commitment to one side of the debate.

McLachlin C.J. suggested that her decision was justifiable because to foster "an atmosphere of tolerance and respect, in accordance with s. 76, the view that a certain lawful way of living is morally questionable cannot become the basis of school policy."[36] This would be a fair observation if the opposing parents had been insisting that books be used in the classroom that represented same-sex parents as living an immoral lifestyle or made stereotypical assessments of the same-sex relationship while positive depictions were excluded. That was not the position of the opposing parents. Moreover, the court's statement appeared to suggest that any legal mode of living must be taught in the schools as a moral way of living. Obviously, that cannot be the case. Many people engage in perfectly legal lifestyles of which many others disapprove.[37] Legality and morality may overlap at times, but they are scarcely identical categories. Within the curriculum of the province, it was quite possible simply to allow children to discuss their own families in an atmosphere of tolerance and acceptance. It was not necessary to address the issue of the morality of same-sex parenting on one side or the other to achieve that end.

Considerations of freedom of conscience and religion were, as I have already noted, strangely absent from the majority judgment, although there is no doubt that the conflict was over a significant limitation of parental rights based on conscience.[38] That silence made it possible for the majority to ignore the role which, as independent judges in the absence of express legislation imposing a particular moral view upon citizens, the court should have played. As I have already noted, many conflicts in belief systems are intractable. Later, I will discuss more promising ways of dealing with these conflicts judicially. However, at this point, it is sufficient to note that the court here overstepped its bounds as protector of the fundamental freedoms.

As I noted in the last chapter, Abella J.'s judgment in *Bruker v. Marcovitz*[39] suggested that courts can use concepts of "Canadian values" to limit freedom of conscience and religion, apart from specific legislative authority and thus without reference to the limitations of s. 1 of the Charter. The majority judgment in *Chamberlain* is an example of a similar approach, using an assessment of the "reasonableness" of the decision as a vehicle for limiting parents' freedom of conscience without any legislative mandate to do so. This is an approach that has been rejected in such cases as *Multani*,[40] where the court stated that all limits to the freedoms must be found in the application of s.1, but it appears to survive in more covert forms. Of course, the reader may consider that the requirement of the School Act to teach "tolerance" is such a mandate – the court certainly took that view. But this brings us squarely back to the different usages of the word "tolerance" in two irreconcilable belief systems and the need for the court to step outside the competing belief systems rather than to impose one over the other.

A variety of arguments have been raised by various writers to insist that the court was right in this case because, at least on the subject of gay and lesbian rights, an "even hand" requires a positive affirmation of homosexual behaviour by the courts. Professor Bruce MacDougall, for example, has argued passionately that our courts must declassify homosexuality as a moral issue and that only in so doing can equality rights be realized. Equality for gays and lesbians, he has argued, is not simply a matter of prohibiting acts of discrimination but requires insistence that homosexuality be celebrated, so that gays and lesbians may be included as a valuable group in society.[41] Other arguments suggest that because negative views of homosexuality can lead to violence, courts are justified in requiring those views to be excluded from public discourse.

These arguments fail to grapple with the reality of the underlying dispute. Sexuality and resulting behaviours are regarded as elements of moral concern by all major religions and, indeed, by secular society. It is not possible for courts to classify sexuality and, in particular, sexual conduct as other than a moral issue because that does not reflect the fundamental understanding of all of us. We have widely differing views on how sexual conduct should be governed, but almost no one thinks that there should be no limits on such conduct, even if those limits are to be defined only when the conduct causes harm (as "harm" may be variously defined). The use of the word "should" in this sentence signals that we are discussing a moral issue. The insistence, then, that homosexuality be "celebrated" or that tolerance in this case requires more than an "even hand" (as I have called it) simply puts us back into the same loop of moral disagreement. We cannot solve the problems these differences create by replaying the same song and pretending it is a different one.

5. Same Moral Conflict – Different Resolution

A private university, governed by evangelical Christian principles, sought approval of the B.C. College of Teachers to extend its teacher training program to cover all five years of the baccalaureate program. Up to this time, the university had only offered four years of the program and its students spent the fifth year at Simon Fraser University, a public B.C. university. The B.C. College of Teachers (BCCT) is a statutory body with powers to oversee the education of teachers and their admission to the teaching profession in British Columbia.

The application of Trinity Western University was turned down by the BCCT, primarily on the basis of the university's commitment to evangelical Christian beliefs, including, particularly, the belief that homosexual relations were immoral.[42] Students and faculty at the university were required to sign a pledge of conduct. The pledge required them to abstain from "Biblically condemned sins."[43] Those included sexual sins such as pre-marital sex and homosexual relations. The position of the BCCT was that the pledge was evidence of discriminatory attitudes towards persons of non-heterosexual orientation and that it was not in the interests of the public school system to allow an institution with those beliefs to provide the entire program of teacher education.

BCCT's position was replete with the underlying and unexpressed beliefs that characterize moral conflicts as, of course, was the position of Trinity Western University. As in the *Chamberlain* case, the parties were divided not simply on conclusions about the morality of a particular kind of behaviour but on the nature of discrimination and tolerance and, indeed, the nature of human beings and the sources of moral authority. Of course, the implications of accepting BCCT's position were more obvious in this case and could more clearly lead to conclusions that a court would find unacceptable. It is difficult to say that, if Trinity Western University's statement of moral conduct was in itself an example of illegal discrimination, the beliefs of all who hold those views about morality are not also discriminatory. If so, then how could BCCT admit to the teaching profession any evangelical Christian, Roman Catholic, Orthodox Jew, devout Muslim, or, indeed, anyone who shared a negative perspective on homosexual conduct?

And if these persons could not be admitted to the teaching profession, then we have in effect established a faith-based qualification for the profession. This would appear to contravene the protection of freedom of conscience and religion in a way that courts would find unacceptable. The rights to equality of persons of those religious persuasions would certainly have been violated. The issue of religious freedom was thus much more starkly raised by the facts in *Trinity Western University v. BCCT*[44] than it was in *Chamberlain*. Moreover, it is raised in a way that can be conceptualized as a matter of equality rights.

The majority judgment adopted the traditional language with which courts are familiar of characterizing the problem as one of balancing conflicting rights. Was there a way in which the rights to freedom of conscience and religion of Trinity Western University and its students could be balanced with the right of non-heterosexual students to be free from discrimination in the public school system? The court held that there was, by splitting the freedom to believe from the freedom to practise one's beliefs.[45] There was no evidence, the majority held, that graduates of Trinity Western University would discriminate in the classroom against gay and lesbian students. If an individual teacher did commit acts of discrimination, then the teacher could be disciplined by the BCCT under its statutory powers. But until such an event occurred, there was no reason to interfere with the freedom of conscience and religion of Trinity Western University or for BCCT to refuse approval of its fifth-year program. The court also pointed out that there was no evidence that a year at SFU would necessarily change the minds or the attitudes of Trinity Western graduates. The remedy BCCT was proposing for their concern was not a reasonable one.[46]

The majority judgment had the merit of holding an even hand between the two sides of the moral conflict. However, it performed this feat by avoiding the issue. While not prepared to go so far as to say that some expression of disapproval of homosexual relationships constituted illegal discrimination, the court left entirely open what conduct would cross this line. Must every teacher in the school system be supportive of students' homosexual relationships? Or must they avoid open disapproval? Or would a teacher have to make some actual difference in his or her treatment of a student to be found to have discriminated? We will look more closely at these unanswered questions in the next segment of this chapter.

Rather than avoiding the main conflict in the case, L'Heureux-Dubé J., in her dissenting judgment, illustrated the reasoning of a judge who enters the conflict on one side of the fray.[47] She would have held that BCCT was justified in its position because of the need to provide a supportive environment for gay and lesbian students in the school system.[48] While not stating outright that disapproval of homosexual relationships was, of itself, an act of illegal discrimination, she made clear her discomfort with the idea that a teacher could disapprove of such relationships but not discriminate against the students.[49] She did not seem to have considered the implications of a school system that would exclude from the teaching profession substantial segments of Canadian society on the basis of conscientious or religious belief.[50]

6. A Tale of Two Teachers

Several cases have directly dealt with the question of how far teachers can go in expressing controversial views arising out of their own belief systems before crossing the line of discriminatory conduct. In these cases, freedom of expression and freedom of conscience and religion are typically raised in defence of the teacher's rights. In this segment, we will review two of those decisions in some detail. Before we do so, however, we should briefly consider the place of the public school in a climate of moral conflict.

The decisions in *Chamberlain* and *Trinity Western University* illustrate what we all know: in our public school system, we will find a wide variety of belief systems, many of which are incompatible with each other. Yet, perhaps coming out of the more unified community standards of a simpler age when the phrase was less contested, our schools are entrusted with "inculcating the highest morality." And in a social climate where few children will live in what once might have been considered a "traditional" Canadian family with a mother at home and a father in the work force, schools are often thought of as required to fill the gaps in moral teaching that parents no longer have the time to provide. This appears to set up an impossible situation in which we have little common understanding of many moral issues but a requirement that morality be taught; little agreement on our fundamental beliefs but a requirement that the moral fruit of these beliefs be the same.

Without tools to solve this central problem, however, courts have had to grapple with issues of teachers disciplined by school boards or by their professional bodies for expressing divergent beliefs that caused concern among other segments of the school population. In looking at these cases and the outcomes, I suggest that we can view them as efforts by the courts to try to maintain the neutrality of the school system in the face of moral conflicts within the population. This aim is a reasonable one. Indeed, as we review the cases, I will suggest that an overt recognition of a principle of neutrality could provide a satisfactory answer to the problem earlier posed of how the legal system could handle cases of moral conflict while fully respecting the freedom of conscience and religion of both sides.

But without articulation of this aim, the decisions can appear confusing and in some cases a burden upon freedom of expression and freedom of conscience and religion that is hard to justify without appealing to the judges' own belief systems. This may lead to a concern that the courts are in fact imposing a particular social agenda upon Canadians. I will suggest rather that the problem is in the courts' failure to recognize the problem of moral conflict and to explicitly commit to their democratic role of protecting public spaces, not as value-free or religion-free, but as zones in which care must be taken to limit proselytizing to situations in which options are available and free debate can take place. Such conditions usually do not characterize the public school classroom, in which the ideas are presented by the teacher who stands in a position of authority.

Mr Ross held opinions that most Canadians find abhorrent. He was a Holocaust-denier who had written several books, pamphlets, and articles and had appeared on local television promoting his belief in a worldwide Jewish conspiracy. Mr Ross was also a teacher. The local school board had received many complaints about Mr Ross's views and had even placed his teaching under supervision for a time. No evidence was presented that suggested any discriminatory conduct by him in the school; his activities were confined to his off-duty time. Mr Ross had received disciplinary warnings from the school board, but no more stringent discipline had been imposed. In 1988, a parent who self-identified as Jewish filed a complaint with the New Brunswick Human Rights Commission, not attacking the activities of Mr Ross directly, but claiming that the failure of the school board to deal effectively with Mr Ross's activities constituted discrimination under the Human Rights Act. A Board of Inquiry was constituted by the Commission.

The Board of Inquiry found that the school board's failure to either restrain Mr Ross or remove him as a teacher constituted discrimination under the Act. The school board was ordered to place Mr Ross on an eighteen-month suspension without pay and to offer him any available non-teaching positions in the district. Failing the availability of such position or his acceptance of it, Mr Ross was to be fired. In addition, the Board of Inquiry ordered that if, at any time during his suspension or during his employment in a non-teaching position, he published further works or distributed his currently available works relating to the supposed Zionist conspiracy, he should be immediately fired. Mr Ross appealed on the basis that the orders violated his freedom of expression and his freedom of conscience and religion.[51]

The Supreme Court had no difficulty accepting the proposition that teachers may be disciplined for conduct that is off duty.[52] However, the court spent considerable time analysing why Mr Ross's off-duty conduct might reasonably be expected to have a deleterious effect on his ability as a teacher. The Board of Inquiry had before it evidence that the school had suffered from a number of anti-Semitic incidents perpetrated by students against Jewish students. It found, on the basis of unchallenged evidence, that there was a poisoned environment in the school. Although Mr Ross could not be shown to have directly contributed to the incidents or the climate, the Board of Inquiry inferred that his aggressive and notorious views had contributed to the problem.[53]

This inference was obviously problematic for the Supreme Court. Nonetheless, they upheld the right of the board to draw such conclusions. This is the point at which the decision is potentially worrisome. If teacher A believes X, which is an unpopular belief, considered perhaps even outrageous or immoral by some, and students in the school also show evidence of believing X, this does not mean that A's influence has been at work. The Supreme Court made a very careful analysis of when it is acceptable to make the linkage between the teacher's beliefs and the negative behaviour of students or the existence of a poisoned environment in the school. Quoting from a judgment of Dickson C.J., the court held that "when the nature of the occupation is important and sensitive and when the substance, form and content of the employee's comments are extreme, an inference of impairment [to carry out the employee's functions] may be sufficient."[54]

These limited circumstances were, the court held, present in this case. Turning to the question of whether the order of the Board of Inquiry contravened Mr Ross's freedom of conscience and religion, the court held that it did.[55] However, applying the provisions of s. 1 of the Charter, the court found much of the board's order to be justifiable as a limit imposed by law (the board's own order) in a free and democratic society. The exception to this was the final part of the order requiring Mr Ross to be fired if, during his suspension or during his employment in a non-teaching capacity, he continued to disseminate his publications and his opinions. The court found this to be an unjustified restriction on Mr Ross's freedom of expression and his freedom of conscience and religion,[56] as it limited his freedoms when he was no longer teaching in the schools and could not therefore be justified as protecting the integrity of the school system.[57]

Because both freedom of expression and freedom of conscience and religion were argued to defend Mr Ross's right to say what he pleased about Jews, it is interesting to note how the court approached the two freedoms. The court understood freedom of expression to be a protection for the core of the democratic process. In keeping with this understanding, it was less prepared to extend vigorous protection to expression that had as its purpose impeding participation in the political process by an identifiable group.[58] Much less attention was given to freedom of conscience and religion. However, the court expressed the view that "any religious belief that denigrates and defames the religious beliefs of others erodes the very basis of the guarantee in s. 2(a) – a basis that guarantees that every individual is free to hold and manifest the beliefs dictated by one's conscience."[59]

The court did not seem to acknowledge the role of s. 2(a) in a democratic state or its role in preserving the roots of that democracy. Still, its view that there is a range of available protection for conscience and religion, ending perhaps when protecting the belief would require denying the rights of others to the same protection, illustrates a similar approach to the range of protection for freedom of expression. The idea that some manifestations of freedom of conscience and religion are more worthy of protection than others is a potentially useful way of looking at the problem if we are to regard this freedom, as I have argued, as being also a crucial component of democracy. Conscientious or religious beliefs that would deny others access to public debate (as Mr Ross's views did) certainly lie outside that central justification for the freedom.

Despite the fact that there was no direct evidence connecting Mr Ross's out-of-school activities to his classroom conduct, he was clearly engaged in proselytizing for his anti-Semitism. His books, letters, and pamphlets were all directed towards converting others to a belief in a worldwide Jewish conspiracy. It seemed to be the notoriety and aggressive nature of his campaign that linked his off-duty expressions to his role as teacher and made reasonable an inference that he contributed to the anti-Semitism in the school. Teachers are in a position to indoctrinate in a way that is unique in our society. The court expressed this in a positive light: teachers are models whose general lives serve as a "medium" for the "message" the school system wishes to deliver.[60]

This positive way of framing the teacher's role is, I would suggest, a dangerous one. It can too easily be interpreted as ignoring the moral conflict within our society and providing a warrant for assuming that the school system has, in all cases, a unified "message" that it is to impart. La Forest J. partially acknowledged this difficulty when, speaking for the court, he qualified those remarks by stating that he did "not wish to be understood as advocating an approach that subjects the entire lives of teachers to inordinate scrutiny on the basis of more onerous moral standards of behaviour."[61] While it is less inspiring to frame this decision as a prohibition against proselytizing a captive audience, it is certainly more reasonable than to suggest that we will need to agree in all cases on what constitutes moral behaviour and whether or not a particular teacher exemplifies it.

The question of limiting teachers' rights to free expression of unpopular beliefs arising from their conscience was also carefully analysed in the decision of the B.C. Court of Appeal in *Kempling v. BC College of Teachers*.[62] Mr Kempling, a teacher and school counsellor in a small British Columbia community, wrote a series of letters to the editor in the local paper condemning homosexual relationships. The B.C. College of Teachers disciplined him for "conduct unbecoming" a teacher and ordered his teaching certificate suspended for a month. Mr Kempling's primary ground of appeal was that the order to the College violated his freedom of expression. Only in the Court of Appeal did he seek to add freedom of conscience and religion to his argument. The Court of Appeal held that it was then too late to do so, as there was no evidentiary foundation on which the argument that he was exercising his rights to freedom of conscience and religion in writing to the paper could be established.[63]

This basis for dismissing the freedom of conscience and religion argument seems disingenuous. It was obvious from the letters that Mr Kempling believed that homosexual relationships were immoral and against Christian moral teaching. Having Mr Kempling affirm this in court seemed superfluous. It was unfortunate that the court did not give fair hearing to this right. But the argument of the court as it dealt with the issue of freedom of expression would probably have equally applied to the protection of freedom of religion and conscience. Looked at in that light, the court's judgment in *Kempling* provided some helpful comments on the issues we have been discussing.

The court drew a distinction between statements critical of a particular way of life or denouncing a particular lifestyle and statements that revealed a willingness to treat people on the basis of stereotypical judgments about a particular group. The first category of statement is not illegal discrimination; the second is.[64] While the court found that "in his more restrained" passages, Mr Kempling was engaging in appropriate and legally protected expressions of moral or political opinion, in several places he crossed the line into stereotyping individuals in a way that violated their dignity and their right to be treated as individuals rather than as mere representatives of a group.[65] This is a difficult distinction to make. However, despite the fact that the line between these two modes of expression may be fine at times, this characterization of the problem was, I suggest, an enlightening one.

I have already pointed out that "equality rights" and how we would define and apply those rights is very much dependent upon our own belief system. Equality rights are often thought to be in conflict with freedoms such as freedom of expression or of belief and conscience. Yet if we focus on the concept of human dignity, which is the foundation of all human rights, we may be able to realize that protection of human dignity requires both freedom and equality – held perhaps in a difficult and creative balance, but of necessity operating together. The court's introduction of this concept into the decision allowed it to find a way in which conscientious beliefs can be expressed as part of the democratic process where free debate can produce either a broad consensus on some issues or a respectful disagreement on others.

Mr Kempling had also made it clear in his letters that he intended to use his position as a school counsellor to advance his beliefs and to convert others to them.[66] Here the court turned to the traditional language of tolerance and the need to provide an environment free of discrimination for all to hold that his expressed intention violated the integrity of the school system. The problem with this language was, as I have already pointed out, that it is heard by both sides of the moral conflict in widely different ways. Those who share Mr Kempling's beliefs about homosexual relationships will hear the court saying that Mr Kempling's opinions should be repressed and accuse the court of hypocrisy in showing tolerance of every opinion but theirs. Those who oppose Mr Kempling's moral position will hear the court saying that tolerance means approval of the morality of homosexual relationships and that expression of any form of disapproval amounts to discrimination.

In fact, the court's decision made it quite clear that it intended to adopt neither of these positions. Had Mr Kempling confined himself to more reasoned debate on the subject, it did not appear that the court would have considered his conduct illegal or subject to disciplinary action by the college even if he condemned homosexual relationships as immoral.[67] The court's comments on individual dignity as the touchstone of whether or not conduct is discriminatory could have provided a way for it to express its reasoning as to why Mr Kempling's letters violated the integrity of the school system without adopting language to which each side in the conflict could assign its own meaning.

Whatever one's beliefs, a commitment to free and open debate in our society requires respect for the dignity of all persons, whether or not we agree with their belief systems. Certainly Mr Kempling was entitled to try to convince others of the truth of his moral beliefs, but not in a situation in which they cannot participate in the debate on even ground. The public school classroom or counselling room is such a situation of limited engagement. In a society of deep moral conflicts, respecting the dignity of the children and the rights of their parents to bring them up in their own belief systems requires that the public school remain neutral in the conflict. Mr Kempling's letters rejected that role as inimical to his beliefs.[68] Such a rejection does indeed undermine the democracy that the freedoms of both expression and of conscience and religion are intended to protect and therefore can reasonably be limited by the state. It is unfortunate that the court, having initiated a discussion of human dignity that could have led to a solution to the moral conflict at hand, failed to follow through with the concept, but fell back into contested categories that did not advance the debate.

While I have suggested that courts are right to protect the public schools as essentially neutral territory in handling issues where moral conflict is pervasive, despite the inadequacy of the language they have generally used in arriving at their decisions, entirely different considerations must apply where the conflict is carried out in the wider community. In those cases, the legislature has sometimes taken a hand and the role of the courts has been to determine whether the legislation has gone too far in limiting citizens' rights. Where the legislature has not limited citizens' expressions of belief, efforts have sometimes been made before other bodies, such as disciplinary professional groups or human rights tribunals, to repress opinions unpopular with others. We will now look at a variety of cases in this area and see what they can tell us about the role of freedom of conscience and religion in fostering democratic debate in more public settings.

7. The Protest Cases

In matters of public debate, protest is considered a democratic right. Usually, we think of this right to protest a variety of state or private actions as an example of our freedom of expression. However, almost every protest has, at its roots, a matter of conscientious or religious belief. Sometimes freedom of conscience and religion is also raised in support of the right to engage in direct political action; even where it is not, however, it is clear that the actions of protesters are an expression of belief, and limits on their rights are limits on the right to act upon our beliefs in the political realm.

Courts have often been generous in their protections of this kind of political action. Perhaps because of the long tradition of protest in the West and its role in some of the most significant social revolutions of the last century, such as women's rights and racial equality, courts are seemingly comfortable in giving protesters considerable latitude. In some of the cases, the courts have recognized this type of expression as part of the core function of Charter protection: to protect democratic debate, even when its manifestations may be unpleasant or unpalatable. Limitations have more commonly come from the legislatures, particularly in the area of limits to abortion protests within a fixed distance from abortion clinics. In those cases, as we shall see, courts have invariably been deferential to the legislatures' rights to limit political action in certain circumstances.

Throughout this discussion, I have argued that if freedom of conscience and religion is to be adequately protected, the role of the courts is not to impose, in the absence of legislative mandate, one belief system upon another. As well, I have suggested that where the issue before the courts involves matters of moral conflict, they should avoid attempting to find the solution to the problem in the morally contested language of the problem itself. Instead, courts need to find concepts that overarch the contested issues in ways that can allow both sides to express their views, live according to their own principles, and participate in our society to the greatest extent mutually possible.

In earlier chapters, as well as in this one, I have used the concept of open democratic debate as one of those guiding concepts; I have also considered the related need to protect freedom to choose and reject other belief systems as a second. In this chapter, I have argued for courts to see themselves as protectors of what we might call "rules of fair engagement" in both sides' efforts at proselytizing for their own views. In the last section of this chapter, I suggested that protection of human dignity might be another such concept that could prove useful, requiring as it does both ideas of freedom and of equality. As we look at the protest cases, I suggest that we will find examples of the courts using these ideas, although not always referencing them directly, to solve the issues before them.

A somewhat unusual form of protest occurred when Mr Owens[69] took out an ad in the local paper. His ad was meant to provide a counterbalance to a gay pride parade that was being promoted in his community. The ad consisted of four biblical references by chapter and verse (all condemning homosexual conduct),[70] an equals sign, and a circle surrounding two stick figures touching hands and superimposed with a slash running from the two o'clock to the eight o'clock position. Mr Owens stated that the purpose of the ad was to state that God does not approve of homosexual conduct. Three gay men complained about the ad to the Saskatchewan Human Rights Commission claiming that the ad violated s. 14(1) of the Human Rights Code,[71] which prohibits the publication of any material that "exposes or tends to expose to hatred, ridicules, belittles or otherwise affronts the dignity of any person or class of persons on the basis of a prohibited ground."[72] One prohibited ground is sexual orientation.[73] A Board of Inquiry found that Mr Owens's ad violated the code. On appeal to the Court of Queen's Bench, the decision was upheld.[74]

In the first chapter, I mentioned that many of the human rights codes in Canada contain some language dealing with discriminatory publications. This is the first case in which we have encountered these provisions, so I will briefly set them in some context at this stage, although we will return to the controversy surrounding this type of legislation in a later chapter. Obviously, provisions such as that cited here have potentially a great impact upon freedom of expression and freedom of conscience and belief. The degree to which this impact exists depends upon the interpretation of the words such as "tends to expose to hatred," "ridicules," and "affronts the dignity of." If we interpret these words on the basis of how a person targeted feels, I may feel my dignity affronted by very little. Any negative criticism of my conduct could then potentially trigger this section.

If this is all that is required, freedom of expression and freedom of conscience and religion would be dramatically limited. However, in the decision *Canada (Canadian Human Rights Commission) v. Taylor*,[75] the Supreme Court of Canada was asked to consider whether a similar section was unconstitutional as being a violation of the fundamental freedoms. The court upheld the constitutionality of the section, but only under certain limitations. The court held that to pass constitutional muster, the section must be read as directed only towards communications that aroused feelings "of an ardent and extreme nature" of "detestation, calumny and vilification." Although the words of the section appear to prohibit speech that is much milder than this, an earlier decision of the Saskatchewan Court of Appeal had held that "ridicule" and "affront to dignity" also had to be interpreted as evoking these extreme reactions.

In overturning the decision of the lower court and the board, the Court of Appeal applied these principles.[76] Looking at Mr Owens's ad from an objective viewpoint, the court found that it was jarring and might indeed be offensive, but that this was not the test. Although the scriptural texts cited were extreme (specifying that homosexuals be put to death in one instance), the court recognized that in dealing with foundational religious texts, a court had to be cautious about their context. It acknowledged that biblical interpretations varied and that the Bible, when taken more holistically, was open to more than one reading.[77] Importantly, the court also placed the ad in the context of the democratic debate about gay rights which was very much in the public eye at the time.[78] Ultimately, the court held that Mr Owens's actions did not meet the test required by *Taylor*.

Even situations of more overtly offensive protest have been protected by the courts and protestors shielded from at least some consequences of their actions, usually through assertion of a right to freedom of expression. In *Whatcott v. Saskatchewan Association of Licensed Practical Nurses*,[79] for example, an abortion protestor who carried defamatory and offensive signs outside a Planned Parenthood Clinic was protected from discipline by his licensing board on the basis that he was exercising his rights to free speech. In that case, while his signs might have been false and defamatory (and he was not protected from the civil consequences of defamation), the Saskatchewan Court of Appeal held that the interference with his freedom of expression by a finding of professional misconduct could not be justified in a free and democratic society. The association's decision to suspend his licence had no rational connection with the aims of their statutory right to impose discipline for professional misconduct because Mr Whatcott had been acting on his own time without any connection to his role as a nurse.

While this case did not raise freedom of conscience and religion issues directly, it illustrated courts' understanding that public debate must normally be given protection, even when it offends. It also provided an interesting contrast to *Kempling* and *Ross*, discussed earlier. In *Whatcott*,[80] the protest was carried out in circumstances in which the protestor could be ignored or even approached and confronted by opponents. The *Owens* case made the same point. Indeed, the restrictions on discriminatory publication provisions of the Human Rights Code imposed by *Taylor* indicate the courts' concern to protect freedom of expression and freedom of conscience and religion when they are exercised in the realm of political debate.

In contrast, legislatures have enacted some restrictions on protest activities, particularly within a certain distance of abortion clinics. In *R. v. Lewis*,[81] a protestor was arrested for violating a "bubble zone" around a clinic. He argued that the legislation[82] was invalid as an infringement of both his Charter right to freedom of expression and his right to freedom of conscience and religion. The B.C. Supreme Court agreed that both his s. 2(a) and 2(b) rights were infringed by the legislation. Nonetheless, the court upheld the restrictions as justifiable in a free and democratic society. Mr Lewis died before his case could be appealed to the B.C. Court of Appeal. However, the issue was revisited in *R. v. Watson and Spratt*[83] and the Court of Appeal in that case agreed with the holding in *Lewis*.

In finding the limit justifiable, the court referred to the principle that a right to free expression does not entail a right to a captive audience.[84] In the case of women seeking access to an abortion clinic or staff working in the clinic, there was no reasonable way to avoid the message. Mr Spratt and Mr Watson, on the other hand, were quite free to express their views in many other situations or indeed even to carry protest signs in other venues. While this discussion was carried on primarily in the context of free speech, it would seem also applicable to freedom of conscience and religion. Freedom of conscience and religion must entail the right to try to convince others that one's beliefs are better or truer than those of others. Democratic debate requires precisely that. However, there are situations in which proselytizing others should be constrained. One of these situations is the vulnerable or captive audience.

This is the same principle of neutrality that I argued ought also to be applied to the public schools in cases such as *Chamberlain, Zylberberg*,[85] *Ross*, and *Kempling* discussed earlier. In those cases, I suggested that freedom of conscience and religion could be protected by a range of solutions, including granting the other side equal opportunity for debate, exemption from hearing the presentation of one side, or requiring all parties to eschew the debate in the particular circumstances. Outside an abortion clinic, obviously the only feasible solution is to require all parties to refrain from attempting to convince others. Access to abortion is an area of moral conflict in which public opinion is deeply divided. Courts in these cases have acted reasonably in upholding the legislative restrictions on freedom of expression and freedom of conscience and religion in light of the ongoing debate.

8. When the Legislature Has Spoken

In earlier chapters, we have seen a few examples in which legislation has been passed in an area where moral conflict exists and those who remain opposed to the solution have challenged the legislation as violating their freedom of conscience and religion. *Big M Drug Mart*[86] was an example of this situation, although the legislation was very old and the challenger was perhaps more concerned with its revenue than with its conscience. On similar facts in *Edwards Books and Art*,[87] however, it was those whose religion required observance of Saturday as a holy day who challenged a statute requiring Sunday closing. We also considered what might be the outcome of a potential challenge to legislation prohibiting the use of religious law in private arbitrations of family disputes and examined a ruling upholding legislation criminalizing polygamy.

I have asserted previously, as well, that legislatures must be held entitled to pass legislation even where public debate is still divided. If, of course, the government has misread the public mood, the issue may contribute to its defeat in the next election. But elections are seldom fought on single issues. Small minorities, as well, may have little political clout and indeed even significant segments of the population may oppose particular political choices without being able to effect democratic change, at least in the short run. This is where the Charter becomes particularly important. The courts have the ability to strike down legislation that unjustifiably restrains the religious and conscientious rights of minorities. It is thus crucial to the continued flourishing of diverse belief communities that this protection be extended in a predictable and robust way, even though protecting the freedom results in constraining, to an extent, the legislative will. In this way, too, freedom of conscience and religion interweaves with the political process.

In *Alberta v. Hutterian Brethren of Wilson Colony*,[88] a narrow majority[89] of the Supreme Court of Canada appeared to cast some doubt upon its willingness to protect this aspect of the process, even where little social harm would apparently follow if it did so. The Hutterites, as the reader may know, live in agricultural communes that place a religious value upon their self-sufficiency and simplicity of life. They also give the Bible a literalist meaning and believe that being knowingly photographed is a violation of the second commandment, which prohibits making images of anything. For many years, the Alberta driver licensing system accommodated this belief by allowing Hutterites to obtain driver's licences without photos. However, to expand its facial recognition database with the aim of reducing the opportunity for driver's licences to be used in identity fraud, the government of Alberta amended its regulations to eliminate this exemption.

A period of negotiation followed in which the government offered to allow Hutterites to carry photo-free licences, provided a photograph was taken and stored in the database. Clearly, this did not satisfy the religious beliefs of the Hutterites as it still required a photograph to be made and an image to be stored. Hutterites offered to carry non-photo licences that would be stamped "Not for Identification Purposes." This was unacceptable to the government. When negotiations broke down, the Wilson Colony challenged the new regulation on the grounds that it unjustifiably violated Hutterites' freedom of conscience and religion. Both the Alberta Court of Queen's Bench[90] and Court of Appeal[91] agreed.

While expressing some doubt as to whether the regulation interfered with the Hutterites' religious beliefs or practices in a manner that was sufficient to engage Charter protection,[92] McLachlin C.J., writing for the majority of the Supreme Court of Canada, proceeded to consider whether the interference was "justifiable in a free and democratic society." In doing so, she turned to the *Oakes* test under s. 1 of the Charter, which we have already set out and discussed in some earlier chapters. She had no difficulty in deciding that the government objective of limiting the risk of driver's licences being used to perpetrate identity fraud was pressing and substantial.[93] She also found that the requirement of a photograph for everyone was rationally connected to the objective.[94]

The difficulty with the decision, and the area in which it appeared to strike out into new territory for Canadian courts, lay in the interpretation given by McLachlin C.J. to the "minimal impairment" part of the test. Drawing heavily upon an article in the 2007 issue of the *University of Toronto Law Review*,[95] she accepted the formulation of this part of the test put forward by the President of the Israeli Supreme Court. In his analysis, the requirement for minimal impairment meant only that the government had to show that its objective could not be achieved by less drastic means.

Obviously, the first step in applying this test was to determine what the government's objective actually had been. McLachlin C.J. commented that a court should be wary of allowing the government objective to be formulated in such a precise way that the law would be immunized from challenge.[96] But when she turned to the government objective in this case, she framed it principally as an intention to protect the "integrity" of the driver licensing system.[97] "Integrity" is defined as "undivided or unbroken completeness or totality with nothing wanting" by Princeton University's WordNet. Under this definition, of course, any lack of uniformity in licensing processes would damage, indeed destroy, the "integrity of the licensing system." It is perhaps not surprising that McLachlin C.J. went on to hold that exempting Hutterites from the photo requirement would "significantly compromise" the government's objective.[98]

Yet, the purpose of preserving the "integrity" of the licensing system was not simply that some ideal of "completeness" be aesthetically

achieved. One would think it preposterous if a government could justify its actions through adopting a goal unconnected with the public
good. The purpose of the regulation, as McLachlin C.J. also recognized, although usually in tandem with "integrity," was to reduce the
use of driver's licences in identity theft.[99] If we frame the issue in that
way, we can then go on to ask the question whether the existence of
an exemption for about 250 Hutterites (the number who had claimed
the exemption in the past) would significantly undermine the govern
ment's objective.

As the lower courts, and the minority of the Supreme Court, all
pointed out, 700,000 Albertans did not hold driver's licences and were
therefore not represented in the facial recognition database; thus it
would seem highly improbable, and indeed the government presented
no evidence to suggest, that the addition of another 250 missing photos would significantly undermine efforts to reduce identity theft.[100] In
addition, as the Court of Appeal pointed out, the licensing information
would contain considerable personal data that could be used for the
identification of an unphotographed driver.[101] Even more, the government had proposed no other identification measures that might have
satisfied both their goals and those of the Hutterites.[102] In light of these
facts, it seemed untenable to hold – as McLachlin C.J. did – that there
was no less infringing solution to the problem than requiring universal photography of drivers unless one accepts that the government's
goal was to achieve perfection and nothing short would therefore oat
isfy it.[103]

At this point, the reader may be wondering what has happened to
our duty to accommodate minority religious practice. In *Multani*,[104] as
we discussed earlier in chapter 3, the Supreme Court had found that
"minimal impairment" required a concept similar to accommodation in
that administrative rules had to be modified to preserve religious freedom up to the point at which the goal of the rule would be defeated.
McLachlin C.J. in the *Hutterian Brethren* decision drew a firm line between cases such as *Multani*, in which we were dealing with administrative practice or state action, and cases in which we were dealing with
legislation (or regulations made pursuant to legislation). In these latter
cases, she held, the concept of accommodation had no place. Laws of
general application were not required to be tailored to take account of
individual religious practice. McLachlin C.J. suggested in fact that it
would be almost impossible, in our highly regulated society, for governments to meet this obligation.[105]

Of course, governments cannot be expected to be aware of every unusual religious belief that may be affected by a particular piece of legislation. However, McLachlin C.J. badly overstated the problem. In the case before the court, the government was well aware of the religious objections before it changed the regulation. It was not required to speculate on the practices of obscure, unknown sects. In addition, we may be sceptical of the assertion that "it is inevitable that some religious practices will come into conflict with laws of general application"[106] and that therefore these conflicts are "inevitable." Few laws of general application have impact upon people's religious practices; most are in fact neutral. Where they are not, it is no answer to say that we must simply accept the outcome where a simple and reasonable exemption or "accommodation" would relieve the problem. That is precisely the role which the Charter grants to the courts.

The perspective that McLachlin C.J. adopted appears to absolve government from any requirement that its legislation take into consideration possible exemptions for those whose religious practices may be affected by it. In a comment on the case, Professor Richard Moon suggested that "It is not obvious that religious practices should be accommodated – that the state should be required to compromise its policy to make space for a religious practice."[107] I have earlier considered the difficulty that arises when cases can be brought either under provincial human rights legislation or under the Charter. Under human rights legislation, accommodation is required. It may give rise to inconsistency of result if similar cases, when brought under the Charter against government, give rise to no similar duty. I have also considered, in discussing the *Reference* on polygamy, that criminalizing conduct leaves no room for accommodation. However, apart from criminal law, few initiatives of the legislature have to be universally applied to preserve their intended effect. In such cases, it is difficult to see why accommodation should not be required, particularly when we consider freedom of religion and conscience to be key to the democratic system. Protection of freedom of conscience and religion by reasonable accommodation where it can be done without serious detriment to the legislative scheme is not only desirable; it is essential. The Supreme Court seems to have ignored these issues.

Moreover, the stance of the Supreme Court is in conflict with its earlier decision in *Edwards Books and Art*.[108] In that case, you will recall, the legislation contained a provision to ameliorate the effect of compulsory Sunday closing on Saturday-observing groups. The question of whether the measure was sufficient to constitute the legislation's scheme as meeting the minimal impairment test was considered at some length. In the course of that discussion, Dickson J. considered the American case law on Sunday closing laws in which the U.S. Supreme Court held that no exemptions were required to make the legislation constitutional. Dickson J. commented,

> Having said this, however, I do not share the views of the majority of the United States Supreme Court that no legislative effort need be made to accommodate the interests of any Saturday-observing retailers … In my view, the principles articulated in *Oakes* make it incumbent on a legislature which enacts Sunday closing laws to attempt very seriously to alleviate the effects of those laws on Saturday observers.[109]

It seems clear from this that the views of McLachlin C.J. about what is required for a law to meet the test of minimal impairment are very far from the previous approach of our courts.

Having found that the law met the tests of pressing objective, rational connection, and minimal impairment, McLachlin C.J. turned to the final stage of determining whether the law was proportional in its effects. This is the only place in the *Oakes* analysis,[110] according to the interpretation by the President of the Israeli court and adopted by McLachlin C.J., in which the judge is to examine the actual harm to the claimants.[111] In this step, the judge must look at the salutary effects of the law and balance them against the harm.

McLachlin C.J. was unconvinced that much harm would be done to the Hutterite colony if none of its members could have drivers' licences and they were therefore required to rely on hired transportation.[112] She described the effect as simply an increased cost in practising their religion, not a serious impediment.[113] In contrast, she distinguished the *Multani* case by stating that the school board's refusal to allow Mr Multani to carry his kirpan created a barrier that effectively precluded him from practising his faith. In fact, at the time Mr Multani's appeal was heard by the Supreme Court, he was attending a private school at which his kirpan was allowed.[114] Thus, for an increased cost, he was indeed able to practise his faith. Upon closer examination, therefore, it would not seem that the analysis on which McLachlin C.J. based her distinction between the cases can be supported.

What was completely missing from the analysis of the majority was the understanding that there is anything at stake in this case other than the preferences of a small minority about their religious practices. Yet this decision will clearly contribute to the isolation of those with differing beliefs from the social networks of Canadian life. While it may be possible to hire drivers to transport goods to market or perform a number of similar, economically valuable tasks, anyone who has lived in a rural community knows the difficulty of any social interactions without being able to drive. The decision of the court seems at odds in many ways with the previously generous treatment of minority interests that we observed in earlier chapters. However, it was quite consistent with the courts' general lack of concern to support the public practice of religious difference in ways that foster communication and democratic participation.

9. Conclusion

Courts' neglect of any dimension to freedom of conscience and religion other than the private has led to difficulties in many areas in which religion seems to impinge on the public square. Although the court in *Chamberlain* expressed sympathy for participation of people with varying motivations (religious or not) in public life and recognized the inevitability of that dimension of public debate, the decision itself failed to take the next step of recognizing a role for the court in holding an even hand between competing beliefs. While courts have had to struggle with conflict in the public school system over teachers who express unpopular or abhorrent beliefs, even on their own time, they have not been able to derive principles that would help them make justifiable choices in areas where moral worlds clash. Only in the more straightforward protest cases have courts seemed able to recognize any value to preserving open processes in which belief systems can be displayed, debated, and challenged. And in those cases, the courts have leaned more heavily upon freedom of expression, with its more obvious connections to public life, than on freedom of conscience and religion.

Other than in the protest cases, the only area in which courts' decisions seem regularly to have promoted public understanding and acceptance of difference in belief has been in the cases of accommodation of minority religious practice. As we saw in chapter 3, this has not been done without exciting public criticism, and courts' justifications for their accommodations under the head of equality have apparently proved unconvincing to many. The decision in *Hutterian Brethren Colony of Wilson* may signal a change in that approach, certainly where the government action under attack is legislative in nature. How far have the courts been influenced by negative public opinion? Of course, one cannot say with any degree of certainty. However, the exclusionary tendency of many of the decisions we have looked at may be now nudging the court in the same direction in considering minority rights. If so, it would seem to be a retreat from a concept of openly lived plurality of beliefs that will have unhappy consequences on our democratic life. Unable to justify that concept to the public satisfaction in their decisions, our courts may perhaps be simply retreating from the ideal.

The cases such as *Multani*,[115] *Amselem*,[116] and *Grant*[117] that we looked at in chapter 3 relied to a certain extent upon ideas drawn from principles developed in litigation over legal interpretations of human rights codes. The idea that accommodation of difference was required of government as well as of private citizens had a powerful influence on these decisions. The Supreme Court, in *Hutterian Brethren*, seems to have tried to differentiate more starkly the duties of government and private citizens in that regard and seems to have done so at the expense of protecting citizens against government overreach. However, cases under human rights codes have presented their own difficulties as citizens' rights often seem to come into conflict with one another and courts are often at a loss as to how to reconcile the conflicts. How freedom of religion and conscience has fared in such conflicts and how this, in turn, impacts the vigour of our democratic debate will be the topic of the next two chapters.

Chapter Five

Human Rights: A Zero Sum Game?

1. Introduction

Up to this point, we have discussed primarily freedom of conscience and religion as protected by the Charter of Rights and Freedoms.[1] Most of the cases we have reviewed have been assertions of citizens' rights against the reach of the state, although we have looked at parallels with rights of individuals against each other and, in a couple of cases, have made a brief sortie into that field.[2]

In this chapter we will turn to a direct consideration of provincial and Federal human rights legislation that governs the interaction of private citizens. In chapter 1, I briefly outlined the structure of these legislative schemes. We will look at representative samples of human rights statutes in more detail in the next few pages. Also in chapter 1, I made the observation that human rights legislation protects rights to conscience and religion less directly than does the fundamental freedom of conscience and religion in the Charter. The right to believe and express openly one's beliefs is indirectly protected by ensuring access to important social goods by persons of all beliefs. It will be much more difficult for me to practise my Muslim faith if no landlord will rent accommodation to a Muslim. Similarly, if I am shut out of employment or denied common services because of my faith, it will diminish my participation in society. It is protection against these kinds of barriers that human rights statutes extend.

But the conferral on citizens of these rights that can be enforced against other citizens in private transactions has led to considerable controversy. Suppose I want to hire a nanny for my three-year-old. A woman applies and makes no secret of the fact that she is an atheist. I want my child raised as a Jew. I doubt that someone who is not a practising Jew will have the understanding, sympathy, and attitude that I want communicated to my child. Can I refuse to employ her? What if, rather than in a private home, the position is in a Jewish nursery school? Should that make a difference? Why? Suppose I am an Evangelical Christian who firmly opposes gay marriage. Should I be required to rent my hall to celebrate a same-sex wedding? Should I be required to perform the wedding ceremony if I am licensed to do so?

Human rights legislation has to deal with just such difficult questions. But the first thing we should note is that the prohibitions on discrimination in the private sphere are conferred by statute and, because the subject matter of the statute usually deals with matters of provincial jurisdiction within a province, each province has its own legislation, which may have different provisions. There is also a Federal human rights act[3] which is applicable to ventures (such as broadcasting or the military) that fall within Federal domain. It too has a slightly different organization and different wording from some of the provincial acts.

Little is more boring than a provision-by-provision comparison of legislation. But before we turn to the case law, we should be aware of some of the similarities and some of the differences in these separate regimes. First, all provincial statutes and the Federal act identify specific grounds on which certain kinds of discrimination are prohibited. As I noted in chapter 1, these uniformly include religion or creed. Also uniformly protected are race, sex, and sexual orientation. However, some differences in the enumerated grounds are also present, such as the protection in Manitoba[4] of political belief, which is absent from most other regimes. Criminal conviction is also treated differently in different provinces.

Second, they all prohibit discrimination on these grounds in specified transactions. Employment, provision of services commonly available to the public, rental and purchase of accommodation, and membership in trade unions are common transactions in which citizens can expect protection from private discriminatory treatment. However, differences exist here as well. Saskatchewan,[5] for example, also prohibits discrimination in the contracting process and has a specific section dealing with education, although under the other provincial statutes education would be treated as a "service commonly available to the public."

Finally, all the statutes contain some provisions relieving or exempting certain instances of discrimination from being held illegal. For example, in employment, the statutes all allow discrimination, at least on certain grounds, where the characteristic on which the discrimination is made would be a fair requirement for the job. But some of the statues have broader defences than do others. For example, the B.C. statute exempts any bona fide occupational requirement,[6] but the Saskatchewan code exempts only discrimination where "sex, ability or age is a reasonable occupational qualification and requirement for the position."[7] British Columbia provides a general exemption for preferences given to members of certain groups by charitable or religious organizations that are providing a service to a group identified by physical or mental disability, race, religion, age, sex, marital status, political belief, colour, ancestry, or place of origin.[8] Other provinces do not have such a general provision, but may provide specific instances where a preference may be given.[9]

In earlier chapters, we also considered the requirement under both some Charter cases and human rights legislation that accommodation for difference could be refused where the accommodation would result in undue hardship. In some provinces, such as British Columbia, the human rights legislation makes no reference to this concept. Rather, it refers to a bona fide and reasonable justification for discrimination under certain sections of the act. Courts have interpreted this to mean that for the discrimination to be allowable, the respondent must show that the protected characteristic could not be accommodated without undue hardship. Some provinces, such as Ontario,[10] however, expressly refer to the undue hardship defence in their legislation and even list factors for consideration in determining whether undue hardship has been shown.

Even where the provisions seem substantially similar, there are differences in the organization of the statutes and in the wording of some of the sections that may or may not be significant. It is not my purpose here to conduct a detailed analysis of these statutes, but only to point out some of the broad differences among them and to note that when we discuss the case law decided under these statutes, we will need to pay close attention to the wording of the statutory provisions. What constitutes illegal discrimination in one province or what is a defence to a claim of discrimination in one province may not always be in another.

Although many services and goods are provided by the private sector, government is also heavily involved in the lives of most citizens through social programs and through regulation. Just as protection from discrimination on the basis of religion in the private sector facilitates the practice of religion by ensuring the inclusion of those with differing beliefs in our social life, equal access to government programs and to equal legal treatment is ensured in part under human rights acts, but also under s. 15 of the Charter. Section 15 is not structured in quite the same way as human rights statutes. For one thing, the grounds on which discrimination is prohibited are not extensively enumerated; analogous grounds can be and have been read into the section.[11] We will look at s. 15 in more detail in the next section of this chapter.

2. What Is "Discrimination"?

Almost everything we do requires us to recognize differences, evaluate those differences, and choose one set of differing characteristics over another. I want dessert. Cheesecake is creamy and sweet but it has more calories than fruit salad. I consider the differences, evaluate their importance to me, and discriminate between the two possibilities on the basis of my current evaluation of those differences. Similarly, although there will normally be more rational criteria than taste, if I am hiring someone, I will be presented with a variety of skill sets that I may consider more or less desirable for the job I have at hand. Between applicants, I will weigh the differing skills and determine which I prefer for the position I am going to fill. Sometimes, there may be a very logical connection; but not always. I may just like candidate A better than candidate B. In fact, usually, my instinctive like or dislike will weigh in my mind and there is no legal reason why it should not.

Many of the prohibited grounds of discrimination under human rights legislation can be characterized as prohibiting choices made on the basis of grounds that are both irrelevant and that our society has come to believe are socially harmful. We do not believe, in hiring, for example, that a person's race or colour should be relevant; furthermore, we believe that to distinguish people based upon these kinds of characteristics is socially harmful and immoral. It is an affront to their human dignity to believe that simply because of race or colour, a person is more capable of performing a certain job than someone of another race or colour.

But not every difference or distinction fits this pattern, even if it is based upon personal characteristics that in some circumstances we would consider an unfair basis for decision. If I select Katy for my law firm as the new associate lawyer rather than John because Katy's law school grades were all A's and John's were all C's, I am certainly distinguishing between them on the basis of their abilities. Possibly John is simply not as intelligent as Katy. However, we would not think it unfair for me to pick Katy in this case. On the other hand, if I were renting an apartment to John or Katy, we would not be so tolerant towards my discrimination against John on the basis of his lack of intellectual ability. Or, for another example, while we generally want to eliminate discrimination on the basis of sex, a symbol of a man on a washroom door should not be illegal where one washroom is reserved for men and another for women.

The question of when making a difference between people might be justified, even where the basis for the distinction is a personal characteristic that should often be irrelevant, is a particular problem for government programs. These programs typically differentiate on the basis of age, ability or disability, socio-economic, family, or marital status, and a wide range of other personal characteristics or behaviours. Governments, which are in the business of providing a vast number of social programs including such varying services as medical care, education, tax rebates for certain activities, basic financial support for the poor, community services for the elderly, and subsidized housing, make these distinctions daily. Government programs may be challenged on the basis of human rights legislation as services commonly available to the public. They may also be challenged under s. 15 of the Charter, which provides that Canadians are entitled to equal treatment under the law and to equal protection and benefit of the law "without discrimination" on the basis of the familiar categories of race, colour, religion, age, or disability.

Challenges to these programs have led the courts to give careful consideration to how we can characterize cases where there should be a legal remedy and cases where there should not. One approach under s. 15 of the Charter would be to classify any difference on the basis of an enumerated or analogous ground as a violation of equality. Then, it would be up to the government to justify that difference under s. 1 by showing it was justifiable in a free and democratic society. This approach has been rejected by the courts, who have instead tried to narrow the definition of discrimination in such a way as to exclude some cases where a difference is made.

The leading case, *Law v. Canada (Minister of Immigration and Employment)*,[12] recommitted the courts to the concept of substantive equality as the fundamental purpose underlying s. 15: that is, equality in the effects of the law on people in differing circumstances rather than a law that on its surface simply makes no differences between persons or groups. We have already discussed this idea briefly in chapter 3. The court held that this commitment to substantive equality arose because s. 15 was intended to:

> prevent the violation of essential human dignity and freedom through the imposition of disadvantage, stereotyping or political or social prejudice and to promote a society in which all persons enjoy equal recognition at law as human beings ... equally capable and equally deserving of concern, respect, and consideration.[13]

Although the decision in *Law* did not involve discrimination on the basis of religion but of age, it is worth briefly considering the case and its outcome as a foundation for our later discussion in this and the next chapter.

Ms Law was the widow of a contributor to the Canada Pension Plan. She was denied a survivor's pension because the plan did not provide this benefit to widows or widowers under the age of thirty-five unless some special circumstances existed. Ms Law was thirty. She challenged the constitutionality of the law on the basis that it violated s. 15, which prohibits discrimination on the basis of age. We can probably all see why CPP denies a pension to young, able-bodied people. However, it is more difficult to develop legal standards that will tell us why this should not be illegal discrimination in this case and, in the future, how other cases should be decided.

The Supreme Court of Canada in *Law* held that for a law to constitute discriminatory treatment under s. 15, the claimants must show that it made a difference in the sense of withholding a benefit or imposing a burden upon them, that this distinction was made on the basis of an enumerated or analogous ground, and that it discriminated against them in a substantive sense, taking into account the purposes of s. 15. The court identified four factors to consider in determining whether there was discrimination. These included whether the claimant was a member of a group that had some pre-existing disadvantage or was the target of stereotyping or prejudice; what correspondence existed between the grounds on which the claim was based and need, capacity, or circumstance; whether the law had an ameliorative purpose or effect on more disadvantaged groups; and what was the nature of the interests affected by the law.[14] Using these factors, the court held that the denial of a pension to Ms Law was not a violation of s. 15.

The decision in *Law* has been criticized by numerous scholars, first on its insistence that s. 15 does not apply to all instances of formal

inequality based on protected grounds, and second, even by scholars who support this basic approach, on the basis that the concept of
human dignity is not suitable as a legal tool for analysing discrimination.[15] I will have considerably more to say on this matter later.
However, the Supreme Court itself seems to have recognized the difficulties with the *Law* test. While not calling the authority of the decision into question, the court in its later decision *R. v. Kapp*[16] articulated
the view that while "human dignity" was a fundamental concept underlying the s. 15 equality guarantee, the concept was too abstract to
be useful as a legal test. The court warned against applying *Law* as if
the test set out in it was itself a piece of legislation to be applied in
every aspect to every case.[17]

When government programs are not in issue, but we are dealing
with the relationships among private citizens under human rights
legislation, the question arises as to whether the approach the court
took in *Law* has any place. Certainly, there must be some question as
to whether human rights legislation is intended to mould our society
along the egalitarian lines that courts have found inherent in the Charter equality rights provision. We are not talking about general social
programs and aims of government bureaucracy but rather about one
individual's treatment of another. While such individual treatment certainly may contribute to or detract from social peace, harmony, and a
personal sense of belonging and worth, it is not expected to ameliorate
social ills in the same way as are government actions.

Moreover, as we have seen in the preceding section, human rights
statutes already have defences built into the scheme of things in which
the legislature has apparently recognized that making some differences
can be permitted without being illegal discrimination. Provisions such
as "bona fide occupational requirement" in the context of employment
or "bona fide and reasonable justification" in the context of services
available to the public provide ways of differentiating conduct that is
illegal from conduct that the legislature has decided will be tolerated.
Requiring that another hurdle be crossed by human rights complainants before they can show that their complaint fits within the statute
does not appear to fit with the general structure of human rights legislation. Moreover, adding such discretionary factors as membership in
disadvantaged groups, stereotyping, or taking account of need or individualized circumstances provides more opportunities for subjective
judgments on the part of tribunals and courts. Such uncertain subjective judgments are already part of Charter jurisprudence, as we have

seen in our various discussions of s. 1. Without necessity, it might be wise to leave them out of consideration in people's private dealings.

Despite all this, it appears that the *Law* test will apply in certain circumstances to human rights acts. In some cases, human rights statutes prohibit particular actions, whether or not they are "discriminatory." For example, Alberta prohibits refusing employment to someone on the basis of one of the prohibited grounds. The word "discrimination" is not mentioned in this context, but only in the following paragraph, which makes it also illegal to "discriminate against any person with regard to employment."[18] In British Columbia the Human Rights Code has a similar structure, but the statute also defines as "discrimination" the act of refusing to employ someone on one of the enumerated grounds.[19] Where it is not necessary to prove "discrimination" or where the statute itself defines what is discrimination, it would seem that the test in *Law* should be inapplicable.[20] However, the Supreme Court of Canada has signalled that where human rights legislation requires a consideration of what constitutes discrimination, *Law* is applicable.[21] The B.C. Court of Appeal in *International Forest Products v. Sandhu*[22] has applied this test to rule that the prima facie case for discrimination may require an examination of the factors in *Law*.

3. How Does This Affect Discrimination on the Basis of Religion?

Where a claim is made under s. 15 of the Charter that there has been a denial of equal treatment under the law based upon religion, the test for discrimination will require something more than simply showing that the law provided a different treatment of the claimant as a result of the claimant's religious beliefs. We have already spent considerable time on the Supreme Court of Canada's decision in *Hutterian Brethren of Wilson Colony*[23] in the context of the claim that the colony members' rights to freedom of conscience and religion were denied by the regulation. But as well as the claim for violation of the Hutterites' freedom of religion, the Colony also advanced the claim that the law discriminated against them on the basis of their religion, contrary to s. 15 of the Charter.

McLachlin C.J. noted that the s. 15 claim had not been considered in detail by the lower courts. She dismissed the claim in only a few short paragraphs.[24] Of course, since she found that the limitation on freedom of conscience and religion was justifiable under s. 1 of the Charter, she could have applied the same reasoning to any violation of equality rights under s. 15. However, she also observed that the distinction made did not "arise from any demeaning stereotype, but from a neutral and rationally defensible policy choice."[25] She therefore found that there was no breach of s. 15(1); the hurdle for demonstrating discrimination had not been met.

This short disposal of the s. 15 claim illustrates the difficulties with the factors in *Law* and in *Kapp* as applied to religion. If the purpose of s. 15 is to promote substantive equality, then the impact of the law must be examined. The question is not simply whether the law appears neutral, but whether in its effects it is so. There is no doubt that the requirement for photo drivers' licences had a different impact on Hutterites than on the average citizen and there is no doubt that this impact was due to the Hutterites' religious beliefs. However, the court was able to say that the impact was not due to any "demeaning stereotype" and that therefore the law did not violate s. 15. This creates a logical problem for s. 15. Substantive equality (supposedly the aim of s. 15) means that the intent of the law is not relevant – the fact that the framer did not intend to target a particular group does not matter if the law impacts that group adversely. Yet it is impossible to see how a law could arise from stereotypical conceptions of a religious group unless it was to some degree directly targeted at that group. To arise from a demeaning stereotype, the law would have to contain or address some preconceived, generalized attribute of the religious group. Yet the very claim of a violation of substantive equality is that the law as written does not appear to be discriminatory; only in its application does it become so. Chief Justice McLachlin's approach would appear to contradict the very foundations that the court has provided for s. 15.

Most cases of religious discrimination, whether as a result of a law and thus subject to challenge under s. 15 of the Charter or as a result of private dealings and thus subject to proceedings under human rights legislation, arise from indirect effects of general rules. These rules do not contain any stereotypical assumptions about a particular religion; they simply affect members of a particular belief system differently, usually in a way that was unforeseen. In addition, it is often arguable whether or not a particular religious group is historically disadvantaged. Certainly at one time in our history, we could point to legally entrenched discrimination against certain beliefs. For example, even today, a Catholic cannot ascend to the British throne. Civil disadvantage once attached to membership in specific religious groups, particularly in England, where the Church of England is an established church.

Religious tolerance has a long history in Canada,[26] even if the law often ran ahead of popular practice. However, it would now be a matter of heated debate with little chance of objective resolution as to which religious or belief systems, if any, in Canada bear the mark of historical disadvantage.

The effort of the courts to find some way to distinguish between different treatment for which there should be a legal remedy and different treatment for which no legal remedy should be available has thus the potential to undermine protections particularly against discrimination on the basis of belief. In addition, the open-textured nature of the requirements set out in *Law*, even as interpreted in *Kapp*, allow substantial judicial discretion to focus on or ignore factors that are crucial to the outcome. In the next section of this chapter, I will review a number of cases in which claims of discrimination on the basis of religion or creed have been considered by the courts. We will see that this emerging problem has not yet been adequately addressed.

First, however, I will add a word about the debate on human dignity and its place in Charter and human rights jurisprudence.

4. What's Being Human Got to Do with It?

Contrary to the views of the Supreme Court of Canada in *Kapp* and the views of a number of commentators, I intend to argue in this section of the chapter that the concept of human dignity, while not a precise legal tool, is both an essential idea in the interpretation of human rights and a useful one that can help us solve some of the difficulties that human rights cases present, particularly with respect to organizing belief systems.[27] The courts have not paid adequate attention to the possibilities inherent in this idea.

Most of us want to believe that our human rights are not just something that the state confers and can, should it be so minded, take away at its whim. For these reasons, we enshrine human rights in constitutional documents and even, when the rights are conferred by statute, protect and regulate those statutes by constitutional means. For these reasons, we have international statements of human rights, such as the U.N. Declaration of Human Rights, developed and adopted after the atrocities of the Second World War. Yet it is very difficult to find a theory that we can agree upon to support the idea of universal human rights. Legal philosophers have proposed various theories. If one is a theist, the matter may be quite simple because one can believe that the

Creator has endowed humans with basic natural rights. Without the-
ism, however, the matter becomes more difficult.[28]

The idea that, however we derive it, human beings have a basic dignity that must be respected, simply because they are human, is a mediating idea that can be adopted by people of many varying beliefs.
One can believe this arose through natural evolutionary processes, was
conferred by an all-powerful Creator, or is simply a convention that we
will and that therefore has validity for us. The idea of human dignity
thus provides a place from which we can all agree to start, whatever
may lie behind our adoption of that place, and on which we can rest the
fundamental idea that there are some things that must be done to other
human beings and some things that must not be done. This does not,
of course, solve all or even the most pressing problems. Who counts as
"human"? What is human dignity? What rights will flow from the recognition of human dignity? All these questions are still up for debate.
But we at least have an agreed-upon starting place where our belief systems overlap to a large degree.

The court in *Kapp* thought that the idea of human dignity was too
"subjective" to be useful.[29] It is true that Iacobucci J. in *Law* treated the
idea of human dignity as a largely subjective idea.[30] However, that is
not necessarily the case. We can think of dignity as only being something we feel and thus something that will vary from person to person.
On the other hand, we can think of it as something that is an objective
fact about ourselves, not at all dependent upon our feelings. For example, consider an elderly woman in a nursing home who is no longer
able to have much grasp of her surroundings. When she is sedated and
tied to a chair for the convenience of the nursing staff, she may well not
feel that her dignity has been offended. However, I would suggest that
most of us would consider this treatment to be a violation of her human
dignity. Even more convincing is the idea that most of us, and most cultures, hold that we must not disrespect the body of a dead person. The
dead person does not likely appreciate that his or her dignity is being
damaged, but we still believe that certain things must not be done to
the dead because the body was once a human being.

This is not to say that it is easy to agree upon the exact meaning of
human dignity; only that the content is not wholly subjective and, indeed, need not be treated by the courts as simply depending upon how
we feel. Courts are very used to dealing with vague concepts and giving them meaning. The fact is that although we may not be able to say

with certainty everything about what human dignity implies, we can say some things about it and those things can be useful.

The first way we can demonstrate this utility is to think about the problem of discrimination on the basis of religion that I pointed out in the last section of this chapter. It would seem that a law that does not directly target a religious group cannot be discriminatory under the test in *Hutterian Brethren of Wilson Colony*. Yet the whole idea of substantive equality, which has been frequently held to be the aim of s. 15, requires that laws not directly targeted against particular groups can still be discriminatory. The problem arose from the finding of McLachlin C.J. that some form of stereotyping had to be inherent in the legislation for it to have a discriminatory effect.

If the court had considered the broader question of whether the legislation offended the human dignity of the Hutterite Colony members, it would have been able to maintain a test for discrimination that involved more than a simple distinction on a prohibited ground, but that still allowed the effects of the law to determine whether or not it was discriminatory. The effect of the regulation requiring photo driver licences excluded the Hutterite colony members from normal participation in an activity that our society generally considers a right for those of mature age and sufficient skill and knowledge. It also tended to exclude the colony members from interactions in our social structure that we consider part of Canadian life. Of course, stereotyping offends human dignity. But it is not the only thing that does so. Religious discrimination, as we will see in the next section of this chapter, has the effect of exclusion from important social goods that are generally available to all. It thus violates the respect that we owe to one another as human beings.

Another criticism of the use of the concept of human dignity in legal cases has been that it promotes individualism and is thus at odds with the idea of equality and a more communitarian value system.[31] This neglects the fact that it is only the concept of human dignity that can provide a relational aspect to human rights. We may frequently be irritated by groups demanding their "rights" which seem to conflict with or limit the rights of others. It often seems that if I have my rights, you must be deprived of yours. In other words, the assertion of human rights results in a struggle that amounts to a "zero sum." Various proposals to balance rights or limit rights are put forward by both the courts and commentators. We will look at this problem of conflicting rights particularly in the next chapter. But for the moment, we will consider the idea of conflicting rights in the abstract.

If my rights depend upon my human dignity, and nothing else, then it is obvious that you (and all others I acknowledge as sharing in human dignity) have the same rights, for the same reason. If my behaviour deprives you of your human dignity, then I have also denied myself human dignity and the rights that would flow from it. That is because I have by my actions against you rejected the idea that human rights depend upon a dignity that attaches to a person by virtue of being human. At this point, I am no longer entitled to human rights either because either we all have them or none do. What this means is that if I purport to assert a human right that would, if recognized, violate your human dignity and thus your human rights, I am asserting no right at all. My human rights must include treating you with the dignity proper to a human being. I do not have any human right that does not include this feature.[32]

Let's take the common notion of how rights conflict expressed in the old proverb "My right to swing my fist ends where your face begins." This proverb expresses the "zero sum" idea of human rights. I have the right to mobility, but I cannot exercise that right if my mobility right would injure you, violating your right to safety. But if I hit you, I am clearly violating your right to be free from unprovoked violence. By inflicting this violence on you, I am not exercising my right but rather denying that human beings have a right to be free from unprovoked violence by virtue of their humanity. I am denying the very basis of my own right to free mobility. It is more accurate, therefore, to say that my right to swing my fist requires your right to be free from unprovoked violent attack. In the same way, your right to be free from violence requires my right to move freely. Our rights are therefore not in conflict but are interdependent, and one cannot be defined without understanding the other.

In this way, an objective conception of human dignity as the foundation for human rights can lead to an alternative conception of what a human right is. In the next chapter, I will return to this conception as we look more directly at cases in which human rights appear to be in conflict and courts struggle to find some way in which this conflict can be resolved. In the meantime, however, we will turn to some of the cases in which claimants have sought to protect the practices of their beliefs (usually religious beliefs) through claims of discrimination under human rights law. In this context, we will look at how and to what extent claims of religious discrimination have facilitated the practice of varying belief systems and the participation in society of those holding them.

5. Claims of Religious Discrimination

We will start with an examination of three foundational decisions of the Supreme Court of Canada on issues of religious discrimination. The first, *Ontario Human Rights Commission et al. v. Simpsons Sears*,[33] arose from a complaint brought by Ms O'Malley that her employer had discriminated against her on the basis of her religion. Ms O'Malley had converted to the Seventh Day Adventist church, which required strict observance of the Sabbath from sunset Friday until sunset Saturday. As an employee of Simpsons Sears, she was required to work on Saturdays. She was willing to leave her employment, but Simpsons Sears offered her instead part-time work that did not require work on Saturday. The employer also offered to try to find her another position with them that did not require Saturday work, but during the relevant time, the only position of that sort that became available was one for which she was not qualified. Eventually, on her marriage, Ms O'Malley decided she only wanted to work part time, but she brought a human rights complaint seeking to be reimbursed for the loss of earnings between full- and part-time employment up to the time she decided to voluntarily accept part-time status.

This case was decided in 1985 when the law relating to human rights was just being shaped by the courts. The Board of Inquiry under the act, the Ontario Divisional Court, and the Court of Appeal all dismissed Ms O'Malley's complaint. The Board held that there had been discrimination, but that the employer had acted reasonably in seeking to accommodate her.[34] The Divisional Court and Court of Appeal upheld the dismissal because the requirement to work Saturdays was a general rule that applied to all employees in similar positions. Her religion was not singled out and thus the rule was not discriminatory.[35] We are aware from earlier discussions that this is not how the law developed, and in this case, the Supreme Court of Canada clearly laid down the principle that discrimination need not be overt; discriminatory effects of the rule were sufficient to violate Ms O'Malley's human rights. At the time, the court referred to this as "adverse effect" discrimination and for some time there was discussion about whether the same principles applied to both direct and indirect instances of discriminatory conduct.[36]

The case also answered the question of how conduct that was prima facie discriminatory could be legally defended. If we allow that a seemingly neutral rule constitutes discrimination because it operates differently on one group to that group's detriment and that this effect is caused by the group's protected characteristic under the statute, such as religion, then we have opened a very wide door indeed. Arguably, any difference would be prohibited; yet, as we have analysed in other contexts, there may be facts upon which the distinctions are not blameworthy and, indeed, may be almost inescapable. To identify these cases, the Supreme Court introduced the concepts of accommodation and undue hardship.[37] These concepts were borrowed from American jurisprudence and, as we know, have since flourished in Canada.

Simpsons Sears was found to have discriminated against Ms O'Malley on the basis of her religion. Discrimination under the act, the court held, did not require an intent to discriminate. Once discrimination was found, Simpsons Sears had the duty to accommodate Ms O'Malley up to the point of undue hardship. There was no evidence that Simpsons Sears had discharged that duty.

In *Central Okanagan School District No. 23 v. Renaud*,[38] the Supreme Court of Canada elaborated on the duty to accommodate. The complainant was a Seventh Day Adventist who worked as a caretaker in a school. As part of the collective agreement, he was required to work Friday evening. The union resisted any scheduling change, and, after some attempts to reach an accommodation agreement, the employer fired the complainant when he failed to show up for his Friday evening shift. The Supreme Court held that the requirements of a collective agreement must give way to the requirements of human rights legislation and that the union also had a duty to try to accommodate Mr Renaud. The court did note that significant disruption in the employer's business could be a factor in finding undue hardship, as could concerns that rights of other employees would be seriously affected. However, simply the insistence that the collective agreement be adhered to, irrespective of its discriminatory effect, was not to be considered.[39]

The third case, *Commission scholaire regionale de Chambly v. Bergevin*,[40] again illustrated adverse discriminatory effects of a standard policy and the requirements for accommodation. Jewish teachers who wished to observe Yom Kippur took the day as an unpaid day of leave and then filed a grievance claiming that they should be paid, since Christmas and Good Friday were allowed Christians without financial penalty to celebrate their religious holidays. The court held that the school calendar did discriminate against the Jewish teachers and that they were entitled to accommodation, which meant that they should be allowed the day off with pay. The school district did not lead evidence that paying the teachers for this day constituted undue hardship.

This case was later considered by the Ontario Court of Appeal in *Ontario v. Grievance Settlement Board*.[41] There, the employer had a policy on religious observance which allowed two paid days to be taken annually for religious reasons. The employee, Mr Tratnyek, however, belonged to a minority faith that required eleven days off in the year. He requested the days with pay but was told that he could not have more than the two provided for in the policy. However, the employer's policy also allowed employees requiring more days for religious reasons to be accommodated through scheduling changes. One of these changes allowed the employee to compress fifteen work days into fourteen and take the fifteenth day in the three-week cycle free from work without any financial penalty. While this policy did not completely solve Mr Tratnyek's problem, because the policy required the days to be taken as single days in the three-week period while the employee's religion often required contiguous days for celebration, the employer was willing to adjust this policy and allow the employee to bank his days off.

The Court of Appeal distinguished *Chambly* on the basis that scheduling changes were not available on the school calendar. It found that this employer (the Ontario government) had properly accommodated Mr Tratnyek by allowing him to arrange his work so that his religious obligations could be satisfied. Paid days off were not the only reasonable accommodation that was acceptable to the law.

All of these cases, with the exception of the Ontario Court of Appeal's decision in *Ontario v. Grievance Settlement Board*, were decided previous to *Law*.[42] None suggested that any factor other than showing that the rule in question affected the complainant differently and to her detriment because of her religious commitments was required to found a claim of discrimination. Of course, it was open to the defendant, even if the claim of discrimination was made out, to rebut the claim by proving that it had accommodated the claimant up to the point of undue hardship. The questions of stereotyping, disadvantage, or prejudice were not addressed by any of these courts.

However, this is not surprising if the courts had, at least prior to *Law* and *Kapp*,[43] accepted the common-sense notion that unreasonably excluding someone from an important social good because of his or her religious faith is in itself an affront to human dignity. The right to follow one's conscience in the pursuit of truth is surely an obvious component of human dignity. Similarly, the idea of accommodation up to the point of undue hardship also reflects the courts' instinctive grasp of what human dignity requires. While a person must be free to follow his or her conscience, nothing requires that this path be free from difficulty or even from burden. However, the relational aspect of human dignity does require that others, who are in a position to do so, must not impede another's religious observances or impose penalties for those observances unless all reasonable alternatives have been exhausted.

A recent decision of the Alberta Court of Queen's Bench directly faced the issue raised by *Law* in a religious discrimination case.[44] The complainant was a dairy farmer. When he had purchased his farm, he was aware that Alberta Milk, the corporation to which he sold his milk under provincial law, scheduled pickups every two days, resulting in a Sunday pickup every two weeks. However, he was apparently told that this schedule could be altered. Mr Van Der Smit objected to the Sunday pickup on the basis of his religion. When Alberta Milk refused to accommodate his religious beliefs, he brought a complaint against them on the grounds that they had discriminated against him on the basis of religion.

Alberta Milk argued that Mr Van Der Smit had not made out a case of discrimination. They argued that he had shown no prejudice or stereotyping in Alberta Milk's treatment of him and that his human dignity had not been offended because their schedule did not imply in any way that Mr van der Smit was a less valued member of Canadian society. The judge did not directly meet these arguments. Rather, he found, based upon *Law*, that he could take judicial notice of the fact that the distinction was discriminatory within the meaning of the provision. He relied upon a paragraph in *Law* in which Iacobucci J. observed, after enumerating several of the factors that would support a finding that differential treatment amounted to discrimination, that when the distinction was based upon an enumerated ground, it would not always be necessary to adduce evidence to prove a violation of human dignity. Rather, it would be evident from "judicial notice and logical reasoning that the provision was discriminatory."[45]

This, I suggest, is correct, but only if the concept of human dignity is retained as an important element of the test. The protection of human dignity reaches beyond the factors of stereotyping, disadvantage, and prejudice outlined in *Law* and *Kapp* and can be extended to include a person's right to practise his faith without interference and without exclusion from normally available social processes. That did not seem to be the approach favoured in *Hutterian Brethren of Wilson Colony*,[46] nor does it seem feasible if the concept of human dignity is to be discarded by the courts in their legal analysis.

In the end, Mr Van Der Smit was still unsuccessful in his claim against Alberta Milk. Having found that he had been discriminated against, the court turned to the question of whether the treatment was reasonable and justifiable, a defence provided in the statute. The court accepted that to show that Alberta Milk's refusal was reasonable and justifiable, the corporation had to prove that it had tried to accommodate Mr Van Der Smit up to the point of undue hardship. Alberta Milk had indeed made a detailed study of what was required to alter the pickup of milk to avoid Sunday.

There were twenty-four producers who requested this change and Alberta Milk introduced evidence showing that many more would likely request it as well if it became available. Because regulations required milk pickup every two days at the longest, the logistics of avoiding Sunday were complex. Moreover, the new routes would have significant impacts on milk haulers, processors, and other producers in the area. More staff would likely be required and would have to work longer hours on Saturday and Monday. The resulting unevenness in the milk supply would cause difficulties and might cause some milk to have to be turned into powdered milk, thus affecting the fresh milk supply. Changing the pickups to allow more than a day between would create health and quality concerns. The court was convinced that it would be undue hardship to accommodate Mr Van Der Smit.[47]

6. Religious Discrimination Claims to Advance Religious Goals

The cases we examined in the last section of this chapter, which are typical of the vast majority of claims of religious discrimination, were cases of a complainant seeking some accommodation that would ameliorate the negative effect of a seemingly neutral rule on his or her religious practice. Claims of religious discrimination have also been used, in a few cases, to attempt to defend a particular religion or to advance its purposes directly. In the next few pages, we will consider two instances of this type of claim: the contest between pro-life student clubs and university student unions and the claims of Islamic believers to have their religion protected from certain forms of negative comment.

We have already looked at the controversial area of abortion politics when considering protest cases in the last chapter. While unregulated abortion access has been a feature of Canadian society for almost thirty years, the controversy has not subsided. In a democracy, as I have noted earlier, no political decision is ever final. To make it so would be to defeat the very essence of a democracy in which people's opinions and beliefs may change and in which those opinions and beliefs can influence or direct public policy in new ways as the shifts occur.

University student organizations are generally committed to a pro-choice policy, in keeping with the stance of Canadian Federation of Students to which many of the organizations belong.[48] However, while that may reflect the views of the majority of students, it obviously does not represent universal opinion. Yet university students generally have no choice about belonging to the campus student organization; fees for the organization are collected by the university administration and are compulsory. The student organization, in turn, supports a large number of student clubs, giving them access to services, space, and often funding.[49] In several high-profile cases, these umbrella organizations have denied club status to pro-life student clubs and have been met with a claim that the refusal constituted illegal discrimination.

Three British Columbia cases provided interesting insights on the issue of how claims of discrimination may be made in support of finding a voice for religious ideas in the public square. In 2005, Ms Bartram filed a complaint on behalf of herself and others against the Okanagan College Students' Association. She claimed that the association had refused to grant club status to her organization on the basis of the club's political beliefs, which consisted of pro-life views. The claim was brought under s. 14 of the B.C. Human Rights Code, which prohibits a trade union, employers' organization, or occupational association from discriminating against anyone on the basis of the listed grounds, including political belief. The claim was dismissed at a preliminary stage on the grounds that the Okanagan College Students' Association was not a trade union, employers' organization, or occupational association.[50] The tribunal found that the term "occupational association" did not include a student union because it was confined to organizations in which membership was required to practise a particular trade or profession. The tribunal noted that the association was a service provider within the meaning of s. 8 of the code, but that s. 8 did not prohibit discrimination on the basis of political belief.

The next two cases were decided by the B.C. Human Rights Tribunal within four days of each other. Both involved claims by pro-life clubs that their respective student associations had discriminated against them in refusing to provide services commonly available to the public on the basis of religion. In one case, however, the complaint was dismissed at a preliminary stage; that dismissal was upheld by the B.C. Supreme Court. In the second case, the tribunal refused to dismiss the case, and the matter subsequently was settled with the complainants' being granted club status.

In the successful claim where settlement was reached, Ms Macapagal brought a complaint against the Capilano College Students' Union on behalf of herself and the other members of the Heartbeat Club, a pro-life student organization.[51] The Heartbeat Club had twice been denied club status by the Capilano College Students' Association. The association admitted that it denied the club status because of its own pro-choice commitment, but argued that the claim should be dismissed at a preliminary stage because the code had not been contravened and there was no reasonable chance that the complaint would succeed. In support of both grounds, the Students' Association argued that there had been no discrimination on the basis of religion. The tribunal found that there was a nexus between the religious beliefs of the members of the club and their pro-life position. Even if religion had not been discussed in the meetings held to consider the club's status (and the tribunal member in fact found that it had been discussed), that did not settle the issue because club members asserted that their pro-life beliefs arose from their religious beliefs. Thus the tribunal found that a nexus existed between the club's aims and religion. That was sufficient to show that the association's conduct could contravene the code and that the claim might be able to succeed.

The case never proceeded to a full hearing. Thus it is not possible to know whether, when the evidence was presented, the tribunal would have found discrimination on the basis of religion. However, the fact that the tribunal decided that there was a sufficient connection between religion and the club members' pro-life beliefs to indicate that the code could have been contravened strongly suggests that the case might have succeeded. The Students' Association did not seem to have asserted any basis for its refusal to grant the club status other than the club's pro-life mandate.

The contrasting decision in *Gray v. UBC Okanagan Students' Union*[52] had slightly different facts. The club in question had been granted club status by the Students' Union for one year. It had then participated in an advertising program called the "Genocidal Awareness Project" which showed graphic pictures of aborted fetuses and drew parallels between abortion and the Holocaust. The Students' Union asserted, and the tribunal accepted, that some of this material was found offensive by some students and complaints were received by the Union. The next year, the Students' Union refused to ratify the club.

The tribunal found that the claim to discrimination on the basis of religion was belied by the fact that the club had been funded in the previous year. Thus something other than the club's pro-life views accounted for the change in approach. As well, other religious clubs on campus were funded. For these reasons, the tribunal held that the complaint had no reasonable prospect of success. This did not seem to be a supportable conclusion. The fact that other religious clubs were approved does not have any bearing on the case. That I do not discriminate against some religions or some expressions of religion does not mean I do not discriminate against others. The fact that other religious clubs were funded does not have any probative value about the reasons for not funding this one.

As well, although it may well be the case that material the Students' Union found offensive accounted for the change in policy, the tribunal failed to consider whether discriminating against the club on the basis of this material constituted discrimination on the basis of religion. Prohibited discrimination is not confined to interference with the beliefs of a particular group, but also extends to interference with actions taken in furtherance of those beliefs. If I were to be denied a service because I distributed copies of the Qur'an, it seems likely I would have been discriminated against on the basis of religion, even though the Qur'an might offend some people. This is not to say that the claim would ultimately have succeeded, as the student union might have been able to show a "bona fide and reasonable justification" for their action which the act allows as a defence; however, the issue should have been addressed and it was not.

On an application for judicial review of the tribunal's decision, Wong J. upheld the decision.[53] The standard for review of a Human Rights Tribunal in British Columbia is that the decision must be upheld unless it is patently unreasonable. Wong J. found that the decision did not meet that test. However, he also adopted some comments by counsel that merit some consideration. Counsel had argued that a line had to be drawn between protecting the right of people to practise their faith and allowing religious freedom to "become a sword by which religious groups are able to secure advantages not possessed by similarly situated secular groups."[54] Counsel urged that the pro-life club was entitled and remained entitled to meet, express its views, and act to promote those views. At issue was whether they were entitled to force the students' society to fund them in the furtherance of those views.

This strikes at a significant issue in human rights cases. As earlier discussed, human rights legislation does not apply to all interactions among citizens. I am, for example, allowed to choose my own friends. If I do not like people of certain races, creeds, or gender, the law does not compel me to include them in my social circle, however despicable many of us would consider someone who would draw such distinctions to be. It may be a matter of morality; but our statutes do not make it a matter of law. The claim of the pro-life students was based upon the assertion that in funding clubs, student societies are providing a "service commonly available to the public." The reader may be pardoned for wondering if students' society activities really are services commonly available to the public in that they are available only to a very select class of people: university students. If they are not, then, just as I can choose my friends, student societies would legally be able to choose their form of discrimination.

However, the jurisprudence has generally taken an expansive view of what a "service commonly available to the public" means. For example, the Supreme Court of Canada has decided that the facilities and services provided by a university to its graduate student population constituted "services commonly available to the public."[55] In making that decision, the court rejected the idea that "public" must mean a broad cross-section of the population. Every service, the court noted, "has its public." Thus, once the qualifications for a particular segment of the "public" were met, the prohibition against discrimination within that public came into effect.[56]

As I have already noted, B.C. student societies are recognized by statute and membership in them is compulsory; there seems little doubt that under the established jurisprudence, the provision of funding, space, and official sanction to clubs is a "service commonly available to the public." That being the case, the students' society cannot discriminate on the basis of any of the prohibited grounds in any of the services it provides, which include recognition and support of clubs. Religion is one of those prohibited grounds, as are race and sex; political belief (in British Columbia, though, as discussed earlier, the provinces are not consistent on this issue) is not. It would seem to follow, therefore, that if the society's decision to refuse club status turns on religion or affects religious groups more than non-religious ones, it is discriminating illegally. A B.C. students' society could refuse to recognize the Young Liberals, but apparently could not refuse to recognize the Muslim Students' Association.

This combination of what is meant by a "service commonly available to the public" together with the restricted grounds on which discrimination is prohibited under the human rights codes does indeed appear to provide opportunities for religious groups to use discrimination suits to obtain positive benefits, not simply to protect themselves from incursions into their religious practices. We may question, therefore, whether *Gray v. UBC Okanagan Students' Union* was correctly decided.

In none of these cases was the issue of whether the student societies' refusal to recognize the pro-life student clubs constituted "discrimination" in the specialized sense used in *Law* discussed. It is interesting to notice, however, that in *Macapagal*, the complainant's counsel had alleged facts that could have satisfied the *Law* test. Ms Macapagal presented evidence that at a meeting at which the club's status was debated, the student members had been the subject of stereotyping and demeaning comments which asserted that members of a pro-life club were misogynist.

A second example of human rights legislation being used to do more than protect individual religious practice can be found in the cases brought against *Maclean's* magazine arising out of its publication of an excerpt from Mark Steyn's provocative book *America Alone*.[57] Unlike sections of the human rights statutes that protect the distribution of services commonly available to the public, however, the sections on which these actions were based clearly have as their intention the protection of certain social groups from particular kinds of negative comment. Thus, there is no question that these provisions are intended to be used directly to limit certain kinds of speech and provide advantages to the protected groups (which include religious groups) that other organizations or groups would not enjoy.

As a result of the publication of the article, Islamic complainants filed human rights complaints against *Maclean's* in three different jurisdictions: in Ontario and British Columbia, and with the Federal Human Rights Commission. In all three, the complaints failed, although for somewhat differing reasons and with somewhat differing results. The complaints attracted a firestorm of criticism against the sections in human rights codes that limit free speech as well as against the human rights enforcement machinery that has been set up in all provinces and at the Federal level to serve as specialized adjudication systems for human rights violations.[58] The protection of religious and ethnic groups from criticism, even harsh criticism, at the expense of free speech in the media did not meet with public approval. As part of the aftermath of the highly publicized cases, Professor Richard Moon was asked to review s. 13 of the Canada Human Rights Act, under which the complaint was made in the Federal jurisdiction. He recommended that the section be repealed.[59]

Before turning to an assessment of s. 13 and similar legislation as a tool for protecting religious groups, we will briefly examine the three complaints against *Maclean's* and their outcomes. Ontario legislation applies to the display of any "notice, sign, symbol or emblem" that announces an intention to discriminate or incites discrimination prohibited by the Act.[60] The Ontario Human Rights Commission decided that under this legislation, its jurisdiction did not extend to the content of magazine articles. However, in a *Statement Concerning Issues Raised by Complaints against Maclean's Magazine*,[61] the Commission expressed disapproval of what it called "Islamophobic" aspects of the article and general racism in our society of which it found the magazine article to be part.

The Canada Human Rights Act[62] contains section 13, which applies to prohibit telecommunications (including postings on websites over the internet) that are "likely to expose a person or group of persons to hatred or contempt by reason of the fact that that person or those persons are identifiable on the basis of a prohibited ground of discrimination." We have already examined some of the jurisprudence applicable to similar sections when we considered Mr Owens's protest against same-sex marriage in Saskatchewan.[63] Following the judgment of the Supreme Court of Canada in *Taylor*,[64] the Canada Human Rights Commission found that s. 13 of the Canada Human Rights Act was engaged only when the communication aroused feelings of an extreme nature.[65] While the Commission found that the excerpt published by *Maclean's* was intended to be provocative and even offensive to some, it did not meet the *Taylor* test.[66]

The British Columbia Human Rights Code[67] contains s. 7 prohibiting publication of any "statement, publication, notice, sign, symbol, emblem or other representation" that either indicates an intention to discriminate or is likely to expose a person or class of persons to hatred or contempt on the basis of one of the prohibited grounds of discrimination. It is thus broader than either the Ontario or Federal statutes in its coverage of kinds of communications. The chair of the B.C. Human

Rights Tribunal conducted an inquiry into the complaints against *Maclean's*. Her decision was the longest and most thorough of all three. In it, she reviewed the content of the published excerpt and expert testimony that decried the excerpt as being inaccurate and presenting stereotypical views of Islam and of Muslims.[68]

Mr Steyn's views of Islam and those who follow it were certainly far from flattering. Islam was portrayed as having world domination as part of its goal. The spectre of Muslim domination of Europe was raised, based upon demographics of both Muslim and Western European populations, the supposed weakness of Europe and its social welfare system, and the vigour and aggression of the younger Muslim population. However, employing the test set out in *Taylor* and citing the *Owens* decision, Ms MacNaughton, the chair of the B.C. tribunal, found that the article did not inspire "detestation, calumny and vilification" as it would have to do to fall within the scope of s. 7. Also following *Owens*, she commented on the importance of contextual factors such as whether the statements were true and whether they formed a part of public debate.

Further public attention was directed towards these and similar provisions in human rights legislation in Alberta by complaints lodged against the then-publisher of the *Western Standard*, Ezra Levant. In his capacity as publisher, Mr Levant had been responsible for reprinting a series of cartoons depicting Islam and the Prophet Mohammed in a satirical vein. These cartoons had originally been published in Denmark, where they inflamed controversy and even violence. Many newspapers, although reporting on the controversy, had refused to publish the cartoons. When Mr Levant's paper did so, a complaint was brought against him to the Alberta Human Rights Commission. The tribunal did not proceed with the complaint. However, Mr Levant used his clash with the commission to form the basis of a book highly critical of the discriminatory publication laws in human rights statutes.[69]

These cases suggest that the use of sections of human rights legislation that restrict speech to protect the reputation of a particular religion and its followers faces serious obstacles. These obstacles have been decried by some. Certainly, the statement of the Ontario Human Rights Commission noted above expressed its concern with the fact that the case fell outside its jurisdiction and affirmed its commitment to a mandate of preventing racism that extended beyond the legal prohibitions.[70] In the same vein, although Professor Moon recommended the repeal of s. 13 of the Canada Human Rights Act, he did so primarily for practical reasons.[71] He discussed efforts to control "speech that stereotypes or de-fames the members of an identifiable group" and decided that to do so through the legal system would "require extraordinary intervention by the state and would dramatically compromise the public commitment to freedom of expression."[72] For this reason, he recommended that pro-hibited speech be confined to criminalization of speech that "threatens, advocates or justifies violence." But he also recommended the develop-ment of other methods of social control on less extreme forms of publi-cation, such as the establishment of press councils that would have as their mandate the enforcement of professional standards and would receive and deal with complaints.[73] A private member's bill, Bill C-304, to repeal s. 13 has passed the House of Commons and is, at time of writ-ing, before the Senate. Provincial legislatures do not seem to have fol-lowed suit in acting to repeal their similar legislation.

In the context of freedom of conscience and religion, we may ask whether belief systems, including, of course, religious belief systems, and those who hold them ought to have the right to be free from nega-tive, perhaps slanderous or stereotypical comment and portrayal. As a practical matter, we can note that if religious groups are successful in claiming this right, the same right can be turned against them by other groups claiming protection from the negative attitudes of some religions to certain protected categories. In the next chapter, when our focus will be on cases in which apparently conflicting rights come be-fore the courts or tribunals, we will look at some examples of this. The willingness of religious groups to prosecute claims under human rights legislation limiting negative speech may be, in light of those decisions, a case of "be careful what you wish for."

But since I have suggested that human rights have their foundation in a concept of human dignity, we will consider this question from the perspective of whether human dignity is diminished by allowing nega-tive, even extremely negative, publication about belief. We can start by stating that no one has a human right not to be called wrong. The right to hold and practise varying beliefs requires that we draw this conclu-sion because all belief, by its nature, presents itself as true and excludes at least some contrary beliefs as false. Even if we assume a belief sys-tem that considered all beliefs equally true, the adherents of that belief system must consider false those beliefs that deny the truth of other beliefs. But, of course, even if you are not protected from others con-demning your beliefs as wrong, there might be limits on how those con-demnations are expressed.

The question of these limits raises the relational aspect of human rights grounded in human dignity that I discussed above. My right to freedom of belief cannot be defended unless I also defend your right to freedom of belief (including the belief that my commitments are wrong) and your right to freely express that belief. Provided that your expression does not exclude me from participation in democratic life, your disapproval, criticism, even contempt can exist in concert with my right to freedom of belief and practice. If your condemnation of my beliefs involves shutting me out of important parts of social life, including participation in democratic debate, or threatens my life or safety, then of course we can agree that my human dignity is violated. But short of that, criticism, condemnation, and contempt do not interfere with the practice of my beliefs, nor do they appear to interfere with any right that I might have other than, arguably, my right to feel that my beliefs are respected.

The core problem with restraint on speech critical of belief systems is not that freedom of expression must be balanced against my rights to believe. Rather, it is that they may repress freedom of expression in circumstances in which it does not in fact interfere with my rights to believe or practise my beliefs. Does it interfere with my human dignity? Even though I may find certain portrayals of my beliefs offensive or even emotionally hurtful, this need not limit my commitments to those beliefs or to their practice, nor does it appear to interfere with my participation in society. These offensive portrayals may interfere with my feelings of self-worth, but this returns us to the question of whether interference with my feelings is sufficient to constitute an interference with my human dignity.

In an earlier chapter, I commented that for the law to recognize a right to be free from offence would lead us down a very difficult path. We can now see additional reasons why this would be so. My human rights exist only because I am prepared to recognize that you also have rights founded upon your dignity as a human being. If this means that we all have a human right to feel some particular emotion, we will find insurmountable difficulties in our legal system that recognizes this right. My reaction to your behaviour may be quite unpredictable; it will certainly vary with my culture, my previous experiences, and my state of health. The law will be required to make multitudinous adjustments for what offends various cultures and various individuals within those cultures. While our society does accept some variations and accommodations for cultural differences, we also retain the ideal that, by and large, the law should have certain standards applied to all. This would be impossible to sustain in the area of human rights if human dignity is a subjective idea. Moreover, there is no way to test whether I will be truthful about my reaction to what you have written; if it is to my advantage to lie, I cannot be prevented from doing so, nor can I be contradicted, since the matter depends upon my internal state of mind, which only I can know.

Rather than adopt this impossible social construction, we must conclude that human dignity is not a subjective feeling of worth, but rather the real recognition of worth that comes from full participation in our society, in its goods, its services, its democratic processes, and its debates. Human rights codes are rightly concerned with such factors. When they appear to include within their scope limitations of expression of opinion that do not constitute these acts of exclusion, they risk introducing subjective elements into the equation and risk encouraging groups to pursue human rights complaints to protect their feelings rather than their rights to participate in our society. This will inevitably risk undermining the very rights these commissions are supposed to protect.

The test set out in *Taylor* and applied in some of the cases we have just reviewed provides something of a proxy for a concept of human rights that would avoid this conflict. When published opinions arouse extreme feelings of animosity and hatred, one can perhaps reasonably assume that exclusion from participation in society may be a real threat. However, human rights statutes already contain protections against that next step. This leaves these provisions in human rights statutes as at best redundant and at worst an encouragement to use human rights claims to stifle human rights while not protecting any right of the complainant that our legal system can reasonably recognize. In the next chapter, we will consider these ideas in more detail as we turn to the difficult cases in which rights appear to be in direct conflict.

At this point, however, we will return to a case we considered in chapter 2 and revisit the question of what the dissenting judgment of Lacourcière J.A. in *Zylberberg v. Sudbury Board of Education*[74] can illustrate about claims of discrimination on the basis of religion. We will then turn to a more recent example of issues of religious discrimination in the school context.

7. *Zylberberg* Revisited

The reader will recall that in *Zylberberg v. Sudbury Board of Education*, a group of parents were attacking the constitutionality of a regulation

under the Ontario Schools Act that required the school day to open
with prayer and religious reading. While some school boards, such
as Toronto, had devised a multi-faith program of prayers drawn from
many traditions and readings from many perspectives, including that
of atheism, the Sudbury School Board persisted in presenting only the
Lord's Prayer and readings from the Bible. The majority of the court
held the regulation to be unconstitutional as a violation of the complainants' freedom of religion and conscience.[75] I argued that this ruling was incorrect.

The dissenting judge, however, while he found that the regulation
was not a violation of the Charter rights of freedom of conscience and
religion, also held that the practice of the Sudbury School Board was
discriminatory.[76] This was not a case of alleged discrimination under
the provincial human rights legislation, although had the parents
wanted simply to attack the practice of the Sudbury School Board, the
case could have been brought under that statute. But as Lacourcière
J.A. commented, the parents did not simply want the practice changed;
rather, they wanted all religious practice removed from the school.[77]
The claim of discrimination was therefore also brought under the Charter and, as part of the case, the parents alleged that the regulation was a
violation of their equality rights under s. 15.

Lacourcière J.A. found that the regulation did not violate s. 15, but
that the practice of the Sudbury School Board did. His judgment on
this aspect of the case was brief.[78] However, we can consider the decision in light of the various principles about discrimination that we have
discussed throughout this chapter. First, we can note that the students
of differing beliefs were treated differently. Christian students had the
opportunity to hear their religious material proclaimed at the beginning of each school day; students of other faiths did not. This would
certainly suggest discrimination against the non-Christian students. A
question might be raised as to whether the discrimination met the test
in *Law*, but, as I have discussed, that issue is problematic for almost all
claims of discrimination on the basis of religion. But in this case, the discrimination was not a result of an apparently neutral rule, but rather a
direct singling out of one religious tradition over others. Even differing
treatment, however, is not enough to constitute prohibited discrimination under s. 15 unless the procedure either affected the excluded children detrimentally or denied them a benefit to which the others had
access.

The benefit which the Christian children arguably received and which was denied to others was the opportunity to have a brief worship period in their own tradition.[79] Having established that denial, we can conclude that the practice of the school board was discriminatory. The question then remains whether it might be justified under s. 1 of the Charter. This was not an issue considered by Lacourcière J.A. Here we must return to the issue of when accommodation is relevant to a claim of discrimination under s. 15. McLachlin C.J. in her majority judgment in *Hutterian Brethren*[80] considered that the test for justification under s. 1 was parallel to the human rights considerations of accommodation up to the point of undue hardship only when the practice attacked under s. 15 was an administrative one. That certainly was the situation here.

This case is clearly one in which accommodation must be the deciding factor in considering whether the practice was sustainable under s. 1 of the Charter, even if discriminatory. I have already noted that the claim could have been brought under provincial human rights legislation. Then, quite clearly, the question of reasonable accommodation would have been central and would have been the deciding issue as to whether the claim of discrimination would be upheld. To eliminate the question of accommodation from a s. 15 challenge under these circumstances would mean that the outcome on the same facts and for the same issue might be very different depending on whether the claim was brought under the Charter or under human rights legislation. That would be a very disturbing result.[91]

The statute, and presumably the practice of the Sudbury School Board, provided an exemption, allowing students, upon request, to leave the classroom during the opening exercise. In some cases of alleged discrimination, this would be sufficient to save the practice as it would amount to an accommodation for the students of other beliefs. However, the voluntary exclusion for those in another religious tradition did not give them any opportunity for worship in their own faith, although it would seem that this opportunity could, with very little more effort on the part of the school, have been provided. If a large majority of the schoolchildren were Christian and if their parents wanted to provide the opportunity for worship for those children, there seems no reason why the spiritual needs of the other children could not also have been addressed, even if only by encouraging them to bring their own religious texts or prayers to separate rooms. Thus the rule allowing children to be excused does not seem to have been an accommodation up to the point of undue hardship and would probably not be an adequate accommodation for non-Christian children, although a right to be excused combined with some alternative religious opportunity might be.

The Toronto School Board's solution also might be a reasonable accommodation for the varying beliefs of the students, although it would result in those from the various traditions receiving only sporadic opportunity to worship in their own faith rather than on a daily basis. This could arguably be thought to defeat the original purpose of the regulation, turning it into a praiseworthy effort to expose children to varying traditions, but away from its original purpose of providing a worship opportunity.

Zylberberg stands as an interesting example of the role of freedom of conscience and religion in combination with the law related to religious discrimination. Just as in the discriminatory publication cases we considered earlier, the claimants in *Zylberberg* were attempting to use provisions guaranteeing the protection of rights of belief to suppress public expression of others' views. We would have little tolerance for this suppression if it had been directed towards political statements, racial prejudices, or gender roles. Imagine a claimant before the court seeking to eliminate women from the university because he found their presence offensive and consider public reaction. Perhaps the analogy is not perfect, but nonetheless, a review of some of the cases we have discussed suggests that courts and our society have a higher tolerance for intolerance of belief than for other forms of exclusionary claims. The question is whether in our multi-belief society, we can afford such an attitude or whether, as in the case of civil rights for racial minorities, we need to consider seriously a reform of our public perceptions.

8. Religious Discrimination in the Pursuit of "Neutrality"

I have argued in earlier chapters that the public school system needs to maintain a neutral position in the face of moral and religious conflicts in the schools. Yet, the presentation of apparently neutral programs about religion can also discriminate against those with particular religious commitments. "Neutrality" can be taken by the state to mean "secular," rather than a true effort simply to keep out of the controversy. "Secular" frequently involves the tacit or express assumption that all religions are the same and that it is "neutral" to teach not simply that people holding a wide variety of beliefs need to be respected, but that tolerance in our society can only be achieved if one accepts a wide variety of beliefs as equally valid. This is a subtle, but crucial, difference. Given the premises with which this book opened, the reader can appreciate that this is not the kind of "even hand" to which I suggest the public school system must commit.

The problem becomes even more acute where a legally established, private school based on religious affiliation is confronted with government demands to teach secular-based courses that conflict with its commitments to its religious principles. Canadian provinces have, in many cases, given state support to various denominational schools, either (as in Ontario) through constitutional protection of Catholic schools or (as in British Columbia) through legislative provision for partial support for any private school of any religion that will meet governmental standards. In these cases, the entire *raison d'être* of the private school may be the parents' wishes that their children be educated in a particular religious milieu. What, then, is the status of freedom of religion where the school's beliefs apparently conflict with the beliefs of the government?

Loyola High School and John Zucchi v. Minister of Education, Recreation and Sports[82] was a case in which the Quebec government insisted on a private, denominational school, established pursuant to statute, teaching a state-mandated course, Ethics and Religious Culture (ERC). The course content and pedagogy were mandatory, and, according to the unchallenged expert testimony of Professor Douglas Farrow, the aims of the course were not, in fact, neutral, but were intended to inculcate a particular pluralistic view of religious beliefs.[83] Other expert testimony informed the court that the ethics component of the course made a categorical error by mixing a variety of sources of moral judgments and thereby discredited religious ethical perspectives.[84] The legislation itself provided for an exemption from the program if the school offered a program of studies "equivalent" to the required course.

The Catholic school requested this exemption, providing the minister with evidence that they taught the same topics as the ERC program, but acknowledging that they did so from an expressly Catholic perspective, which was made clear to the students. The minister denied the exemption based upon an evaluation from a staff member that the Loyola course was not "equivalent" because it did not adopt the same perspective as the ERC course.

The high school and a parent (Mr Zucchi) challenged the minister's decision on a number of grounds, including improper exercise of discretion under administrative law principles and a violation of their Charter right to freedom of conscience and religion. On the administrative

law issue, the court found that the minister did not have the jurisdiction
to decide on the basis of criteria selected by her whether she found a
program "equivalent." Rather, she was to apply the word in its normal
meaning. She did not have the authority to create the criteria on which
an exemption, made automatic by the statute for equivalent programs,
was granted. The court further found that the minister had applied er-
roneous criteria by requiring exclusion of denominational programs.

On the issue of freedom of religion, the court held, first, that Loyola
High School was entitled to invoke both the Canadian and Quebec charters as a legal person, even though it was not an individual. No doubt
concerns about this issue were what caused the plaintiffs to include an
individual plaintiff. However, the court had no difficulty, referring back
to *Big M Drug Mart*, in concluding that the charters apply to juridical
persons. Second, the court held that Loyola's religious beliefs were seriously infringed by the requirement that it teach the pluralistic and relativistic ERC program rather than presenting the material from its own
belief perspective. Finally, the court held that the minister's decision
could not be saved by section 9.1 of the Quebec Charter, nor could it be
saved by s. 1 of the Canadian Charter. The minister's decision failed the
test of minimal impairment because the solution of allowing Loyola to
teach its own equivalent course would have been available. In addition,
the court held, the deleterious effects far exceeded the beneficial. However, as we shall see shortly, the trial judgment was reversed on appeal
by the Quebec Court of Appeal.

The *Loyola High School* case did not deal with the rights of students
in the public system to resist imposition of state-sponsored religious
and moral education that violates their own beliefs. The ERC program
was also challenged in a separate action by a group of Catholic parents
in the public school system on the basis that the course interfered with
their rights to teach their children their own religion. The claim was
dismissed by the Supreme Court of Canada in *S.L. and D.J. v. Commission Scholaire des Chênes and Attorney General of Quebec*.[85] While the court
accepted the sincerity of the parents' religious beliefs, it held that the
test of whether those beliefs were infringed was an objective one. The
parents submitted material in which they stated that they believed that
the curriculum was not in fact "neutral," but "relativistic" in nature.
They also submitted the textbook for the program. Unlike the plaintiffs
in the *Loyola High School* case, it does not appear that they presented any
expert evidence about the perspective of the program, whether it was

genuinely neutral or whether it implicitly taught the relativistic position that all religions are equally true (or false).

The court held that the subjective belief of the parents did not discharge the burden of proving that the program actually interfered with their ability to teach their faith to their children. Neutral presentation of facts about other religions, even if those religions were contradictory to the religious beliefs of the parents, was not a violation of the parents' religious beliefs. The court found that they had no evidence, other than the parents' subjective beliefs, that the curriculum had been instituted to teach a relativistic view of religions "to influence young people's specific beliefs."[86] Two members of the court, though concurring with the majority view, also held that the decision did not rule out the possibility that the ERC interfered with freedom of religion; but they agreed that the case was not made out.

The court's emphasis on an objective basis for determining whether or not religious freedom was infringed appears contradictory to other jurisprudence on the matter of religious freedom. As we saw in chapter 2, the court in Big M Drug Mart[87] held that religious freedom was infringed because the original religious purpose of the statute was a reminder of the majority view and offensive to those who were not Sunday-observing Christians. In Zylberberg, which we have just revisited, it was again the subjective feelings the court imagined non-Christian children to have that were the foundation of the majority decision. The same was true for the case in which the town mayor was required to refrain from using the Lord's Prayer to open council meetings.[88] The Supreme Court cited both Big M Drug Mart and Zylberberg in this decision. However, they seemed oblivious to the essentially subjective nature of the claims in both those cases. No actual interference with the practice of anyone's religion was demonstrated in any of these cases.[89] The Supreme Court in the this decision explained these earlier decisions as simply exemplifying the requirement that the state treat all religions equally. But as we have seen, a close analysis of the cases does not support this as the decisive factor in the judgments.[90]

I have argued, of course, that feelings of offence are not an adequate basis for determining that one's freedom of religion has been infringed. This case provides an object lesson as to why this is so. As I stated in chapter 2, of necessity the sense of offence of some groups will be privileged over others. Here, despite the long history of allowing religious practices to be curtailed because of the offence to groups not sharing the majority sentiments, the court considered the offence visited on the Catholic parents by having their children taught the material in the ERC program was insufficient to found a claim that their religious beliefs had been infringed. This leaves the observer wondering why the feelings of one group are important while those of another are apparently not.

However, the fact that I would argue that the parents' feelings ought not to have been a sufficient objection does not dispose of their claim. The parents objected to the program because they argued that it was not, in fact, neutral. The court commented that neutrality was not an easy position to achieve. It recognized, reasonably one would think, that holding an even hand among all religions and treating all with respect is the appropriate position for the state and for the public schools.[91] But although the parents had filed the textbook for the program, the court did not appear to undertake any analysis of whether the material was, indeed, neutral in simply presenting facts and emphasizing the need to respect those with a wide variety of beliefs or whether it promoted the belief that all religions are equal in terms of their truth, in direct contradiction to the parents' beliefs that their religion is the one true faith.

This was the question the court needed to answer. Whether the material was "intended" to influence children's beliefs is not really relevant. The question was whether it in fact taught that the parents' and children's religion was by implication false. Pluralistic views of religion that present all religious beliefs as having equal validity can do so only if they treat all religious belief as untrue. Since religions contradict one another over many points of belief, they cannot all be true; so if all are of equal worth, then they must all be untrue. If the ERC program, by design or otherwise, taught that the parents' and children's religion was untrue, it would seem incontrovertible that it violated their freedom of religion, not because it caused them offence but because a state institution was officially promoting the belief that their faith was false.

There is, in fact, little indication that the court understood the point at issue. Rather, the court adopted the proposition that neutrality in matters of religion is not achievable. In support, they cited Richard Moon's comment that "With the growth of agnosticism and atheism, religious neutrality in the public sphere may have become impossible."[92] Relying on a single scholarly article to dismiss the claims of school neutrality as a legitimate goal seems in itself almost contemptuous of the parents' concerns. But having adopted this comment as correct, the court proceeded to hold the state to a much lower test that it neither "favour nor hinder any particular religious belief."[93] This test would make the pluralistic approach acceptable, despite its obvious curtailment of religious freedom. A pluralistic view can be said neither to "favour nor hinder any particular religious belief"; rather, it discredits them all equally. The Supreme Court's reasoning was thus seriously flawed.

It is impossible to tell from the decision whether the court was simply unaware of its own biases and beliefs and so was unable to grasp the problem with pluralism; alternatively, perhaps this court was influenced by its own excessively deferential stance to legislation (as we have seen in the *Wilson Colony* decision). As well, the evidence of pluralism was less well established than in the *Loyola* case, since apparently little evidence was put forward by the parents about the way the program was actually delivered and, as noted, expert evidence was not submitted. But the fact that the court paid so little attention the text, coupled with their sudden adoption of an objective test for infringement of religious freedom and the further creation of a test for state conduct that seems likely to permit a school to teach the falsity of religious belief without being held accountable for violating students' religious freedom, all suggests an unwillingness to analyse the problem thoroughly. If that is the case, the decision bodes ill for religious freedom in the schools in the face of state hostility. If, as the court accepted, neutrality is not possible in presenting religious material in the public schools (and it hardly seems conclusively established that is so), the even-handed approach would be to leave such material to the home. Children can still be taught respect for others without needing to teach them any views of religion at all.

The decision in the *Loyola High School* case was reversed, as noted, by the Quebec Court of Appeal.[94] In its decision, the Court of Appeal determined that the trial judge had not properly applied the standard for administrative review of the minister's decision. The statute gave her a discretion which she had exercised in a reasonable manner and was thus not subject to judicial review. On the matter of freedom of religion, the appeal court relied upon the Supreme Court of Canada decision in *Chênes*, discussed above, to hold that such infringement of religious freedom as was created by the ERC was insignificant and did not attract the protection of the Charter. The court does not seem to have accepted that the evidentiary differences in the two cases should have any effect. Leave to appeal to the Supreme Court of Canada is under consideration. If it is allowed, perhaps the Supreme Court will have the opportunity to reconsider some of the inconsistencies in the *Chênes* decision;

certainly it will be required to consider the issues with a more extensive evidentiary basis for holding that the ERC was not, in fact, neutral.

In the next chapter, we will see the issues intensified as we deal directly with cases in which human rights of one group appear to collide with those of another and the courts and tribunals try to find a balance between competing claims. In this chapter, I have outlined some of the principles with which I will critique these efforts. We will then be in a better position to draw together some final observations and conclusions about the state of protection of varying beliefs in Canada and how it might be reimagined.

Chapter Six

Conflicting Rights: A Balancing Act?

1. Introduction

In the last chapter, I suggested a way of conceptualizing human rights that avoided viewing them as unlimited entitlements curtailed only when they come into conflict with the equally unlimited rights of others. In this chapter, we will further continue this analysis as we examine cases in which courts have found that rights of one person are in direct conflict with those of another. As we have seen, courts have consistently stated that there is no "hierarchy" of human rights.[1] Rather, they have suggested that in cases of conflicting rights, a balancing process must be undertaken. This judicial commitment to balancing assumes that the conflict between rights is an appropriate way to describe the situation. It further assumes that courts can, in fact, balance rights. In my opinion, both these assumptions are wrong and likely to perpetuate polarization of differing segments of the population whose belief systems conflict.

I will start this chapter by analysing what happens when a court purports to balance parties' conflicting rights. The first thing to remind ourselves is that in a human rights complaint or in a Charter action, there are at least two parties before the tribunal and they are arguing for mutually exclusive results. One of these results will normally be approved by the court. The situation does not admit of any form of compromise in the result because a court does not devise the remedy for the parties in isolation from or in opposition to what the parties themselves have requested. The court (or human rights tribunal) simply picks one of the solutions before it and, as noted, that solution will exclude the solution for which the other party has argued.[2]

Given this structure, it is difficult to see how any "balance" is possible. One "right" will be vindicated and the other made subservient to the right of the winner in the particular fact pattern at hand. Thus, when a court or tribunal speaks of balancing rights, it does not mean what most of us think of as a "balance." Typically we speak of a balance when both parties receive some recognition for their position and some compromise between them is achieved. However, as a court "balances" rights, we are speaking of only a method by which one right is, in the circumstances of the case, going to be preferred over the other.

An interesting paper published on the website of the Ontario Human Rights Commission in 2005[3] analysed in some detail what courts and tribunals do when they speak of "balancing" rights. The author (whose name is not given on the website) suggested that there are two methods that courts use, often in the same case, to balance rights. One is a pragmatic approach; the other, a principled approach. The pragmatic approach is described as an analysis of the particular circumstances of the case and an attempt to find a compromise position. It is particular to the case before the court and does not lay down any general guidance for future cases (other than those with highly similar facts). The principled approach, on the other hand, is described as drawing on values of human rights law, both at a Federal and provincial level. It establishes general principles on which further cases can be decided.

What I have already said will lead the reader no doubt to appreciate that I find the description of the pragmatic approach puzzling. As noted, compromise positions are not usually achieved by legal action. A court will sometimes modify the remedy requested, as, for example, when it finds damages for the plaintiff but in a lesser amount than claimed. Sometimes it may qualify its findings to ensure that future cases will not expand the implications of the decision. But neither of these activities is a "compromise." Further, the legal doctrine of *stare decisis* stipulates that every case is fact-specific. Yes, courts do refer to general principles which they draw from the circumstances of the decided cases and use to guide future decisions. But simply because a case deals with fact-specific matters has never, in the past, prevented common law courts from using it to establish general principles for later cases.

The principled approach also presents difficulties. The author of the paper suggested that these principles are found in both Charter "values" and in the purposes of human rights legislation. But the author then took this analysis in a strange direction. He or she made no mention, for example, of the underlying Charter values of preserving freedom and democracy, but made extensive reference to climates of understanding and inclusion, equality and dignity of each person. This is the problem, of course, that we have identified earlier when courts or tribunals attempt to use values rather than statute or legal principle to decide cases before them. Such decisions inevitably call upon the decision maker's own belief systems to prefer one value to another. While all decision making before courts and tribunals has always involved elements of this preference, it becomes highly problematic in cases where the central issue is a fundamental moral conflict. In such cases, it encourages the decision maker to impose his or her beliefs on the parties, stifling the participation in public debate of one side or the other and violating the very fundamental premises of the democratic state.

Yet despite the framework, which seems open to serious criticism, when the author of this paper looked at the decided cases, he or she seemed to reach both the principled and the pragmatic conclusion that a court's first step must be to analyse the scope of each party's rights. This, indeed, fits very nicely with the idea that human rights are only legitimate insofar as they make room for the human rights of others. But it is not really a matter of conflicting rights, and the balance that must be found between them is not a mode of preferring one to the other, but of finding the point at which each can leave space for the other to operate.

With these points in mind, we will now turn to consider a specific case in which the courts are said to have balanced the parties' rights. After analysing this case in detail, we will turn, first, to statutory efforts to delineate the scope of rights in the light of the rights of others and then to some of the other cases in which conflicts seem to occur. In the next chapter, we will use what we have observed about these cases to consider situations in which conscience is in the foreground. Those cases perhaps present the greatest challenge to our understanding of human rights, and, arguably, the traditional concepts of conflict and balancing are inadequate to resolve them in a manner that leaves intact our democratic ideals.

2. *Trinity Western University* and Conflicting Rights

In an earlier chapter, I reviewed the case of *Trinity Western University v. College of Teachers (British Columbia)*.[4] We will now turn back to this case and look at it from a slightly different perspective. The case has been held up as a paradigmatic example of conflicting rights and of courts' balancing processes. A major principle that is said to emerge from the case is that "The proper place to draw the line is generally between belief and conduct. The freedom to hold beliefs is broader than the freedom to act on them."[5] These sentences have been cited by many subsequent decisions.

In one way, this statement is self-evident and hardly deserves the name of a principle. As long as I keep my beliefs completely internal, I am, of course, perfectly "free" to hold them in the sense that my mind is always free because no one can determine what is in it but me. We may speak jokingly of "thought police," but indeed, until some method to read minds is discovered, efforts to limit our thoughts will be (as they always have been) restricted to socialization processes and persuasion to convince citizens to exercise internal self-censorship. As soon, however, as I express my belief to the outside world, by any degree of conduct including speech, writing, or some other physical act, I have "acted" on my belief. The only legal point is: When and to what extent can I act on any belief? That is the only question that decides the scope of my right, and the characterization of the Supreme Court is useless for determining it. Indeed, the Supreme Court's statement is tautological and, like most tautologies, has no implications for any other conclusion than that contained in the statement.

The reader may recall that the dispute in *Trinity Western University* was over whether a private evangelical Christian university could provide its students with the full teacher education program to qualify them to teach in British Columbia. As an evangelical Christian institution, Trinity Western University required its staff, faculty, and students to adhere to a code of conduct, which they were required to sign and by which they agreed to abstain from a range of behaviour that evangelical Christians consider immoral. This included sexual activities such as pre-marital sex, adultery, and homosexual behaviour. The B.C. College of Teachers refused to approve Trinity Western's application to offer all four years of the teacher education program on the grounds that it was not in the public interest to allow the education program to be offered in an atmosphere of discrimination. Trinity Western students were therefore to be required to take their last year of education at a secular university.

There was no doubt that Trinity Western University had acted on its beliefs. It had expressed them in a code of conduct and it required members of its community to sign and presumably to observe this code. The students had also acted on their beliefs by signing the code.

Thus there was no question of this simply being a case of freedom to hold beliefs. There is also no doubt that the moral strictures of the code, certainly as they implied that homosexual relations were immoral, and perhaps in other respects too, were offensive to those in the B.C. College of Teachers who decided that Trinity Western's application to offer the full teacher education program should be denied. The Supreme Court, after pronouncing the principle just reviewed, decided that there was no evidence that graduates of Trinity Western University's education program would conduct themselves in the classroom in a way that violated the rights of others.[6] Certainly, B.C. school students had a right to receive an education in an atmosphere that was free from discrimination. However, there was no evidence that a Trinity Western graduate could not or would not provide such a service.

The reasoning of the decision was unsatisfactory. It appeared to establish no workable principles for determining future cases. It vindicated the right of Trinity Western to have a full teacher education program and, as I have observed elsewhere, it avoided the inevitable consequence of the opposite decision, which might easily have been interpreted to allow a faith-based test for work as a public school teacher. But it left open many insoluble problems. What evidence would have been enough to show that graduates of Trinity Western University were discriminating against gay and lesbian students?[7] Would the action of one or two graduates have been enough? And what of other, more established teacher education programs? Would evidence of the misbehaviour of their students (or of certain kinds of misbehaviour) leave open to doubt whether their certification with the B.C. College of Teachers could continue?

Rather than opening these unanswerable questions, the court could have focused on the rights of students in B.C. schools and the rights of students at Trinity Western University and considered them together as mutually dependent. Students in the public school system certainly have the right to receive from their teachers an education that treats them with dignity and respect and that does not differentiate between them on any prohibited ground. That does not mean that they have the right to be taught only by those who accept their belief systems and moral codes.[8] The consequences of concluding otherwise would be to require schools to become impossibly ghettoized, with differing interest groups and belief systems taught only by those who share those beliefs. Freedom of conscience and religion might be preserved by such a structure, but only at the expense of the democratic value of recognizing and respecting a plurality of belief systems. Does that mean that the students in the school system can be subjected to harangues from teachers who disagree with their (or their parents') beliefs or disapprove of their conduct? Of course it does not. In an earlier chapter, we have already considered the requirement that schools remain neutral in proselytizing efforts where fundamental moral conflicts are at issue.

Turning to Trinity Western University and its students, the logical implications of acting on a belief that homosexuality is immoral do not extend beyond the right to say so (in appropriate circumstances), to refrain oneself from such conduct, and to exclude from one's faith community those who are not prepared to agree. None of this requires, compels, or even implies that teachers who hold this belief system treat those in the school system who do not in a different way from those who do. Can teachers be expected to make these differentiations? The answer, I think, is that they must do so, for their own rights to hold (and act upon) their evangelical beliefs depend upon their ability to treat all students equitably and fairly regardless of the students' compliance with the teachers' moral or religious beliefs. That is the treatment to which the students have a right. Individual teachers who demonstrably cannot do so have negated the basis for their own rights and can be subject to discipline and dismissal notwithstanding that arguably the basis for that discipline or dismissal is religious belief. Students, however, cannot expect to have every teacher actively offer them support in circumstances which would require the teacher to transgress his or her own beliefs.

The problem with the position of the B.C. College of Teachers was not lack of evidence that graduates of Trinity Western University were more likely to discriminate against gay and lesbian students than graduates of any other program, but that nothing in Trinity Western University's code of conduct implied that they would or should. On the other hand, the implications of the position of the B.C. College of Teachers would have been disastrous both for freedom of belief and for democratic plurality in the school system. The Supreme Court in *Trinity Western University* did not balance rights. It gave Trinity Western University the relief it sought; but it did nothing to delineate the boundaries of the rights of the university, its students, or the students in the public school system.

The decision is often thought of as a victory for freedom of religion. As a result, the decision is often criticized by those who would prefer what they define as the rights of gay and lesbian students in the school system over rights of belief in principles which they hold to be immoral.[9] The decision was praised in comments from orthodox religious perspectives.[10] But it left troubling questions. Did the decision mean that evangelical (or other similarly believing) Christians could teach in the public schools only if they were not identified as evangelicals and thus no suspicion about their moral views emerged? And what are the rights of children in the public school system who may be gay or lesbian or who may believe same-sex sexual relationships to be either positive in nature or, at least, morally neutral? In contrast to the approach taken by the Supreme Court, a close analysis of the rights of each party as they must exist in harmony together could be used to avoid either making decisions on the basis of the judge's own moral judgment about a matter on which there is intransigent moral conflict or leaving the consequences of the decision unclear.

3. Exemptions in Human Rights Codes and Conflicting Rights

We have already seen that provincial human rights statutes confer upon individuals a right to be treated without distinctions based upon prohibited grounds of discrimination in certain particular situations. I have also mentioned that the statutes establish some defences to a claim of illegal discrimination and contain some sections that provide exemptions to legal liability in certain cases. These defences and exemptions are often characterized as exceptions to the general rules. The suggestion has been made that they should be interpreted narrowly because they are cases in which the prevailing prohibitions against discrimination have been suspended in deference to personal, religious, or ideological sensibilities.[11] Not surprisingly, given this characterization of the problem, human rights commissions have often appeared to be jealously guarding the "right" to be free of discrimination in all circumstances while giving the "rights" of the party seeking an exemption as little scope as the words of the statute allow.[12]

This was not the approach taken by the Supreme Court of Canada in an early case analysing one exemption commonly found in human rights legislation across the country. In *Caldwell v. Stuart*,[13] the Supreme Court adjudicated a complaint brought by a woman whose contract of employment had not been renewed by a Catholic school in British Columbia. Mrs Caldwell had been teaching in the school since 1973 on annual contracts, subject to renewal. In 1977, she married a divorced man in a civil ceremony. Although she had been brought up in the Catholic faith and had been hired to teach at the Catholic school only after presenting evidence that she was a practising Catholic, her marriage was in violation of the teachings of the Catholic Church. When the circumstances of her marriage came to light, the school board gave her notice and refused to renew her teaching contract. She claimed that she had been wrongfully discriminated against under the B.C. Human Rights Code on the basis of religion and marital status.

The B.C. Human Rights Code[14] contained two provisions that were argued in defence of the Catholic school's right to refuse to continue Mrs Caldwell's employment. In the section prohibiting discrimination in employment on the basis of certain characteristics (including religion and marital status),[15] there appeared to be an exception for anything that constituted a "bona fide qualification" for the employment. This exception still exists in the B.C. statute,[16] although the section is now structured slightly differently from how it was when *Caldwell* was decided.[17] The second defence was based on a section common to most human rights codes that permits organizations that primarily serve the interests of members of a particular group identified by a characteristic that would normally be a prohibited ground of discrimination to give a preference in employment to persons who are also members of that group.[18]

The Supreme Court reviewed the purposes and objectives of the Catholic school. It found that the school was dedicated not simply to conveying the requirements of the B.C. education curriculum, but also to teaching and fostering the Catholic faith in its students. It was certainly the case that not all teachers at the school were Catholic and that those who were not Catholic were not required to live by the teachings of the Catholic Church. However, they were expected to maintain the standards of their own religion. Catholic teachers, on the other hand, were expected to illustrate with their lives the precepts of Catholic teaching.

The court found that Mrs Caldwell, by marrying a divorced man outside the Church, in contravention of Catholic teaching, had lost a bona fide qualification of her position.[19] Thus, although the school had fired her for religious reasons, she was not entitled to the protection of the section prohibiting discrimination. They further found that the Catholic school was primarily engaged in serving the interests of Catholic students and was therefore entitled to exercise the statutorily permitted preference for employing persons who were practising Catholics.[20] On both grounds, Mrs Caldwell's complaint was dismissed.

In reviewing the defences raised by the school, the court spoke, as one might expect, in the language of conflicting rights. However, it also refused to view the defences, and particularly that raised by s. 22 of the code – permitting a preference in employment to be given by groups identified by one of the prohibited grounds of discrimination and serving their own group of the population to those belonging to that group – as an "exception" to the normal non-discrimination rule. Rather, the court understood that this exemption protected freedom of association which would otherwise be undermined by the statute.[21] Thus, in effect, we are dealing with a right (the right to employment unaffected by grounds that are normally irrelevant and thus a prohibited basis for discrimination) which must take account of the existence of another right (the right to associate with members of one's own group for benefit to that group). This is a much more reasonable way to view the defences provided by human rights legislation than to see them as barely tolerated exceptions to the moral order enacted by the code.

That is because – except for the inclusion of hate speech sections, which have already been noted in earlier chapters and will be referred to again later in this one – Federal and provincial human rights legislation deals only with one aspect of human rights: the right to be free from certain kinds of discrimination.[22] Those involved in the industries produced by human rights commissions and tribunals may perhaps be pardoned for understanding the moral universe only in terms of issues of discrimination and equality. However, as we know, that is not a realistic view. A regime of perfect equality is not necessarily a regime of perfect human rights. Freedom of conscience, religion, expression, and association are not the subject matter of these statutes. That does not mean, however, that those rights can be ignored in the interpretation of anti-discrimination laws.

Where the enforcement of rights to be free of discrimination would obliterate or seriously undermine the human rights of others, there is a strong case for interpreting those rights as having to operate consistently with the exercise of human rights by others. In this case, Mrs Caldwell had a general right to be free from discrimination in employment on the basis of her religion and her marital status. However, that could not be interpreted to override the right of the Catholic school to exercise its freedom of religion to provide education in the Catholic faith. That educational environment required it to employ teachers who exemplified fidelity to the moral code of conduct of their chosen belief systems. This right of the Catholic school was recognized by those sections of the Human Rights Code that allowed discrimination on the basis of bona fide qualifications and that protected the freedom of association of religious and philanthropic bodies.

An enlightening contrast to this case was the recent *Heintz v. Christian Horizons*,[23] a decision of the Ontario Human Rights Tribunal which was overturned in part by the Ontario Divisional Court.[24] We should first note that there are some differences between the Ontario Human Rights Code[25] and that of British Columbia in the defences that they provide in these kinds of cases. While the B.C. code still retains a general exemption from discrimination in employment on the basis of a bona fide qualification for the work, the Ontario statute allows such discrimination only where the ground of discrimination is age, sex, marital status, or record of offences.[26] It is arguable therefore that had Mrs Caldwell been dismissed in Ontario for the same reasons, her change of religious practice could not have been relied upon as a bona fide employment qualification. However, the Ontario statute contains an exemption in very similar language to that of B.C. allowing a preference in employment to be given by organizations primarily engaged in serving special groups to members of those groups. The section contains the additional requirement that the qualification is reasonable and bona fide considering the nature of the employment.[27] It seems probable that *Caldwell v. Stuart* could have been decided the same way under this provision as it was under the B.C. statute, although perhaps on only one of the two grounds relied upon by the Supreme Court.

Ms Heintz was employed as a support worker in a home run by an evangelical Christian organization for people with developmental disabilities. All members of the organization and all its employees were obliged to subscribe to a code of conduct which expressed the religious and moral commitments of the organization. The code went far beyond workplace conduct and included adherence to a particular lifestyle. It contained a prohibition on several forms of sexual behaviour, and, in particular, homosexual activity. Ms Heintz accepted employment with Christian Horizons and signed the code of conduct as part of her employment contract. Some years after her employment commenced, Ms Heintz entered into a lesbian relationship. When her employer discovered that relationship, she was confronted with her breach of the employment contract. Ultimately, this led to her resignation from her employment and her claim before the Ontario Human Rights Tribunal that she had been unlawfully discriminated against in her employment on the basis of sexual orientation.

The tribunal found that Christian Horizons was not entitled to the exemption under the code. After a lengthy review of the circumstances in which Christian Horizons was founded, its history, its mission statement, and its approach to the provision of its services, the tribunal had no difficulty in finding that Christian Horizons was a religious organization, thus meeting the first requirement of the statutory exemption.[28] However, the tribunal also found that Christian Horizons was not primarily engaged in serving persons from its own religious group.

This was an interesting argument, because certainly one of the purposes of Christian Horizons was to allow persons with a common Evangelical Christian commitment to have an outlet for their religious impulse in caring for the disadvantaged. It was also the case that another of its purposes was to care for these disadvantaged individuals. While many of the persons residing in the Christian Horizons' homes were from Christian families, and families were able to express a preference for the kind of home and religious orientation that they preferred, Christian Horizons placed no limitation on the faith of those it accepted. The tribunal found that the organization could not have two "primary" purposes. While its commitment to provide the opportunity for Christian service was important, the tribunal held that its primary purpose was to serve developmentally disabled persons from all faith backgrounds.[29]

The Divisional Court overruled the tribunal on this point. The court examined the purposes of the provision and its legislative history. It also compared the English and French versions of the section. The court found that the tribunal had overlooked the purpose of the legislation, which was to protect rights of association of certain groups, including religious groups.[30] The court rejected the view that religious organizations were entitled to the exemption only when they were acting privately within their own communities. Rather, the test of whether the exemption applied required

an analysis of the nature of the particular activity engaged in by a religious organization to determine whether it is seen by the group as fundamentally a religious activity. This must be followed by an assessment of whether that activity furthers the religious purpose of the organization and its members, thus serving the interests of the members of the religious organization.[31]

Christian Horizons was therefore entitled to the protection of the statutory exemption and could be entitled to a preference in hiring co-religionists without being guilty of illegal discrimination. However, that did not conclude the matter.

The tribunal also held that even if its finding on this point were wrong, the requirement of adherence to the morality statement was not a reasonable and bona fide job qualification.[32] The Divisional Court agreed with this determination.[33] Support workers were not expected to convert the residents or to impart to them the organization's evangelical faith. On this basis, the court distinguished such cases as *Caldwell*. The type of care that the support workers provided was not one that required a commitment to an evangelical Christian lifestyle. Since the statutory exemption only protected preferences given where belonging to the particular group was a bona fide requirement to perform the particular duties of the job, Christian Horizons could not claim the exemption in this case.

What the court appeared to widen, by rejecting the tribunal's interpretation of the section as applying only to services delivered to co-religionists, it then significantly narrowed by its interpretation of what was a bona fide qualification for the job. Most of the employees of Christian Horizons were support workers with exactly the same duties as Ms Heintz.[34] There may be a hint of inconsistency in these two holdings. The court accepted that the purpose of the organization was primarily to carry out the evangelical mandate of Christian service to the disadvantaged, even where those it served did not share that faith.[35] Yet apparently the opportunities Christian Horizons offers to its co-religionists directly to engage in serving the disadvantaged must be limited to those who are in supervisory or management positions.[36] Those who do the direct work – engage, in other words, in the traditional types of Christian menial service that date back to Jesus, who washed his disciples' feet – cannot be hired for their religious commitments.

Even if Christian Horizons had been entitled to fire Ms Heintz for her deviation from the moral code, the tribunal would still apparently have found that she had been discriminated against by the creation of a poisoned atmosphere at her workplace. She had been offered counselling to assist her to change her sexual orientation by her supervisor. It was further quite clear on the evidence that Ms Heintz had become a source of conflict in the workplace based upon her sexual orientation. Co-workers were apparently unhappy working with her, given her lifestyle, and seem to have made that apparent. Christian Horizons had not taken adequate steps to address this situation and put an end to the discriminatory treatment.[37] The court found that there was evidence on this point and did not interfere with the tribunal's decision in this respect.[38]

The hearing of the appeal attracted a great deal of public interest. The tribunal member commented that the result of his decision that Christian Horizons did not fall within the exemption under the code seemed to be that a religious organization could not give any preference in hiring to those of its own creed unless it restricted its activities to its own members. That could certainly have weakened the commitment of religious organizations to provide social services. However, the tribunal noted, that appeared to be the policy choice made by the legislature and the consequences of that choice could not influence his decision.[39] While the court's decision avoided the exclusion of religious charities from public good works that the tribunal decision seemed to compel, it did so in a manner that left one puzzled about an exemption that seems to be broad on its face, but rarely will apply in practice. These inconsistencies seem inherent in the wording of the legislation, which in Ontario at least combines the religious element with a requirement of bona fide qualification for the work. Perhaps it is time to take a second look at the nature of the problem and how it might be solved using principles that we have discussed earlier.

The problem presented by the case is a difficult one. No doubt religious organizations do have and must have the right to define their membership, even including the right to exclude people from membership on grounds that many citizens might find repugnant. To hold otherwise would be to destroy the rights of religious organizations to exist and thus to destroy the religious freedom of those who wish to commit themselves to a common creed and way of life. However, at the other end of the scale, members of religious organizations have no right to be protected from living and working, in the broader social environment, beside those who do not share their religious commitments or their moral views. To hold otherwise would be to destroy the free and democratic society which provides both the basis and a primary reason for the existence of religious freedom (as well as other human rights).[40]

We need to analyse carefully what the rights of the religious organization actually are in this context and where they fall along this continuum. If Christian Horizons or other religious groups wish to provide a social service as part of their faith commitment, it would be a breach of their religious freedom to prohibit them from doing so.[41] Their right to provide a social service necessarily includes a right to run their organization on their own principles and to require their staff to comply with the operating principles for their organization while at work. This does not, however, necessarily require that all employees have a personal commitment to those principles. The right to operate a charitable organization in accordance with particular religious principles would certainly require that the staff not undermine those principles in their work environment. But absent some work-related need for a personal commitment (such as for the teacher whose life is expected to be a role model for students of their own faith community), lack of that commitment on the part of some staff does not seem to violate the rights of committed members of the organization to act out their faith in the workplace or the right of the religious organization to operate the workplace in accordance with their principles.[42]

If that is so, then it is difficult to see what right of Christian Horizons was infringed by requiring them to continue to employ Ms Heintz despite her sexual orientation and apparent personal disagreement with the tenets of Christian Horizons' moral beliefs, unless, of course, she had displayed hostility to those beliefs in her work. That was not an issue raised in the case, nor was there evidence that this was the root of the problems in the workplace.[43] However, the right to employment without discrimination must be interpreted consistently with the right of the employer to abide by its own principles and to expect its employees to support those principles while at work. As long as an employee is willing to do this, the employer's rights to religious freedom do not seem to be infringed by requiring the employment of someone whose beliefs differ where those employees are not involved in religious duties.

Readers may object that this in effect requires the employee to live a life of concealment. That is not, however, the case. Someone in Ms Heintz's position would not need to conceal her sexual orientation or her living arrangements from her employer or from her co-workers. As already noted, those co-workers have no rights to work only with those who share their faith. However, neither should the non-conforming employee be allowed to be critical of her employer's beliefs to those the organization serves. He or she must be prepared to support those beliefs in the workplace. To decide otherwise would be to allow his or her rights to extend beyond employment to the destruction of the mission of the employer's business. It would be effectively to prevent a Christian organization (or an organization committed to any other beliefs) from carrying on a social service as part of its belief system. There is no reason why a right to employment without discrimination cannot operate compatibly with the employer organization's rights to practise its religion when the existence of each right is understood as requiring recognition of the rights of the other.

An interesting contrast to and comparison with this case can be found in the recent decision of the U.S. Supreme Court in *Hosanna-Tabor Evangelical Lutheran Church and School v. Equal Opportunity Commission et al.*[44] An Evangelical Lutheran church employed in their school two kinds of teachers, "lay" and "called." "Called" teachers were required to undergo some theological training, were given the title "Minister of Religion," and were given various responsibilities for teaching religious studies classes and leading worship in the school chapel. Ms Pasich was a "called" teacher. She acquired narcolepsy and was on disability leave for a time. When she wanted to return to the school, a dispute arose. The congregation revoked her call and she was fired. She complained to the Equal Opportunity Commission that she had been discriminated against contrary to statute because of her disability.

The U.S. Supreme Court affirmed a "ministerial exception," which, they held, was grounded in the First Amendment guaranteeing the free exercise of religion and prohibiting the establishment of any religion. This exception required, the court further held, that churches be permitted to designate who were their ministers. There was no rigid formula for determining who was a minister, but all factors, including the employee's title, ordination, training, and participation in religious duties had to be weighed. The lower court had considered the amount of time spent on religious duties in isolation. The exception barred suits from ministers against their churches for violating statutes prohibiting discrimination in employment. Ms Pasich could not succeed in her claim.

The American exception appears much broader than that contained in our human rights codes in Canada. However, even it does not apply unless the employee can legitimately be considered as a "minister" in the organization, based upon a range of factors. It seems likely that Ms Heintz, who had no special training and was not expected to carry out any religious duties, would have qualified for the American protection. While the American position protects more broadly religious organizations that fire employees who are violating the religious organization's standards, it does not extend to those who take no part in religious activities.

Other defences and exemptions in human rights legislation also exist. Some are designed to facilitate special social policies that permit affirmative action programs or protections for certain particular groups.[45]

They introduce into the legislation consideration of rights that might otherwise be ignored by the anti-discrimination purposes of the statutes, such as the right to free association. However, they do so in ways that appear to produce inconsistent and problematic results. In the next section of this chapter, we will turn to consider cases of apparently conflicting rights where the human rights codes do not provide an adequate solution within themselves, and we must look to constitutional rights to determine how the problem will be solved.

4. Human Rights Codes versus Constitutional Rights

In this section, we will consider three cases in which a claim of discrimination was met by a claim that enforcement of the human rights legislation would violate the defendant's constitutionally protected right to freedom of religion. Before looking at these cases in some detail, we should recall the way in which Charter rights interact with provincial laws. Charter rights are not enforceable against other individuals in private situations. For example, if an organization refused admission to a person professing Hinduism as their religious belief, it could not be challenged on the basis of freedom of religion under the Charter. There is no aspect of state action involved and the Charter regulates state actions, not those of private citizens. However, the disappointed applicant could possibly bring a claim under the provincial human rights code of illegal discrimination.

To be successful, he or she would have to prove that the organization was operating a service commonly available to the public or some other enterprise (such as provision of housing or employment) where discriminatory treatment is prohibited. Even so, however, the defendant organization could raise the claim that to punish it for its behaviour would be an action of the state through the human rights tribunal and that this punishment would violate its freedom of religion, by using state power to coerce its beliefs. Of course, it would also be open to the complainant to argue that the application of the anti-discrimination laws, even granting that they limited the defendant's religious rights, was justifiable in a free and democratic society. As we know, this process is a complex one and not always rigorously analysed.

But this structure provides precisely the tools that could be used to recognize interdependent rights. It requires the court or tribunal to look carefully at how far the right to be free from discrimination in certain aspects of life extends and how far the religious freedom of the defendant can be exercised in the face of the rights of others. It also provides the opportunity for the court or tribunal to ask itself what decision will better contribute to a free and democratic society, not simply a society that expresses the beliefs of the decision maker. How successfully courts and tribunals have used this opportunity will be considered in our analysis of the cases.

Mr Brockie operated a print shop. He was approached by Mr Brillinger on behalf of a gay and lesbian organization to print some letterhead, envelopes, and business cards for its officers. Mr Brockie refused on the basis that, as an evangelical Christian, he believed the organization to have immoral purposes. Mr Brillinger brought a complaint against Mr Brockie before the Ontario Human Rights Tribunal, which found that Mr Brockie had violated the human rights code in discriminating on the basis of sexual orientation against Mr Brillinger in providing a service commonly available to the public.[46] The case was appealed to the Divisional Court.

The Ontario court performed a classic analysis of the problem.[47] The Ontario Act, unlike that of British Columbia, contained no defence in the statute permitting discrimination where there is a bona fide and reasonable justification. The court further declined to read in such a defence.[48] However, that did not dispose of Mr Brockie's argument that the order of the tribunal requiring him to provide services to Mr Brillinger's organization violated his Charter rights to freedom of conscience and religion. With or without this defence, the question would still have come down to the issue of whether Mr Brockie was entitled to exercise his freedom of religion in these circumstances and whether the state was allowed under the Charter to penalize him for doing so.

The Divisional Court's holding about the extent of Mr Brockie's freedom of religion was somewhat disturbing. It suggested that the exercise of Mr Brockie's freedom of religion in the commercial sphere was "on the fringes of that right."[49] The suggestion that those engaged in commercial activities must leave their beliefs at the door of the workplace cannot be supported. We have already looked at the idea that there are circumstances in which a right claimed can be less or more protected. For example, in *Owens*,[50] the court found that speech contributing to political debate is worthy of stronger protection than speech that is hateful or untrue. But the core of religious belief is not simply acts of worship, but the living of a life in conformity with that belief. Exercise of religious or conscientious belief in the marketplace cannot be considered less worthy of protection than exercise of those beliefs in the church or mosque. To hold otherwise would be to subordinate freedom of conscience and religion to any and all other rights. As discussed in chapter 1, this is antithetical to the role which the Charter assigns freedom of conscience and religion as a fundamental freedom.

The court also trod on problematic territory when it stated that "the freedom to exercise genuine religious belief does not include the right to interfere with the rights of others."[51] This suggested that all other rights are unlimited while freedom of conscience and religion must always give way to another right. Again, this is antithetical to the recognition of freedom of conscience and religion as fundamental. It is also, as I have argued, a failure to recognize that the existence of those other rights depends as well upon the existence of the right to free conscientious and religious belief.

Notwithstanding these troublesome signs in the decision, the court engaged on what it referred to as a "balancing" of the rights of Mr Brockie and those of Mr Brillinger. This case, indeed, is often considered an example of how rights can be balanced. While I object to the terminology of "balancing," what the court did was to try to analyse the scope of the two rights in such a way that they could be exercised in a compatible fashion. It recognized that imposing punishment on Mr Brockie for his actions violated his freedom of conscience and religion. It also recognized the public interest expressed in the human rights code in ensuring that gays and lesbians were treated with dignity and were included in the economic life of society. For these reasons, it held that an order requiring Mr Brockie to print the submitted material was a justifiable infringement on his rights. However, the court also observed that if the material had directly contradicted Mr Brockie's religious beliefs, for example, by advocating for sexual behaviour he found immoral, Mr Brockie would have had a defence. The court found that the order was too broad to meet the proportionality test and therefore limited it to material "not in direct conflict with the core elements of his religious belief or creed."[52]

This decision has sometimes been considered a "compromise" and, to an extent, that is a fair description. Neither Mr Brockie's nor Mr Brillinger's rights were unlimited. While in the circumstances of the case, Mr Brillinger was the successful party, the court made it clear that his rights were not to be applied to virtually extinguish the rights of Mr Brockie. The case also illustrated that the place where two rights meet can be difficult to define. Had the court decided that Mr Brockie needed to give no services at all to Mr Brillinger's organization, it would have risked justifying the exclusion of gay and lesbian groups from numerous aspects of economic life. On the other side, had Mr Brillinger been permitted to require Mr Brockie to print anything Mr Brillinger might have provided, Mr Brockie's right to refuse on religious grounds to support causes he found repugnant would have been extinguished. The boundary between rights may be said to fall where each is required to tolerate the existence of the other, even though, in the circumstances of the particular case, one party will be successful and one will fail.

A case that has some similarities to *Ontario (Human Rights Tribunal) v. Brockie* was decided by the B.C. Human Rights Tribunal in *Smith v. Knights of Columbus*.[53] Ms Smith and Ms Chymyshyn had decided to marry and entered into a contract to rent a hall from the Knights of Columbus for their wedding reception. The Knights of Columbus is a Catholic men's organization which supports and abides by the teachings of the Roman Catholic Church. Among those teachings is the doctrine that marriage is confined to the union between a man and a woman. The Knights' representative who met Ms Smith and Ms Chymyshyn apparently did not realize that the two women were the parties who were to be married. The tribunal heard evidence that there was a misunderstanding that it was Ms Smith's wedding and Ms Chymyshyn was simply present in the role of friend.[54] When the Knights discovered that the wedding was a lesbian wedding, they cancelled the contract with Ms Smith. Ms Smith and Ms Chymyshyn complained to the Human Rights Tribunal that they had been discriminated against on the basis of sexual orientation.

The B.C. Human Rights Code contains, as noted, a defence to the complaint of illegal discrimination in the provision of a service commonly available to the public where there is a bona fide and reasonable justification.[55] The tribunal focused on this defence. However, the justification raised was the Charter right to freedom of conscience and religion. Thus, just as in *Brockie*, the tribunal was required to consider the exercise of that freedom and how it affected the right under the provincial statute to be free from discrimination. Because the tribunal focused on the question of whether rights to freedom of religion constituted, in this case, a bona fide justification for the discriminatory conduct, its process of analysis was quite different from that in *Brockie*. It treated the question as requiring it to consider whether the Knights had adopted a standard in good faith, rationally connected to the purposes it was designed to achieve, and whether the complainants could be accommodated under this standard without causing the defendants undue hardship.

We have already discussed the connection between the requirements to accommodate in cases of discrimination and the standard in s. 1 of the Charter that the rights it confers are limited only by measures imposed by law and justifiable in a free and democratic society. At least in cases of administrative action by the state, the tests produce very similar results.[56] In this case, however, it seems likely that the tribunal should not have ignored the separate issues. One may argue that being required to act against one's conscience ought to constitute a bona fide and reasonable justification for what would otherwise be illegal discrimination. However, that is not an enforcement of a Charter right and the jurisprudence on freedom of conscience and religion is not directly relevant to this issue. The Knights' freedom of religion is not something that can be asserted against private individuals. So in this context, assuming the tribunal was willing to recognize religious principles as a basis for excusing discriminatory conduct, it was correct in analysing whether the Knights could have accommodated Ms Smith without undue hardship.

But after that matter was determined, the tribunal needed to take a further step and determine whether imposing a penalty upon the Knights for their conduct was a state action that violated their freedom of conscience and religion. In this context, it would be necessary to treat separately the question of whether the violation of religious freedom in imposing a penalty for exercising religious beliefs was justifiable under s. 1 of the Charter. However, the tribunal collapsed the two questions by discussing the jurisprudence on freedom of conscience and religion under the heading of the bona fide and reasonable justification test and investigated only the question of accommodation up to the point of undue hardship.

The tribunal held that opposition to same-sex marriages was part of the core religious beliefs of the Knights of Columbus and that they could not be required to violate that belief. Thus the Knights were not required to provide the service of renting the hall to Ms Smith and Ms Chymyshyn. The tribunal found that the Knights had adopted a standard of refusing to rent for purposes that undermined the teaching of the Catholic Church. This standard had been adopted bona fide and was rationally connected to the purposes of the Knights.[57] But the tribunal also found that while it would have constituted undue hardship to the Knights to require them to rent their hall for a reception for a same-sex marriage, there were other steps that the Knights could have taken to accommodate the couple. They could have offered to help find another rental. They could have apologized and they could have offered to pay the expenses wasted by the couple in communicating to their friends that the reception would be held at the Knights of Columbus hall. The Knights had agreed to reimburse those expenses, but had done so only on condition that they received a legal release. The tribunal felt that this had exacerbated the tensions between the parties and should have been handled differently. In the result, the tribunal fined the Knights for their failures in these matters.[58]

Superficially, the decision looks a lot like *Brockie*. However, although it might be called a "compromise" – the Knights did not have to rent out their hall, but had to pay a fine for abiding by their principles – it was not a matter of delineating the rights of both parties such that each had to recognize those of the other and then applying that boundary to the facts at hand. Rather, the decision seems to be a determination that the Knights' freedom of religion was protected, but that they were subject to a fine in any event.

The right given to Ms Smith and Ms Chymyshyn under the Human Rights Code was the right to receive services commonly available to the public without discrimination based upon their sexual orientation. The tribunal found, probably correctly given the jurisprudence, that the hall rental was a "service commonly available to the public." Although the hall was used for parish purposes, it was also freely rented to outside groups without any approval process or restrictions as to faith. It seems probable that had the wedding been between a man and a woman in a Sikh temple, the Knights would have allowed the hall to be used for the reception.

Assuming that a sincere conscientious objection to an act can be a bona fide and reasonable justification for discrimination, we turn to the question of whether any accommodation was possible here without crossing the boundaries of undue hardship. Rental of the hall was the only service being offered. No accommodation could be provided in this situation because either the hall was rented or it was refused. It is unlike situations in which a person with a disability can be accommodated in the workplace by providing special tools or scheduling changes or reorganizing her responsibilities. It is more like the situation in which the employee cannot perform the key functions of the job at all, in which case, accommodation is not required because it would impose undue hardship on the employer. The actions the tribunal found should have been taken were not, in fact, actions of accommodation at all. Rather, they were simply more generous ways of refusing to rent the hall. None of them would have altered the refusal at all.

If we turn to the actual question of the Charter rights in this case, the tribunal held that requiring the Knights to rent the hall would have violated a core belief of their religion. The question then is whether the Knights could be penalized by the state for failing to rent their hall to the complainants. Based upon the *Brockie* decision, the answer would appear to be negative. It was held not demonstrably justifiable in a free and democratic society to require parties to violate a core belief in similar circumstances. The fine, of course, was imposed because the Knights failed to do other things that, short of renting the hall, the tribunal thought should have been done and that would not have violated their core beliefs.

The actions of the Knights for which they were fined, taken after the refusal had been made, had nothing to do with prohibited discrimination under the Human Rights Code. At this point in the process, the Knights had refused to honour what was probably a legally enforceable contract. Leaving aside the human rights issues, they were probably liable for damages for breach of contract. Proceeding upon that basis, it is hardly surprising that both parties, by this time preparing for possible litigation, were wary of each other and treated each other with some degree of suspicion. While it may be admirable to treat one's opponent in such a situation in a generous and open manner, it is hardly a breach of human rights to behave in a less exalted fashion.

The third case we will consider in this context involved Marc Hall, a young man in a Catholic school who wished to invite his boyfriend to the school prom.[59] The school refused to allow the two young men to attend together, citing as their justification the Catholic prohibition on homosexual relations. The case was one in which either an action under the Ontario Human Rights Code or an action for breach of equality rights under s. 15 of the Charter could have been brought. Under the Human Rights Code, the claim would have been that the school discriminated against the student in the provision of education on the basis of sexual orientation. The defence would have been the Charter rights of the school, both under freedom of religion and under s. 93 of the Constitution Act, which protects denominational schools in Ontario. The case was, however, brought as a breach of s. 15 of the Charter. As the reader will know, court cases and cases before provincial human rights tribunals can take years to be heard and decided. The date of the prom would have long passed by the time Mr Hall's case had followed this process. The superior courts can issue injunctions to restrain conduct during the trial process and can act quickly to accomplish this limited result. Mr Hall sought this relief and therefore had to bring his claim in the courts rather than before the tribunal.

Because of the nature of the proceedings, the case did not actually decide whether or not Mr Hall's claim was justified or whether or not the school's defences would have been successful. In granting an inter-locutory injunction, a court only needs to be convinced that there is a serious issue to be tried, that the applicant will suffer irreparable harm if the injunction is not granted, and that, on the balance of convenience, it is more just to issue the injunction than to withhold it.[60] There seemed little doubt that the question of Mr Hall's right to bring a male partner to the prom raised serious issues of human rights. Moreover, if the injunction did not issue, Mr Hall's opportunity to attend the prom would have been lost. The question of the balance of convenience required the court to look also at what harm the school would suffer if Mr Hall attended with his boyfriend. The court found that there was little harm that would flow from it.

The difficulty with the outcome of the injunctive relief process, in this case at least, was that when the injunction was granted, as it was, the issue from Mr Hall's perspective became moot. He was allowed to bring his boyfriend to the prom and the school was prohibited from for-bidding it. Not surprisingly perhaps, Mr Hall applied later to discon-tinue the action against the school. The school objected and asked that the matter proceed to trial. However, the court was not willing to grant this request.[61] This is an unsatisfactory legal outcome: in practical terms, it means that the school will never be allowed to prohibit same-sex cou-ples from attending their functions, because an injunction can be is-sued to prevent the school's prohibition. But the school will likely never be able to obtain any definitive decision on what is legally required of them or what their rights in this case are. This is the kind of "Catch-22" situation that is likely to contribute to hostility rather than resolve it.

Leaving that aside, however, we can look at how the trial judge ana-lysed where the boundaries between Mr Hall's and the school's rights fell. It was clear from the decision that, had the judge been required to make a final finding about that boundary, he would have agreed that Mr Hall had a right to attend the prom and that the school had no right to prevent him doing so. Some of the points made by the judge were questionable. He appeared to suggest that there might be some ques-tion about Roman Catholic teaching as to homosexual conduct, for ex-ample, although he emphasized possible disagreements over pastoral responses rather than the moral issue.[62] He further suggested that to permit the school to ban Mr Hall from the prom with his male date would simply open the door to allowing unrestricted discrimination against gays and lesbians because of personal preference, seemingly ignoring the genuine religious doctrine at issue.[63] These comments were unfortunate.

The judge made the point that there was no Roman Catholic doctrine against same-sex dancing and that boys and girls attending the prom were at different stages of romantic, sexual, or simply friendly relationships with the opposite sex.[64] This, of course, was true. Indeed, a number of boys or girls in the past may have made do with a date for prom night from a close relative where romance had nothing to do with it. Incest is clearly against Roman Catholic teaching, but it is unlikely that the school would have refused a girl the right to attend with her brother, for example, even if they danced together. However, this was disingenuous. Mr Hall and his partner were clearly involved in a romantic relationship. Such relationships do not always lead to sexual relationships or to marriage, but they are precursors to those activities and Mr Hall made no secret of his intention to carry on romantic, sexual, and perhaps eventually marital relationships with other members of his sex.

Looking at *Brockie* and *Smith*, we can ask whether there was any distinguishing difference between those cases and *Hall*. In both *Brockie* and *Smith*, compelling activities that would promote the view that homosexual relationships could be morally justified was held to trespass upon a core belief of the defendants and a refusal to engage in those activities was held to be protected by religious freedom. In allowing Mr Hall to attend the prom with his boyfriend, could the school be said to be in any different position? I have already mentioned that the boundaries between where one right ceases to exist in recognition of the right of another are often difficult to discern. In this case, there are two differences that might be important.

First, unlike the cases of *Brockie* and *Smith*, the defendant was engaged in a long-term relationship with the complainant in which setting the defendant had an ongoing responsibility to him. That might have required more effort on the part of the school to accommodate their student than existed in the cases of *Brockie* or *Smith*. In both those situations, the complainants could have easily obtained the services they sought elsewhere. Separating a student from the school he is attending is a more difficult and more emotionally involved process. The school also had the opportunity to make clear the Catholic religious position to him and to their other students. Unlike the public school system, where I have argued for a position of neutrality on issues of moral conflict, denominational schools have the right to teach their own doctrines and moral beliefs.[65] The public school system is an available option for those who find those beliefs objectionable and do not wish to hear about them.

Both these factors meant that there was a way to preserve the school's religious principles without refusing Mr Hall access to the prom. As the judge held, the school could have (and probably had) informed its students clearly of its views of homosexual relationships. It could also have controlled expressions of physical intimacy on its property at the dance, since it obviously held religious beliefs against such expressions.[66] In neither *Brockie* nor *Smith* were these options open to the defendants. Neither Mr Brockie nor the Knights had any way of expressing their beliefs in these situations other than by refusal. Accommodation was not a practical reality. Arguably, in *Hall*, the school had those methods open to them and Mr Hall might have been accommodated had the school allowed him to attend with his male date on the basis that their behaviour was platonic at the prom and that the students all understood clearly the Church's position on same-sex relationships. The school was not necessarily put in a position of sponsoring or condoning a relationship it believed to be sinful.

But there remain troubling issues in reconciling these three cases. One problem we have seen in defining discrimination is that courts and tribunals have often extended its meaning beyond the simple denial of services. Its definition appears to include delivering those services, but doing so in an unpleasant fashion. For example, when we considered Ms Heintz's position with Christian Horizons, the tribunal found that discrimination existed in the supervisor's offer to arrange counselling for Ms Heintz to help her change her orientation. In *Smith*, the tribunal found that the lack of openness and generosity on the part of the Knights was discriminatory. But in *Hall*, the court seemed to say that while Mr Hall could attend the prom with his boyfriend, the school was entitled to single him out in a way that could have been quite unpleasant, both by communicating Catholic teaching on homosexuality and by limiting his behaviour while at the prom.

Of course, unpleasant behaviour can reach a level at which it effectively becomes a denial of service. Constant persecution can persuade even the bravest soul to give up and go elsewhere for the service or employment that he or she is seeking. In that case, tribunals are justified in claiming that the behaviour amounts to discrimination. In *Heintz*, the conduct of her fellow employees may have reached that level. Certainly, Ms Heintz did resign because of it. In *Smith*, in contrast, the service had already been denied when the unpleasant behaviour took place. The court in *Hall*, however, appreciated that while one is entitled to a service, receiving it without discrimination does not mean that the service provider must conceal its views on what it is required to provide. This is a sensible and necessary distinction. Anti-discrimination provisions cannot be reasonably interpreted to protect a right to feel accepted. Otherwise, we find ourselves back in the hopelessly tangled notions that one has a right not to be offended or not to be told that others believe one to be wrong.

This raises, again, the issue of human dignity as a subjective concept. It may be said that in all three cases, the complainants' subjective feelings of dignity had been affronted; all were publicly refused a service which would have been extended to others. But it may equally be said that if Mr Brockie were required to print pro-gay material, if the Knights were required to have their hall publicly rented to a lesbian couple for their wedding celebration, or if the Catholic school were required to allow a student to attend its prom with a same-sex date without objection, the dignity of these persons would also be affronted. We then descend into a question of "Whose dignity is worth more?" As one comment on the *Hall* case observed, "While an individual cannot achieve self-fulfillment as promised by s. 15 if he is not able to act on, express or have honoured his sexual orientation, Catholics apparently can reach self-fulfillment without always acting as directed by their faith."[67] Or, on the opposing side, Professor MacDougall, writing in approval of the same decision, stated, "Elsewhere I have suggested that in order for there to be real equality for the members of a given group, the state must show towards the members ... compassion, condonation and celebration."[68]

With respect to both sides, these assertions do little more than provide a cheering section for one of the parties whose subjective feelings of worth have been vindicated or quashed. In some senses, human dignity does, of course, have a subjective element. However, what the law must recognize, as opposed to our use of the term in common speech, is the reciprocal nature of human dignity, meaning that I cannot have human dignity if you do not. For this reason, the feeling that your dignity has been affronted may be misleading if, in order to establish that dignity, you require that the dignity of others be damaged. In fact, your apparent vindication is a serious defeat. This leads to the conclusion that unpleasant feelings are, in fact, an essential part of recognition of the dignity of all. We cannot expect to accord dignity to those with whom we passionately disagree without a degree of discomfort; but we cannot fail to accord that dignity if we wish to maintain our rights to it ourselves. Only a careful analysis of where my dignity can extend without defeating yours can solve this problem. One thing we can be certain of: Neither of us will find the limits we must accept to be enjoyable.

5. The Limits of Anti-Discrimination Statutes

While provincial and Federal human rights codes protect freedom of religion by prohibiting discrimination on religious grounds, they also, as we have seen, can produce problems in reconciling freedom of religion with other claims to be free from discrimination. Defences inherent in the statutes appear to recognize that human rights are not simply a matter of being free from discrimination under all circumstances. I have tried to propose a method of analysis that takes into account as being of equal value other human rights that are recognized in our constitution and in our culture.

An inherent conflict between rights is set up, however, when anti-discrimination statutes are interpreted as mandating pleasant, non-offensive, or approving behaviour, as I have discussed in the preceding section. A similar conflict is produced when the statutes include direct limits on expression found in many of their discriminatory publication provisions. We have already spent considerable time on these provisions in earlier chapters. In this section, I want to draw attention to another possible interpretation of these provisions that might make them fit more appropriately into the limited sphere that Federal and provincial human rights codes are designed to address.

Mr Boissoin was an Alberta pastor who was chair of a conservative Christian political organization. He took it upon himself to write to his local paper a lengthy letter condemning homosexual activists and the gay agenda. He attacked homosexual activists as being on the same level as drug dealers and pedophiles, warned of the corruption of children in the school system as a result of their activities, and issued a general "call to war" against the threats to the sanctity of the community's children. The letter caused some controversy in the Letters to the Editor page and several rebuttal letters were received and published.

Dr. Lund, a prominent member of the local gay community, complained to the Alberta Human Rights Commission that Mr Boissoin had violated the human rights statute. He alleged that the letter was a publication "likely to expose to hatred or contempt a person or group of persons" on the basis of their sexual orientation, a prohibited ground of discrimination under the act. As part of the evidence for his case, the complainant presented a newspaper report of a teenager who had been assaulted because of his sexual orientation. The report quoted the young man as stating that he felt unsafe reading anti-gay material and, whether quoted from the young man or an addition by the writer, gave as an example letters "like" the one published in the *Red Deer Advocate* from Mr Boissoin. The human rights panel agreed that Mr Boissoin's letter violated the statute. It ordered him to cease and desist from making "disparaging remarks against gays and homosexuals," ordered him to provide a written apology to Dr. Lund to be published in the paper, and imposed a fine.[69]

Mr Boissoin appealed. In many respects, the appeal judgment of the Alberta Court of Queen's Bench added nothing to what we have already discussed considering similar sections.[70] The court held that the letter did not reach the level of vituperation required by the Supreme Court of Canada in *Taylor*.[71] It did not rouse extreme feelings of hatred and calumny. The court further held that the tribunal had no jurisdiction to issue an order prohibiting "disparaging" remarks about anyone, since such remarks were not contrary to the statute and clearly fell far short of "hatred and contempt."[72]

The court, however, added an interesting and novel requirement to the interpretation of this section of the Act. The court held that the purpose of s. 3(b) of the Act, prohibiting discriminatory publication, was to aid in preventing those acts of discrimination prohibited by the Act. The complainant, therefore, had to show some likelihood that the impugned publication would bring about or encourage discriminatory behaviour contrary to the Act.[73] The court found that evidence as to this linkage was lacking and had not been addressed by the human rights panel. As to the evidence of the attack on the gay teenager, the court found that the panel had no acceptable evidence of the attack before it and had no acceptable evidence that Mr Boissoin's letter had in any way contributed to that attack. The court had some opinion evidence that letters such as that under review could negatively affect "impressionable" youth. However, it noted that it had no evidence that those impressionable youths read the newspaper, and, in particular, letters to the editor.

The court's novel interpretation of the section was rejected on appeal.[74] The Alberta Court of Appeal upheld the result, determining, on a traditional analysis, that the standard in *Taylor* had not been reached. But it also held that the requirement to a linkage between the publication and discriminatory conduct was not justified on a reading of the statute.[75] Having said this, the appeal judgment continued with a highly critical review of inconsistencies and interpretive difficulties with the section.

It is unfortunate that the appeal judgment felt compelled to reject the connection between discriminatory publication and acts of discrimination because such an interpretation could have solved some of the problems with these provisions. Certainly, one of the difficulties these sections present is that they are out of harmony with the other provisions of the provincial and Federal legislation. Although some of these statutes contain preambles or sections delineating the statute's purposes that appear to speak of general rights to be free from discrimination, the legislation is somewhat more modest in reach. The B.C. code, for example, expresses the purpose of "fostering a society ... in which there are no impediments to the full and free participation in the economic, political, social and cultural life ..."[76] But in later paragraphs, it sets out the more modest purposes of preventing and redressing discrimination as "prohibited by the Code."[77] The Ontario code ambitiously acknowledges the need to make everyone "feel a part of the community,"[78] but also limits itself to protect "equal rights and opportunities without discrimination that is contrary to law."[79] As we have seen, the statutes generally address particular classes of transactions, although some of those classes such as "services commonly available to the public" can be very broad. As well, they contain defences that make it clear that not every type of discrimination is intended to be illegal.

Discriminatory publication sections are much more far-reaching than the other parts of the statute. The "discrimination" targeted is not the denial of important necessities of life, but feelings of offence and exclusion. This, in turn, produces inescapable conflicts with other human rights – in particular, rights of free association, expression, religion, and conscience. The problem appears to be that in enacting these sections, legislatures have forgotten the other aspects of human rights that our society must acknowledge in order to have a genuinely free and democratic life. Tying the discriminatory publication provisions to requirements that the publication must make likely the breaches of particular rights given by the statutes would significantly help put the role of these statutes into perspective. It would limit the risk of their misuse as weapons to eradicate the rights of others, contrary to the fundamental human dignity the statutes are meant to preserve.

In short, the Federal and provincial human rights codes and their anti-discrimination provisions are only a part of the scene created by a much broader range of human rights. It is when these statutes purport to be the entire landscape that problems arise. The discriminatory publication sections encourage this myopia. In the next chapter, we will consider a human right that is often ignored or overlooked in both human rights and Charter cases. Freedom of conscience may well be the missing piece of the picture in our discussion. It is rarely given any weight, yet it is arguably the most important human right of all. In the next chapter, I will propose that it is only with an understanding of freedom of conscience that the boundaries between human rights can be drawn and the whole picture brought into better focus. As conflicts in our society deepen, we will continue to ignore this right at our peril.

Chapter Seven

Freedom of Conscience:
The Forgotten Human Right

1. Introduction

Those of us "of a certain age" may remember iconic cartoons in which the main character made his decisions to act after listening to miniature versions of himself hovering in mid-air above his shoulders. One, typically dressed in white with a halo, opposed one dressed in a red devil's suit with horns. Naturally, the little guy in horns often won. But we had no doubt that this represented the struggles of our hero with his conscience. "Conscience," represented by the little white-clad figure with the halo, presented the "right," the "moral" choice.

Throughout this book, we have often coupled "freedom of conscience" with "freedom of religion" because that is how it appears in section 2(a) of the Charter. However, the jurisprudence we have considered has exclusively dealt with "religion," while "conscience" has neither been argued about nor, except in passing, been discussed. Yet, conscience is a more universal part of human nature than is religion. Not everyone has a "religion," at least not as it is commonly understood as a creedal belief system involving the transcendent. In chapter 1, I made the point that even those without belief systems that could be classed as "religious" do operate on a belief system of one sort or the other, whether materialism, secularism, humanism, or the vague yet growing group of those who consider themselves "spiritual, but not religious." Freedom of conscience should protect the moral judgments of those belief systems, as well as the religious.

"Conscience" cannot be limited to religious conscience. The wording of s. 2(a) of the Charter makes that clear. Protection is extended to "freedom of conscience and religion," thus making the protection for conscience primary. Had Parliament intended to protect only religious conscience, the provision would have read "freedom of religion and conscience." Then an argument might have been made that protections of conscience are not intended to stand alone. But the order set out in s. 2(a) forecloses that argument and suggests, as I have done, that the protection for freedom of conscience is intended to be the broader category.

Conscience is related to all types of belief systems, both religious and not. Often, conscience is the reason why a belief system is chosen. Certainly, the chosen belief system then affects one's conscience because most religions have at least an aspect of moral teaching to their belief system. So there is a complex interaction between conscience and belief. Conscience provides a strong intellectual and emotional commitment that some things are morally right and some morally wrong. Almost no one, even the most relativistic thinker in our society, is without some form of conscience. Those who appear to be without conscience we class as sociopaths and consider abnormal.

Conscience is not simply an internal operation of the mind. Perhaps this is where protection for conscience can be more clearly differentiated from protection of religion. We saw earlier, in the *Trinity Western University* case,[1] the Supreme Court drawing a line between the freedom to hold beliefs and the freedom to act on them. I criticized this distinction, when applied to freedom of religion, as meaningless as a guide to application of the Charter protection because one is always free in the operations of one's mind. Thus, if freedom of religion means only that, it means very little indeed. But there is a broad range of the religious sphere that is, in fact, concerned with internal belief. The distinction is wholly inapplicable to conscience. Although connected to belief, as I have observed, conscience is a moral judgment about right and wrong that compels the actor to do something or to avoid doing something. As the Catechism of the Catholic Church defines it, "Moral conscience, present at the heart of the person, enjoins him at the appropriate moment to do good and to avoid evil."[2] The emphasis is on the act.

2. Why Protect Freedom of Conscience?

In both doing "good" and avoiding "evil," actions born of conscience may come into conflict with other people and with the demands of the state. Diversity and multiculturalism, to which Canadian society is committed,[3] guarantee that there will be differences about matters of conscience. We have already seen some of the hot points of those differences in matters of abortion, polygamy, homosexual rights, and appropriate legal systems for marital disputes. While we have usually dealt with those differences as arising from religion, that is largely because, if the conscientious act or objection is connected to religion, courts have ignored the protections for conscience.

Conscience is integral to the human personality. When the Supreme Court of Canada was considering the question of whether sexual orientation was a protected ground under s. 15 of the Charter, even though not enumerated in it, the court based its decision on the fact that sexual orientation is a fundamental part of what it means to be human.[4] For this reason, the court held that anti-discrimination statutes would violate the Charter if they failed to protect persons from discrimination on that basis.[5] Conscience is not listed either in s. 15 or in any anti-discrimination statutes as a protected ground. However, it is clearly as fundamental a part of our nature as is our sexual orientation.[6]

Consider a brief thought experiment. Pick some action that you would consider profoundly wrong. It might be serving as an executioner in a state that allowed capital punishment, or rounding up Jewish children for a Nazi concentration camp, or torturing prisoners at Guantanamo Bay. Now consider your situation if you were ordered by your government to perform that act. Most people's reaction to this thought experiment will reveal how basic decisions of conscience are to our own human nature. While some might capitulate if the pressure were sufficiently strong (such as a severe penalty of prison or death for refusal), others would not and most will likely hope they would not! Of course, we are not often put in a position where we might be forced to violate our consciences. All the examples I suggested are ones that the average citizen in Canada will likely never be forced to confront. But for those forced to confront them, history illustrates that conscience will often exercise a surprisingly strong influence.

Often, people have preferred to suffer disgrace, penalty, or even death rather than violate their consciences. Many of these actions have been motivated by religion, such as the old story told in 2 Maccabees (in the apocryphal books of the Bible) of the seven young men tortured to death for refusing to break their religious objection to eating pork[7] or in later times the story of Christians facing death rather than worship the Roman emperor. But certainly many acts of conscience spring from other motivations. Conscientious objectors to wars, citizens hiding the innocent from persecution, resistors to both Nazi and Stalinist regimes, demonstrators for civil rights, environmentalists protecting old-growth forest – these all have been acts of conscience that crossed religious and philosophical boundaries.

The point of all this is to illustrate that we should not ignore conscience as a central and powerful motivation of our personalities. An attempt to force someone to transgress his or her conscience is a very serious matter indeed. It can result in civil disorder, for one thing. Civil rights demonstrators in the American South in the 1960s were often the centre of violent reprisals; anti-war demonstrators at Kent State University were shot. It can certainly exclude, marginalize, and oppress persons and groups who are the target of efforts to compel their conscience. Hutterites, as we have already seen,[8] have been deprived of their rights to drive on our roads because they will not have their photos taken. In cases of civil disobedience, it can result in depriving the subject of liberty. Ms Linda Gibbons, age sixty-three, has spent nine years in jail for contravening a "bubble" law related to picketing at abortion clinics.[9] I have argued throughout this book that repression of difference in religion and conscience is inimical to a "free and democratic" society, for it disenfranchises those who disagree; in these (admittedly) extreme cases, we can see that it does even more. For these reasons, we should take the protection of conscience by law very seriously and should give particular attention to the impact of laws and policies that might result in placing citizens in the position of being required to violate their conscience or violate the law.

Still, we must acknowledge that the state will interfere with the exercise of conscience from time to time and under some circumstances is justified in doing so. Perhaps I believe I am required by conscience to blow up the Parliament buildings. Obviously, I can be restrained from carrying out this action and can be prosecuted and sent to jail if I attempt it. I have said before that this book is not a work of political theory or philosophy. But the legal system cannot afford the luxury of philosophical speculation and disagreement that has no resolution. Laws regulating our society are considered, made, and enforced. Where laws may interfere with the exercise of conscience, we should have some idea of what limits on this interference are justifiable and where we might want to consider our position more carefully.

Before we tackle current legal issues in which protection of conscience is a key question, we will try to arrive at some general understanding about the significance of various kinds of interference and how they impact individuals. Suppose that you are a vegetarian with a strong belief that killing animals for food is wrong. As a part of this belief, you may think that you should invade a slaughterhouse at dead of night and release the penned animals. Clearly the state will interfere with this plan if it can, and if you carry it out, again, the state will attempt to arrest and convict you of a crime. This is one level of interference with your conscience, but it is perhaps the easiest to justify. We have laws of general application about animals, property rights, and theft. These are not aimed directly at you as a vegetarian but are for the general good, given that our society recognizes private property and considers those animals as property. These principles are accepted by the large majority in Canada. Your treatment is the result of a general commitment to these basic principles of our social structure.

Of somewhat more concern might be the state's collection of income tax used to subsidize the production of meat. This will require you, although indirectly, to support that which offends your conscience. This, of course, commonly occurs as when taxes are applied to fund a war the taxpayer objects to or to promote programs and policies that the taxpayer believes to be wrong. But taxes are collected for many purposes and we do not generally recognize a conscientious objection to taxation; obviously the state's policies could quickly become unmanageable if my tax dollars only go to causes with which I agree. Let's take this a little further again and suggest that because the state decides that the meat industry needs support, it now requires that you purchase meat every week. If you fail to have meat in your shopping basket, you must pay a fine. We often consider that people are not entitled to have a free ride when exercising their consciences, particularly if that exercise contravenes a policy of a duly elected government. You may have your principles, but it is not always unreasonable for you to have to pay for them.

Going even further, suppose the fine for not buying meat is confiscatory or suppose that failure to purchase meat means that you are no longer entitled to government services or to be employed in the civil service. At this stage, we are probably feeling considerably less comfortable about the interference with conscience. We are excluding from participation in society those whose conscience demands that they not eat meat. Finally, to take the extreme case, suppose the government provides that anyone not eating meat will be forcibly confined and force-fed liquid meat products. At this point, most of us would probably find the interference with conscience has gone too far.

This simply illustrates that there is a sliding scale of interference where the state action becomes less justifiable as the violation of conscience becomes greater.[10] Probably the strongest claim to protection of conscience is the claim against being forced to commit an act that one believes wrong by the imposition of serious penalties against those who refuse. Interfering with an act that conscience mandates be carried out rarely appears as disturbing as an effort to force performance of an objectionable act. In most of the historical cases we can think of, our sympathies are most strongly engaged by those who resist the state's efforts to compel them, under pain of serious penalty or death, to perform an action that they believe morally wrong.

3. Conscience: Forgotten or Feared?

We noted in an earlier chapter that use of the criminal law to control actions stemming from different belief systems poses particular problems. Accommodation is not possible, since a fundamental principle of the criminal law requires the law to apply to all or to none. Cases in which freedom of conscience might have been used to attack a criminal statutory provision have generally been argued on other grounds. Even when s. 2(a) has been raised, it has been ignored by the court.

A case in point, in which freedom of conscience might have been relevant, was the well-known decision in *R. v. Latimer*. Mr Latimer was the father of a child, Tracy, who was severely disabled. Ultimately, he killed her, by poisoning her with carbon monoxide. Mr Latimer was tried and convicted of murder. Under the Criminal Code, Mr Latimer was subject to a statutory minimum penalty of ten years without parole. He argued for a constitutional exemption from this minimum, primarily on the basis of s. 7 (security of the person) and s. 12 (cruel and unusual punishment) of the Charter on the grounds that he had committed a "mercy killing," out of compassion. The Saskatchewan Court of Appeal determined that he was not entitled to such an exemption. They considered the arguments, acknowledged that Parliament could have provided for an exception for "mercy killings," but noted that "our society, through its criminal law, may properly decline to make judgments about the quality of life that a particular individual may enjoy and simply assert an unqualified interest in the preservation of human life."[11]

The result might have been the same even if freedom of conscience had been argued, since s. 1 justifications apply to limit all the rights and freedoms granted under the Charter. However, it is interesting to note that apparently no argument was made on the basis of conscience. If, as Mr Latimer alleged and as was certainly publicly credited, he had killed Tracy because of her ongoing and unbearable suffering, he did so as an act of conscience. He testified that he was impelled to commit the crime because of his moral decision that it was worse to allow her to endure the sufferings of her disability rather than end her life. This was an issue for the public, but not for the court.

The reader may consider that this argument presents a "slippery slope," and she may well be right. A similar obliviousness to potential arguments on the basis of conscience was evident in the decision of the Supreme Court of Canada in *Rodriguez v. A.G. for British Columbia*,[12] the case with which we began chapter 1. Ms Rodriguez, suffering from ALS, was seeking the right to be assisted to commit suicide and claimed that the prohibition in the Criminal Code, which would make anyone assisting her guilty of murder, violated her rights to security of the person (s. 7) and equality (s. 15) of the Charter. It also could have been argued that anyone assisting Ms Rodriguez to die would have been acting out of conscience and, therefore, the classification of such an act as criminal was an infringement of freedom of conscience.

The argument was never made. Again, it would likely not have made a difference because the criminal prohibition was upheld under s. 1 of the Charter. The court refused to attempt to create a "right to die," in part, because protection of the vulnerable would require detailed legislative provisions. Simply striking down the section of the criminal law that made assisted suicide an offence could open the door to abuse. The "slippery slope" was a genuine fear. As well, in both these cases, the claim to conscience was an objection to being prevented from performing an act the individual believed himself or herself compelled to do; as we have discussed, this has a lesser claim for protection than being compelled to perform an act one believes immoral.

A freedom of conscience argument was made in the case of *R. v. Morgantaler*.[13] In that case, Dr Morgantaler and several co-defendants attacked the provisions of the Criminal Code that made abortions illegal, except after administrative procedures considering whether the mother's life and health were at risk. The defendants had been charged for operating an abortion clinic and performing abortions. One of the questions posed to the court was whether the provisions of the code violated s. 2(a). Presumably, Dr Morgantaler would have argued that his conscience required him to perform abortions at the request of women, perhaps for a variety of reasons, such as risks to their mental or physical health or the possibility that they would access unsafe "back-street" abortionists if he refused. We know little from the report of the case about this argument because the Supreme Court of Canada failed to consider it. The court struck down the provisions on the basis that they interfered with the security of the person unjustifiably.

Lawyers probably do not like to engage arguments on which there is no precedent. Although freedom of conscience could have been argued in any of the above cases, other arguments seem to have been more likely to succeed, as seen in the *Morgantaler* case. But a consideration of these cases also suggests the potential scope of the conscience provision. Many Canadians would worry about unrestricted rights to die or rights to kill when the killer believed himself or herself morally entitled to do so. No tie to religion must be shown to make a claim of conscience, and therefore claims of conscience seem without limit. As well, many of the actions to which conscience may lay claim are threatening to social order and seriously risk harm to the vulnerable, such as the elderly or those disabled and reliant upon caregivers.

If a robust protection for freedom of religion is often worrisome, robust protection for freedom of conscience is more so. Perhaps it is not surprising that courts and lawyers have simply preferred in general to avoid the issue. With this as background, we will now turn to three examples in our current social conversation that raise these kinds of issues. We will look at how the law seems to ignore claims of conscience, not only when matters of public order are at stake but also in the less defensible cases when these claims are raised against what are characterized as others' rights or where the exercise of conscience is one that many Canadians disapprove. Thus far, the treatment of these issues in the courts and in public discourse has failed to provide the concepts and principles that we need for a nuanced understanding of conscience in its relation to state power. Again we will return to the theme that human rights can flourish only where those rights are exercised in such a way that they recognize the human rights of all and we will see what role claims of freedom of conscience can play in understanding how this interaction can work to support a free and democratic society.

4. "Ban the Burqa"

Recently, a number of countries have expressed an intention to ban or restrict the wearing of a burqa or niqab, dress worn by some Muslim women for reasons of modesty and religious submission that partially reveals only the woman's eyes. As I write this, Belgium has apparently taken legislative steps in that direction.[14] Governments in France and the Netherlands have expressed support for a similar move. Belgium primarily justifies its action on the basis of national security. Local communities already were banning and fining women who wore the full covering. France seems to regard the ban as more a matter of expressing its secular character and promoting women's rights.[15]

In Quebec, Bill 94 was introduced to require all women seeking access to public services to have uncovered faces.[16] This included women working in the civil service, education, or health fields and women attending hospitals, schools, or government offices. The primary justification presented by the Quebec government was that of security. However, Quebec cabinet minister Christine St Pierre referred to the burqa as an "ambulatory prison"[17] while PQ immigration critic Louise Beaudoin characterized all religious head coverings for women as examples of the "submission of women, regression and a subjugation of all our freedoms."[18] Considerable opposition to the bill developed and it was not passed by the Liberal government before its defeat. However, a Canadian ban on face coverings has not been abandoned. In a similar vein, in December 2011, the Federal minister of immigration announced that Muslim women would have to remove their face coverings in order to recite the citizenship oath.[19]

No doubt there are some good reasons why it is important to see the face of the person before you. Ms Naema Ahmed made headlines in Canada when she was removed from her government-sponsored French language course in Quebec because she refused to remove her niqab in a mixed classroom.[20] The teacher claimed that the covering was interfering with the lessons, since Ms Ahmed's face and mouth were not visible and it was therefore difficult to measure her performance. There are also certainly cases in which identification may need to be proved, such as when an exam is being written and it is important to ensure that the person writing is the person enrolled in the course. Safety reasons may also militate against full-face coverage in particular circumstances. In many of these cases, however, a private identity check may be very reasonable. The need to ban the burqa (or other forms of veiling of the face) is questionable. Certainly it is questionable whether the entire civil service and all accessing government services pose a security risk. The reality is that many Canadians find covering the face offensive or unpleasant for one reason or another and do not want it to be a part of our society.

An interesting aspect of the debate is that many Muslims do not consider wearing the burqa or niqab religiously motivated. As Hoda Faleh wrote in a letter to the *Ottawa Citizen* on April 22, 2010,[21] the burqa is a cultural practice, not a part of Islam. This is sometimes used to suggest that a ban is acceptable because it does not violate religious freedom. But the fact is that the burqa or niqab (or other veiling garments) is adopted, by women who wear it, out of a belief that it is immodest for them to appear with their faces uncovered in the presence of men not of their own family. Whether it is religious or cultural, it is a matter of conscience. The press reports and the debate in letters to the editor columns generally have ignored this aspect of the case.

Christopher Hitchens's column in the *National Post* of Wednesday, May 12, 2010 ("In Your Face") illustrated the kinds of arguments that are usually used to support the ban. First, he argued, the burqa violates the "right" of citizens to be "equal before the law and equal in the face of one another." He explained that we have a mutual "right" to see each other's faces. Where he found this "right" or why, even if it is a cultural expectation, the law should enforce it he did not explain. He expressed a thorough distaste for "hooded people," associating them with the Ku Klux Klan. Such an argument has some rhetorical impact, no doubt, but it is hardly a ground for legal action. These arguments, boiled down, were simply arguments from personal preference.

A second argument was that banning the burqa frees women from men who would force them to wear it. We have already considered this kind of argument in considering the Ontario problems with Sharia law in chapter 3. While it may be true that some women wear the burqa because of intimidation, it is clear that this does not extend to all who do so. Other solutions, including cultural pressure, education, and social support, can be used to combat this problem while leaving free those women who choose the burqa voluntarily. Of course, Bill 94, if ever passed, would ensure that women who wore the burqa no longer had access to education or cultural interactions. Nowhere in his analysis did Mr Hitchens grapple with the difficult issue of when the state has the right to override conscience.

Why might that be? First, the burqa and niqab are usually associated with religious commitments, despite the fact that Islamic groups disagree on their necessity. But, second, ignoring the conscience aspects of the situation enables the supporters of the ban to ignore the negative and anti-democratic effects of the action. Women who believe they are by conscience required to adopt this standard of modesty will respond by refusing to comply. In practice, this will mean that they will not access health care or education if, to do so, they must remove the veil in public. They may be unwilling to accept citizenship if they cannot take the oath veiled, thus depriving them of fundamental participation in our democratic system. The alternative will be to require them to violate a key part of their personal integrity. It is unlikely they will be prepared to make that adjustment. It is a feature of the claims of conscience that those subjected to forcible compliance will choose resistance, even at great personal cost. Making the connection with conscience makes it much less acceptable to force compliance or to impose the cost of social exclusion for failing to comply.

It is easy for us to support protection of conscience when it is a cause that we find appealing such as pacifism or racial equality. We would much prefer not to support rights of conscience with which we disagree. Conscientious military objectors, in times of war, have been treated to social ostracism. We would now, in times of peace, find that troubling. I have pointed out elsewhere that a free and democratic society is a necessary foundation for the existence of human rights. Diversity and difference are essential for a free and democratic society. And that means the support of rights of conscience that we do not personally like.

Another interesting aspect of this example of the invisibility of conscience in our understanding of human rights is that wearing the burqa harms no one but, arguably, the wearer. It does not deprive anyone else of their rights or limit the equality rights of others. We can make provisions for proof of identity by other means in necessary cases and for allowing security measures where that is likely an issue (such as boarding airplanes), taking an oath of citizenship, or even perhaps entering banks. Ms Beaudoin's comments that wearing the burqa constitutes "a subjugation of all our freedoms" are rhetorical only, and without logical basis. There is no effect on the freedom of others at all. In the next two sections of this chapter, I will consider issues of conscience where the rights of others may be involved. But in the ban of the burqa, the only right we give up is the "right" not to see those in our society who disagree with our concepts of equality, modesty, and faith.

Would the burqa ban, if proceeded with in Quebec, have survived a constitutional challenge? Would the requirement that the citizenship oath cannot be taken by a veiled woman? Given that any such challenges will be fought most probably on the basis of freedom of religion, and given the Supreme Court of Canada's turn away from the importance of that fundamental freedom as seen in *Hutterian Brethren of Wilson Colony*,[22] they might do so. Whether the "forgotten right" of conscience will be argued in such a challenge is difficult to predict; given the obscurity into which it seems to have fallen, issues of conscience may again be ignored.

5. Medical Ethics and Conscience

Except where legitimate and serious security concerns are in question, wearing the burqa, as we have noted, does not interfere with the rights of others. In some other situations, in contrast, the exercise of conscience can appear to conflict with others' rights. This issue has been particularly difficult in the United States, where courts and legislatures have struggled over the responsibility of medical personnel to provide medical services that, although legal, are against the medical practitioner's conscience. Some American states have passed laws compelling pharmacists to dispense contraceptive and "morning after" drugs. These have been challenged in the courts. Others have passed conscience clauses permitting physicians and pharmacists to act on their conscience in these circumstances. The Bush administration issued directives prohibiting the firing of medical personnel for refusing to aid in abortions; the Obama administration has promised to repeal the rules. Obviously, the issue of protection of conscience is a difficult and contentious one.[23]

A new but related issue arose in the American presidential election campaign of 2012. The recently enacted medical insurance requirements provided that any employer who provided health care insurance for its employees was compelled to include in the insurance plan contraceptive services. An exemption was made, but only for religious institutions that served their own members exclusively, meaning that Catholic hospitals, schools, and charities would be required to include contraceptive services in their insurance plans, in contravention of the moral teachings of the Catholic Church prohibiting artificial contraception or direct sterilization. The American Catholic bishops loudly protested the requirement as a violation of their freedom of religion. However, it could equally be seen as a conscience matter, in which Catholics would be required to pay for what they found immoral. The Obama administration attempted a compromise, allowing religious institutions that objected to delete the services, but only if the insurance company still provided them for free.

The Canadian landscape has been much less troubled until recently. But the Canadian legal situation is complex. Provincial and Federal human rights legislation protects a person from discrimination in employment on the basis of religion or creed. If an employee is fired because of his religious objections to dispensing a prescription or handling abortion cases, and the employee's beliefs could have been accommodated without imposing undue hardship on the employer, the firing would arguably be discriminatory. In a 2002 decision of the B.C. Human Rights Tribunal, Ms C brought a complaint against her employers, three doctors, claiming that she had been fired for her pro-life views.[24] The tribunal found that this was not the cause of her dismissal; but had it been, the tribunal noted, she would have been entitled to redress.

This is not to say, of course, that employers would not be entitled to have a policy requiring employees to abide by the employer's decision to provide abortion, contraceptive, or other morally controversial procedures. We have discussed this distinction in the last chapter when considering the *Christian Horizons*[25] decision. But as long as the employee was prepared to support the employer's policies, even though not actively participating in them herself, she may be protected against being fired for her views and her refusal to take an active part in the process. On the other hand, while this protection is available to employees who found their objections on religious grounds, it would likely not be available to employees with no religious foundation for their beliefs. Conscience is not protected under human rights statutes. Therefore, in dealings between private citizens, whether in employment or other important social transactions, there is no impediment to discriminating against exercises of conscience that are not religious in nature.[26]

A recent case in the United Kingdom provides some interesting insights into the problems that this situation presents. Mr McFarlane was a marriage counsellor who was employed by a British firm, Relate Foundation, to counsel couples in their relationships.[27] Relate was a member of the British Association for Sexual and Relationship Therapy, which had a code of ethics that prohibited discrimination in providing services. Relate also had a non-discrimination policy. Mr McFarlane was a Christian who believed that same-sex sexual activity was immoral. Although he had signed an acknowledgment of his employer's equality policy when hired, he later sought to be exempted from counselling same-sex couples if there was a sexual issue involved. His employer refused his request and eventually he was fired. He brought a claim against Relate under the Employment Equality (Religion or Belief) Regulations[28] alleging that his dismissal was unlawful discrimination on the basis of his religion.

The regulation prohibited both direct discrimination on the basis of religion and indirect discrimination where a rule, although apparently not aimed at a particular religion, treated those of that belief less favourably than those of other beliefs. The regulation also contained a defence if the respondent could show that the discrimination was a proportionate means of furthering a legitimate end. Relate's policy that all couples, whether same-sex or not, receive counselling in all relationship issues, including sexual, from any counsellor was not directly discriminatory. In deciding that the firing was not indirect illegal discrimination, the court held that Relate's policy was a legitimate one. Given that, Lord Justice Laws held, the insistence that every employee be prepared to offer counselling to same-sex couples on sexual matters was a proportionate means to accomplish this end.

The court held that it was bound by an earlier decision of the English Court of Appeal, *London Borough of Islington v. Ladele*.[29] *Ladele* involved a government action, which in Canada would differentiate the claim from that in *McFarlane* because it would make relevant the Canadian Charter. At this point, I am concerned only with the issue of protection of conscience in employment in the private sector. For that reason, we will leave the discussion of government action until later in this chapter. However, the court in *Ladele* had ruled that it was a legitimate objective for the Islington Borough Council to adopt a "dignity for all" policy regarding marriages. It was a proportionate means of accomplishing this policy to require all its officials to be prepared to perform same-sex marriages.

The problem with *McFarlane* is that it appeared to put the law requiring non-discrimination in employment on a collision course with the law requiring non-discrimination in provision of services to the public. An employer is certainly justified in adopting a policy that will make its services available to all without regard to sex, religion, sexual orientation, etc. But why should this perfectly reasonable policy serve as an excuse to discriminate against employees on another prohibited ground unless the employer's policy cannot be carried out otherwise? Mr McFarlane was put in the position where he either had to violate his conscience or be fired. Certainly, losing one's job may not be too great a price to pay for preserving one's conscience, and many people have taken this option in many different circumstances. But it appears inconsistent that an employer was very concerned about some types of discrimination yet willing to inflict others. It suggested an unwillingness to recognize as legitimate conscientious objections with which we do not sympathize.

In Canada, some provinces, such as British Columbia, provide a defence to a claim of discrimination in employment that the quality on which the discrimination is made is a "bona fide and reasonable" qualification for the position.[30] This is a somewhat different test, perhaps, than that the discrimination is a "proportionate means of achieving a legitimate aim." Canadian courts have generally required proof that the complainant could not be accommodated without imposing undue hardship on the employer before that defence is allowed.[31] There was apparently no evidence in *McFarlane v. Relate Avon Limited* that Relate could not have assigned Mr McFarlane only to heterosexual couples, thus accommodating his religious beliefs. Of course, if no counsellors had been available to counsel same-sex couples, undue hardship might have been established.

In Ontario, as we saw in the *Christian Horizons*[32] decision, there is no general defence to a claim of discrimination in employment based upon a bona fide and reasonable qualification. Rather, there is a list of specific exceptions where discrimination would be allowed. One of these, in s. 24(1)(b),[33] is where the discrimination is on the basis of age, sex, record of offences, or marital status if the "age, sex, record of offences or marital status is a reasonable and bona fide qualification because of the nature of the employment." This is narrower than the B.C. statute and does not appear to allow discrimination on the basis of religion at all unless the situation fits within s. 24(1)(a), where a preference in hiring is allowed for religious organizations restricting their services to co-religionists.

This analysis seems to support the statement of the Human Rights Tribunal in *C v. Dr. A, Dr. B and Dr. C*[34] that, had Ms C been fired because of her religiously based pro-life views, she would have been entitled to reinstatement. However, in British Columbia and other provinces that have a general "bona fide qualification" defence, this protection would likely not extend where the employer's policy could not be carried out while accommodating the employee. In that case, those in similar positions to Ms C would pay the price for their consciences by being required to find other work. The protection for conscience based on religious grounds would appear to be stronger in Ontario.

The situation is different where the person raising a conscientious objection is not negotiating with his employer as to the scope of his duties but is providing services commonly available to the public. The most common morally controversial medical procedures are the provision of abortion services and the dispensing of contraceptives or morning-after medications. Obviously, these procedures are all exclusively provided to women. And, as we have discussed earlier, discrimination is not confined to acts that directly target those belonging to a protected group. The fact that the action affects that group principally, exclusively, or differentially is sufficient to constitute discriminatory treatment. Thus, nurses, doctors, medical technicians, and pharmacists who refuse these services to the public may be held to have discriminated illegally against women.

The issue arose in Ontario in 2008 when the Ontario College of Physicians attempted to reform its code of ethics. The Ontario Human Rights Commission made submissions to the College in which it pointed out that a refusal to provide certain medical services to women on the grounds of conscience was prima facie discrimination under the Human Rights Code.[35] It further opined that a defence of freedom of religion might not be successful in all cases as rights needed to be balanced. The draft expressed a preference for the rule that doctors' moral and religious beliefs ought to be "checked at the door" before they exercised their professional roles.[36]

The submission caused substantial controversy in the press and before the College. The Canadian Medical Association president wrote to the editors of national newspapers opposing any measures that appeared to force physicians to violate their consciences.[37] This is in keeping with the position of the American Medical Association as well. The AMA requires timely and frank information to patients about services a doctor will not offer, but does not require the services to be performed. In the end, the code of ethics of the OCP warned doctors of the potential human rights issues but did not make the refusal of services[38] on grounds of conscience unethical.

The apparent disregard of the Ontario Human Rights Commission for issues of conscience is puzzling. "Creed" is a protected quality under the Ontario legislation. It would seem untenable for the Commission to consider that religious beliefs could be excluded completely from the workplace, given that many religions have a primary focus on certain moral conduct in all aspects of the believer's life. It suggests that the Commission has decided to interpret "creed" in an overly narrow sense while giving much broader play to other protected qualities. That interpretation could, of course, resolve some of the apparent conflicts between rights. But it does so by imposing a hierarchy of rights: religious rights are being treated as purely private exercises in worship and belief; other rights extend to both the public and private spheres. Women, for example, are protected not only against discriminatory rules aimed directly at differentiating on the basis of sex but also in areas in which women alone would be the actors, such as seeking contraception or abortion. This establishes effectively a priority of one right over the other and therefore should be contrary to the established juris prudence which holds that rights are not hierarchical.[39]

Had the OCP made it a breach of ethics to refuse certain services on the basis of religious beliefs, as the Commission apparently recommended, substantial difficulties would have resulted. First and most obviously, a physician disciplined by the OCP would have been entitled to argue discrimination on the basis of creed. The disciplinary action would have been directly linked to and caused by the physician's religious commitments. Although not aimed at a particular religion, this would appear discriminatory. In addition, because the OCP is constituted by statute to govern the medical profession in Ontario, it is probable that the disciplinary action could have been considered a violation of the doctor's Charter rights to freedom of both religion and conscience. The Commission appears to have been attempting to combat prima facie discrimination in the denial of some medical services to women by advocating for a position that would almost certainly have also constituted prima facie discrimination on the basis of creed and very likely a breach of the doctor's Charter rights to freedom of conscience and religion.

Second, to return to our comments about conscience, the result of a declaration that refusal of medical services on the grounds of conscience was unethical would have been to deny participation in many branches of the medical profession to certain religious groups. It may not always be unreasonable to require people to suffer some penalty for the exercise of their conscience, as we have seen. An employee, for example, who does not want to dispense the "morning-after" pill may not be entitled to insist on employment where there is only one pharmacy in a remote community and he or she will be required to be on duty alone for much of the week. But there is a substantial difference between that action by a single employer and an action by the governing body of a profession that would exclude large portions of our population from its ranks.

How this issue will resolve itself in Canada is still unclear. Even if associations governing the conduct of nurses, doctors, medical technicians, and pharmacists do not stigmatize religious or conscientious refusal of treatment as unethical, the human rights codes and related jurisprudence do not provide much assurance about how much protection these professionals have. Reflecting back to earlier discussions in this chapter, depriving medical personnel of their professional lives in order to force them to perform acts that are against their conscience appears to be near the extreme end of interference with conscience. It should, therefore, be avoided unless compelling reasons to the contrary exist. Those compelling reasons certainly do not exist where the service is readily available from another practitioner.

The issue of medical services is further complicated by the question of whether, if the service can be legitimately refused, it would be reasonable to impose on the physician or pharmacist a duty to refer the patient to someone who will perform the service. This is not as direct an effort to compel conduct contrary to conscience as is insisting that the service be given. Thus, less compelling reasons for this requirement should be needed. In some cases, however, even the duty to refer has been objected to on the basis that it constitutes aiding in the commission of what the professional believes to be a moral crime.[40] This is the case where a Roman Catholic doctor is asked for an abortion referral. Giving the referral would be considered a mortal sin by the Church. In some cases, as for example in a city where numerous doctors and pharmacies can be quickly contacted by telephone to determine what services and prescriptions they offer, a blanket requirement to refer seems unnecessary and perhaps accomplishes only a form of punishment for insisting on a right of conscience.

The absence from our human rights legislation of any protections for conscience is particularly worrisome here. As we have seen, religious belief by no means accounts for all medical personnel who would object to abortions, for instance, in some circumstances. Many physicians, for example, might object to late-term abortions or to abortions that were for the purpose of gender selection on conscientious, but not religious, grounds. These seem particularly at risk to a claim for discrimination. While they might not be subject to discipline by their professional organization because of Charter protection, they might well be subject to prolonged legal proceedings arising from human rights legislation. While, as we have seen, a Charter right could still be raised in defence to penalties under the legislation, human rights tribunals have not always handled such arguments expeditiously or correctly. The parallel between conscience and sexual orientation drawn in the introduction to this chapter may suggest a case for requiring conscience to be a protected ground both under s. 15 of the Charter and in human rights legislation. In the final chapter, I will reflect on this issue and other amendments to human rights legislation that our review of the landscape may have indicated.

6. Marriage and Conscience

Even though conscience is not a protected ground under human rights legislation, freedom of conscience can be used to control penalties imposed under those statutes, as I have just noted. We have already seen this pattern where an allegation of discrimination is made and the respondent raises as a defence to the imposition of a penalty by the state his or her Charter rights. We have also seen that tribunals have not always handled this pattern of legal argument as thoroughly as they might.[41] In this section of the chapter, we will consider a classic case in which this form of reasoning is applicable. The history and analysis of the jurisprudence in this area illustrate the problems of courts and tribunals trying to deal with claims of conscience with inadequate tools. Conscientious objections to same-sex marriage by those authorized by the state to perform marriages are excellent examples of the shortcomings of our current reasoning about human rights, about rights of conscience in particular, and about ways in which we can live together in a democratic and free state.

First, we need to examine some background to the controversy. After a series of decisions at the provincial level questioning the legitimacy of confining civil marriage to persons of the opposite sex,[42] the Federal government proposed to amend the definition of marriage to require only "two persons," rather than the then-current requirement of a man and woman.[43] Questions were raised about the potential constitutionality of the legislation, given that solemnization of marriage is exclusively within provincial power. Questions were also raised about whether the amendment would force those solemnizing marriages to perform same-sex ceremonies in the face of religious objections. The Federal government referred these questions to the Supreme Court of Canada for an opinion.[44] In a reference of this kind, the government poses specific questions to the court for its opinion. The questions limit the scope of the court's response and may leave questions unanswered if the questions posed are not sufficiently broad.[45]

The questions asked by the Federal government of the Supreme Court were, first, whether the proposed act, amending the definition of marriage, was within the competence of the Federal government. The second question was whether the proposed extension of the right to marry was consistent with the Charter. The third question was whether s. 2(a) of the Charter would protect religious officials from being required to perform same-sex marriages if it was contrary to their religious beliefs.[46] The court answered the first question as yes, in part, and gave affirmative answers to questions two and three.[47] We will spend a few paragraphs on the details of the reasoning of the court. We may first notice that conscience is never raised in either the government's questions or the court's opinion. Again, it was the forgotten right.

The act, as originally proposed by the Federal parliament, had two sections. The first section defined marriage as "the lawful union of two persons to the exclusion of all others." The second section provided that "nothing in this Act affects the freedom of officials of religious groups to refuse to perform marriages that are not in accordance with their religious beliefs."[48] The court held that the first section was within the Federal legislative competence, but the second was not because it impinged upon the province's rights to legislate with regard to the solemnization aspect of marriage. As to whether the first section of the act violated the freedom of religion of various groups opposed to same-sex marriages, the court held, quite reasonably, that the conferral of rights upon one group does not of necessity limit the rights of others.

However, our primary focus here is on the court's answer to the third and final question. The court first pointed out that the proposed statute was limited to "civil marriage" and therefore had no effect on religious marriage.[49] But it went on to consider the question of whether state compulsion on religious officials to perform same-sex marriages in violation of their religious beliefs would offend the Charter. The court found that religious ceremonies were a core part of religious belief. Therefore, state compulsion in this case would violate freedom of religion. The court went on to add that "absent exceptional circumstances which we cannot at present foresee, such a violation could not be justified under s. 1 of the Charter."[50] Finally, the court held that the protection of the Charter would also extend to protect religious organizations from being forced to make places of worship available for the performance of same-sex marriage in violation of the religious beliefs of their owners.[51]

What the Supreme Court did not decide was the position of those other than religious officials who are licensed by provinces to conduct marriages. Provinces appoint and license individuals for the purpose of allowing them to conduct civil marriages as a part of the provinces' power over the solemnization of marriage. These licensed marriage commissioners obviously perform an important service in being able to perform marriages for those with no religious affiliation or for those who, for one reason or another, do not wish a religious ceremony. The complex question then arises as to what rights to freedom of conscience a marriage commissioner might have in refusing to perform a same-sex marriage.

In *M.J. v. Nichols*, the Saskatchewan Human Rights Tribunal decided that Mr Nichols, a marriage commissioner, had unlawfully discriminated against M.J. by refusing to marry him to his same-sex partner.[52] Mr Nichols was a Baptist who believed that he would be violating his religion by performing a same-sex marriage. He apparently recognized that same-sex marriages were a legal fact and seemed to have no objection to others solemnizing them. However, he was not prepared to do so. The Human Rights Tribunal decision was somewhat confused. It spent considerable time trying to analyse how the Supreme Court reference affected the position of marriage commissioners. The Court of Queen's Bench[53] correctly observed that, since the question to the Supreme Court had been confined to religious officials, it had no relevance to this issue.[54] However, the result before the tribunal was upheld by the Court of Queen's Bench. Although later decisions seem to have put a further appeal on "hold," we can gain some insights into the problem by taking a closer look at the reasoning in the case.

The Saskatchewan government made no exceptions in its legislation for marriage commissioners refusing to conduct same-sex marriages.[55] Indeed, it had issued a directive to marriage commissioners instructing them that they would be required to perform same-sex marriages.[56] Applying the provisions of the Saskatchewan Human Rights Code, the court agreed with the tribunal that Mr Nichols had discriminated against M.J. in the provision of a service customarily offered to the public on the prohibited ground of discrimination, contrary to s. 12 of the code.[57] The question then turned to possible defences.

Mr Nichols argued that although there was no "bona fide and reasonable justification" defence set out in the code, the court ought to imply one. The court declined to take this step.[58] His second argument was that he was entitled to accommodation for the practice of his religious beliefs. The problem with this argument, as framed before the court, was that Mr Nichols was not claiming that he had been discriminated against. A duty to accommodate arises only where one party is claiming that a rule is discriminatory in its effect. In this case, M.J. was suing Mr Nichols and this gave rise to no duty on M.J.'s part to accommodate Mr Nichols's beliefs.

In discussing this argument,[59] the court spent extensive time on the argument of the Human Rights Commission that Mr Nichols was not entitled to any accommodation because he was acting as an agent of government, not as an employee. The court agreed with the Commission's position that as a "government actor, he is not entitled to consider his personal religious views while performing his public functions."[60] This argument does not seem strictly relevant to the issues at hand, since, as noted, the question of accommodation did not legitimately arise in this part of the case. However, I will return to this idea later, since it also affected the final argument in the case.

Mr Nichols's third argument was that the application of s. 12 impaired his Charter right to freedom of conscience and religion. Further, he argued, the infringement could not be justified under s. 1. It was perfectly possible for the government of Saskatchewan to provide adequately for the solemnization of same-sex marriages without infringing his right to freedom of religion. Unfortunately, Mr Nichols apparently had not laid an adequate groundwork for this argument. Challenging a section of a statute on the basis that it offends Charter rights requires a notice to be given to the government that a constitutional question will be raised. Moreover, as we know, an argument over whether a particular infringement is justified in a free and democratic society is a complex matter and requires a fairly broad inquiry by the court with evidence submitted in support. Neither of these steps had evidently been taken.[61]

The Commission, however, urged the court to consider the issue of justification under s. 1. The Commission cited passages with which we are familiar in which the Supreme Court of Canada suggested that a distinction generally had to be drawn between belief and conduct. The passage concluded with the words, "For better or worse, tolerance of divergent beliefs is the hallmark of a democratic society."[62] Without noting the irony, the court accepted these general propositions and concluded that "Mr. Nichols in his capacity as a marriage commissioner, acting as government, is not entitled to discriminate, regardless of his private beliefs."[63] The court concluded that if Mr Nichols could not perform same-sex marriages in accordance with his conscience, he could not hold the office of marriage commissioner.[64] The court pointed out that the Saskatchewan Marriage Act allowed commissioners to limit their work to couples of particular religious or ethnic backgrounds. It noted that this section should provide a remedy for marriage commissioners who did not believe they could celebrate certain types of marriage.

The decision had multiple problems. First, I will note some of the legal issues raised by the judgment on the points that were argued. Then we will turn to the broader question of difficulties that the result presents for human rights law. Finally, I will consider whether there is another way to look at this problem that might provide more satisfactory results both in the problem of marriage commissioners and in the broader area of human rights. We will then examine efforts by the Saskatchewan government to resolve the problem by legislation and a very troubling discussion of those efforts by the Saskatchewan Court of Appeal.

a) Problems in the Decision

The judgment adopted the principle that marriage commissioners were not allowed to discriminate in their role, acting as "government." In almost the same breath, however, the court acknowledged the statutory provision that allows commissioners to limit their services to particular religious or ethnic groups.[65] Under the Saskatchewan Human Rights Code, nationality, place of origin, race, religion, and creed are all prohibited grounds of discrimination.[66] The statement, therefore, that marriage commissioners cannot discriminate appears considerably too broad. The statute contained no exemption for marriage commissioners who discriminated on the basis of sexual orientation, although it permitted discrimination on other grounds. So the question was not whether marriage commissioners could discriminate in the performance of their public functions (obviously they could), but whether the protection of conscience and religious rights required recognition of other rights to discriminate as well as those already in the statute. The court did not confront this question. The presence of some permission to discriminate in the statute seems to undermine fatally the court's holding that marriage commissioners could not exercise their private beliefs in the performance of public functions.[67] It therefore fatally undermined the central finding on which the court relied to hold the limits on Mr Nichols's freedom of religion justifiable under s. 1 of the Charter.

A second problem with the decision was the lack of analysis in finding the infringement justifiable under s. 1. Unfortunately, as noted, this issue had apparently not been thoroughly canvassed before the court, although it was the strongest line of defence for Mr Nichols. However, since the court undertook the analysis in any event, it can be open to criticism for having failed to properly handle the question. It is correct to say, as the court did, that Mr Nichols had no claim for accommodation of his beliefs from the complainant, at least based upon the arguments raised. However, the reason Mr Nichols was required to perform same-sex marriages was an administrative order of the government and a refusal of the government to include a provision in the Marriage Act allowing marriage commissioners to limit their services to heterosexual couples. In that case, the test for proportionality under s. 1 of the Charter may be very similar to the test for reasonable accommodation under human rights law. We discussed this similarity in our analysis of the *Multani* decision.[68] The ability of the government to accommodate Mr Nichols's religious beliefs was highly relevant to this consideration. It received no notice by the court.

Another interesting feature of the case is that the Saskatchewan Human Rights Code, unlike those of most other provinces, also contains a "Bill of Rights." This Bill of Rights provides in s. 4 that "every person ... shall enjoy the right of freedom of conscience, opinion and belief and freedom of religious association, practice and worship."[69] In Quebec, as we have seen in some earlier cases,[70] the inclusion of a Charter of Rights in their human rights legislation extends those rights to the interaction of private citizens. Whether the Bill of Rights in the Saskatchewan Human Rights Code might have done the same, we do not know. The matter does not appear to have been argued, nor did the court comment on it. Had the issue been raised, the argument that M.J. should have accommodated Mr Nichols's conscience might not have been so easily dismissed.

b) Consequences of the Decision

The judge appeared to be convinced that because Mr Nichols was acting as an agent of the government, he was not entitled to any protection for his conscience or religious beliefs. This is an easy and simple solution to the problem. Unfortunately, it is also a dangerous one. Do we want to enshrine in law the principle that those who work for government are not allowed the protection of their conscience? If so, we have set up the conditions that applied in Nazi Germany in which people who, in ordinary life, would no doubt have strenuously objected to genocide were convinced that, because the state ordered them to carry out its plans, they were justified in participating in it. Of course, we are not talking about evil actions here. Prevention of discrimination is a good, as we would agree. But the principle that a government actor is not entitled to protection for his or her conscience is not limited to the situation in which the government is doing things we like. Of all the reasons why marriage commissioners should be compelled to marry same-sex couples (and there are quite a number which I will discuss shortly), this is the worst.

A second consequence of the decision is that it may have created a "double bind" for the Saskatchewan government. Mr Nichols originally brought a claim against the government for discrimination on the basis of his religious beliefs, based upon the directive that marriage commissioners could not opt for performing heterosexual marriages only. The action was dismissed.[71] Had it continued, however, the claim would likely have been that the government had discriminated against Mr Nichols in his employment or in the provision of services commonly available to the public.

Mr Nichols, as a marriage commissioner, was not employed by the government in the sense we usually use that word, meaning a regular job with a salary. However, considerable jurisprudence exists that "employment" under human rights law is not limited to the traditional meaning of the word.[72] It has, for example, been held to include agency situations and volunteer work.[73] Alternatively, the government holds itself out as licensing marriage commissioners. Any qualified person may apply. This suggests that the issue of marriage commissioner licences might be a service commonly available to the public. Either of these claims could establish a right of Mr Nichols to be accommodated up to the point of undue hardship by the government.

Could the government have met the undue hardship test? The argument would have to have been that it could not provide adequate service to same-sex couples if it accommodated those whose conscience prohibited them from performing the ceremony. This seems improbable. There is no limit on the number of commissioners the government could appoint, as they are paid by fees and are not salaried.[74] As well, the government's concern for the dignity of same-sex couples could be met through a specification on the lists of its available marriage commissioners as to who was available to perform same-sex marriages. Would it create undue hardship for same-sex couples to realize that there were marriage commissioners who objected to marrying them?

Given the controversy about same-sex marriage, this seems unreasonable. As I have said before, no one has the right not to have others disagree with their morality or their opinions.

It seems quite conceivable that Mr Nichols could have succeeded in a claim for discrimination against the government of Saskatchewan for failing to accommodate his religious beliefs based upon their insistence that all marriage commissioners be available to perform same-sex marriages. So we seem to have arrived at the ridiculous situation in which the court would find Mr Nichols guilty of discrimination if he can act on his religious beliefs and the government guilty of discrimination if he cannot. Arriving at this conclusion suggests strongly that the approach of the court to this case was mistaken. Let us turn to another way to analyse the problem.

c) An Alternative Analysis

What is the problem with protecting Mr Nichols's conscience in this case? A telling comment has been made in discussions over the rights and wrongs of the matter: that marriage commissioners must not discriminate against same-sex couples because, if we are prepared to allow discrimination on this basis, why would we not allow discrimination on, for example, race – a result that most Canadians would find offensive?[75] The comparison with racial discrimination is often made. It is not necessarily a good one. It has been, for example, argued that "race and religion are irrelevant to one's capacity to occupy the office of 'husband' and 'wife,' sex is not."[76] Whether the analogy is apt depends upon whether we believe that we can separate cultural history from the definition of marriage and recognize the right of the state to redefine it.[77] This is again a matter of fundamental and irreconcilable belief conflict. However, the analogy can be useful to allow us to discuss the issues of when interference with conscience can be justified.

First, the comparison suggests that we should only protect conscience when the result is one that our society favours. The Marriage Act already contains provisions for discrimination on the basis of religion and nationality.[78] A marriage commissioner could limit herself, for example, to performing marriages only for Buddhists or only for Ukrainians. Most of us probably do not find this particularly disturbing, although it would mean that a Muslim couple or an Irish couple might have to find another marriage commissioner if they picked the wrong name from the list. More Canadians would find discrimination against same-sex marriages unpalatable. Even more would be disturbed if protection of conscience allowed a marriage commissioner to refuse, for example, to marry Asians or to assist in mixed-race marriages.

Courts and tribunals cannot, however, adopt the position that conscience is worthy of protection only when it leads to a result that the judge or the tribunal member favours as compatible with his or her morality. Conscience, like religion, is protected by the Charter because it is required for a free and democratic society. We have a tendency to see our society as locked in a "culture war" in which "right" and "left" struggle for domination. Each side fears that the other will, if its turn at power should come, impose its moral views on society as a whole. That fear seems to be most often met with a call to suppress the opposing side immediately, before it can gain power. The protection of freedom of conscience and religion in the Charter, however, implies a different response. Rather than repression of the "enemy," it imposes a regime of strengthening the defences against repression, no matter who is in power. If we are afraid of the "right" or the "left" (as we broadly caricature them) then the solution is to ensure that no philosophy can impose without proper democratic safeguards its own conscience on others, not (as the saying goes) to "do unto others, but do it first."

But recognition of this hierarchy in our own moral calculations where some forms of discrimination appear more objectionable than others does lead us to recognize a very real problem with the protection of conscience. If we recognize a right to protection of conscience, even if the moral conclusions on which it is based are repugnant to us, then we must allow discrimination in some cases. And if so, then why, for example, might we not allow a teacher to refuse to desegregate her classroom or a restaurant owner to refuse to serve blacks? While there may be many motivations for racial discrimination, at least some of them are probably conscientious in nature, even if based in a moral view that we do not share. Logically, protection of conscience appears to have the potential to lead to widespread exceptions to anti-discrimination laws, with no way to call a halt to them.

So we return to the question: When can we decide that the state has a right to interfere with conscience? We have already elucidated a number of the factors that need to be considered. The right to be protected from discrimination, like all other human rights, is also dependent upon the requirement that those protected recognize the human rights of others, including the right freely to behave in accordance with their conscience. Those who claim the protection of conscience must also

222 Free to Believe

recognize the rights of others to be free from discrimination. So, in any given circumstance, can both rights be protected? If one right must be limited, how serious is the limitation? Does it consist simply of having to recognize and live with those who disagree with us? Does it in fact deny an important part of social participation to the claimant? Does it exclude from certain professions or occupations wide segments of our society? Does it attempt to compel a person to act against her conscience or only to refrain from committing some act that harms others?

Courts and tribunals have the tools at hand to apply these considerations to cases in which conscience is raised as a defence to a claim of discrimination. As noted, a claim to a defence of conscience in face of an accusation of illegal discrimination requires the court to analyse what limitations on conscience are justifiable in a free and democratic society. The factors I have just enunciated all deal with both freedom and rights to social participation and are therefore highly relevant to that inquiry. The example of marriage commissioners and same-sex marriage is an interesting one. It does appear possible to protect both the commissioner's right to conscience and same-sex couples' rights to marry with dignity. It is simply a case of the government being careful to provide commissioners willing to marry same-sex couples and to notify the public of that availability. This suggests that courts should recognize the marriage commissioner's right to refuse to perform same-sex marriages. This would remove the "double bind" problem we pointed out earlier. While a marriage commissioner refusing to perform a same-sex marriage would be guilty of discrimination contrary to the code, he or she could not be penalized for that action. The government would be compelled to accommodate the marriage commissioner's conscience.

This analysis is also supported by some of the other factors I have listed above. A requirement to marry same-sex couples is a direct effort to compel conscience or impose the penalty of exclusion from the marriage commissioner role. Further, refusal to accommodate the commissioner's rights of conscience will result in excluding from the office of marriage commissioner Roman Catholics, evangelical Protestants, orthodox Jews, Muslims, and several other classes of people who do not support same-sex marriage. Generally, the broader the exclusion, the more difficult it becomes to justify.

However, the office of marriage commissioner is a fairly limited one in our society. While there is a fee to be gained, it is not a full-time employment, nor is there likely much harm done to broad segments of society if the class of marriage commissioner is limited to exclude a number of religions or philosophies of life. No one is probably deprived of a livelihood or refused entry to a calling that constitutes his or her entire professional life. As well, the impact on others of having a lack of diversity among marriage commissioners is likely small. Unlike the role of teacher or physician, marriage commissioners deal with people on a one-time basis for only a very specialized transaction. No one is likely to become less tolerant because a marriage commissioner comes from a restricted group. These factors support the limitation of a marriage commissioner's rights to conscience, although the factors in favour of protection in this case seem weightier.

We can contrast the application of these factors in the case of same-sex marriage to that of racial discrimination. Suppose a marriage commissioner were to object, on grounds of conscience, to performing marriages for visible minorities. First, it would be considerably more difficult to ensure visible minorities had equal access to civil marriage. Rather than a general piece of information about a large number of marriage commissioners who are doubtless quite comfortable with performing same-sex marriage, allowing this objection would seem to require very specific information about a very few commissioners who wished to refuse certain couples. As well, those excluded from the ranks of marriage commissioner by a refusal to permit a conscientious objection on racial grounds would be few. They would also not be characterized by belonging to any protected category such as religion since direct racial prejudice is not confined to any particular religion or belief system, except perhaps the very small category of white supremacists. Therefore excluding these persons would do even less damage to the pattern of diversity in the office of marriage commissioner. Added to these factors, I have already mentioned that the penalty of being excluded from the office of marriage commissioner likely has minimal impact on the individual or on society. The case for prohibiting racial discrimination, even if based on conscience, is much weaker.

But the reader may object that he or she is still convinced that marriage commissioners ought to be required to marry any couple before them legally entitled to marry and that any discrimination in this function is morally objectionable. For consistency, I believe, that position would also require the elimination of the current Saskatchewan provisions allowing ethnic or religious restrictions. However, with that caveat, this is certainly a defensible moral decision, particularly in light of the limited role of marriage commissioner that I have already pointed out. This is clearly an appeal to the moral superiority, at least in the area of marriage commissioners, of a complete prohibition on discrimination, even if it excludes extensive numbers of persons and groups from the function on the grounds of their religion or conscience. It is not, however, up to the courts to effect this moral judgment.

d) A Legislative Intervention?

Moral choices in which one human right is overridden by another belong to the legislatures alone. If the populace is dissatisfied with the moral decisions of its elected representatives, the issues can become election issues and the government can be defeated. Although our democratic system is not perfectly responsive, government policy can be changed, even if only gradually and after much effort, through public pressure. When the legislature acts, the courts are there to take their proper role to ensure that even if a choice in favour of one right is made over another, the result is constrained to a degree to protect those affected by it as much as is consistent with legislative intent.

The central problem with Saskatchewan's (and several other provinces') approach to the issue of conscience for marriage commissioners is that it left the legislation silent about the issue. This is in keeping with our Canadian tradition of legislatures avoiding controversial questions, but if a government has decided that all marriage commissioners should marry same-sex couples, it should be much more successful in accomplishing that policy if the policy is enshrined in legislation. As we know, the Supreme Court of Canada allows government statutory or regulatory amendment to intrude further into rights of conscience and religion than when the government uses administrative policy to achieve the same end. Questions of accommodation, apparently, do not arise in the former case,[79] although they do in the latter. A provision in the Marriage Act that marriage commissioners must marry any couple legally entitled to a civil marriage might withstand the inevitable constitutional challenge, even though it interfered substantially with marriage commissioners' right of conscience.

However, while the *Nichols* case was dormant before the Saskatchewan Court of Appeal, the Saskatchewan government attempted to remedy the situation by legislation. They proposed an amendment to the Marriage Act that would either "grandparent" marriage commissioners appointed prior to 2004 from performing marriages that were contrary to religious belief or allow all marriage commissioners to object to performing marriages that violated their faiths. Before enacting either provision, the Saskatchewan government sent a reference on the constitutionality of the amendment to the Saskatchewan Court of Appeal.[80]

The Court of Appeal decided that the amendments failed to meet the constitutional test under the Charter. They were a violation of s. 15 of the Charter and would cause "personal hurt" of a kind that was "very significant and genuinely offensive."[81] The majority also recognized that the government had a pressing and substantial objective in the amendments: to protect marriage commissioners' freedom of religion, which would be curtailed if the amendments were not enacted. But while this objective was not insubstantial or trivial, it failed the proportionality test. It did not minimally impair the rights of gays and lesbians. The court suggested, as an example of a measure that would be less infringing, the system in place in Ontario, in which there was a single intake for persons wishing the services of a marriage commissioner. If those persons were a same-sex couple, they were not referred to a marriage commissioner who objected to performing same-sex marriages.

I have already suggested a similar process in discussing the *Nichols* case. As far as this part of the decision goes, therefore, the court is likely correct. Even if the government is obliged to accommodate marriage commissioners, I would argue that it has the duty to do it in the least problematic way for same-sex couples who wish to marry. This simply recognizes the need to adopt conflicting rights, where possible, so that each leaves space for the other. Even so, the decision may be at odds with the *Hutterian Brethren of Wilson Colony* case, in which the Supreme Court decided that government did not need to choose the least infringing option, only a reasonable one.

However, the decision went considerably further than that and made some very troublesome comments. First, the court refused to decide that a system of single intake would survive a constitutional challenge. While this may simply reflect a court's unwillingness to prejudge any case in the abstract, it may also be signalling a reluctance to find the religious beliefs of marriage commissioners worthy of protection. We should note that while the court commented upon the "personal hurt" caused to a gay or lesbian couple when a marriage commissioner refuses to marry them, it ignored the "personal hurt" of a long-serving marriage commissioner who is told she is no longer wanted in her job because her beliefs of right and wrong are offensive.

The court also appeared dismissive towards any use of freedom of religion to affect rights of gay and lesbian couples to feel accepted.

Although, as we noted above, the *Reference Re Same-Sex Marriage* had signalled a strong protection for freedom of religion, its views were interpreted by the Saskatchewan court as confined strictly to religious officials.[82] What differentiates priests, clergy, rabbis, or imams from ordinary believers in terms of their constitutional rights was not explained. The court further dismissed the provisions of the Federal Civil Marriage Act[83] guaranteeing freedom of religion and conscience as applying only to Federal law. Again, it is certainly true, as the Supreme Court had held, that the Federal parliament cannot legislate with respect to the provinces. However, the protections of freedom of conscience and religion in the Charter apply to both Federal and provincial legislation; s. 3 of the Civil Marriage Act may do nothing more than restate that reality.

In addition, the court, in balancing the positive effects of the law against its deleterious effects, gave only the narrowest scope to the religious beliefs of the marriage commissioners. The court held that the requirement to marry same-sex couples did not impinge upon the core of religion, which was the right to worship and hold beliefs.[84] This narrow reading of freedom of religion as really simply a freedom of worship does not accord with the earlier cases in the Supreme Court of Canada that granted a much broader scope to religious freedom. It also, recalling our discussion in chapter 2, leaves almost no scope for the exercise of religious freedom in a free and democratic society. The court then returned to stress the negative feelings of gay and lesbian couples, ignoring once again the negative effects on marriage commissioners.[85]

Of particular concern is the fact that neither the court nor the government considered the possibility that what needed protection here was not simply religious belief but also conscience. The question whether same-sex marriage is acceptable is a moral question, and the issue of whether a serious penalty can be imposed upon an official for refusing to act against his or her moral beliefs is thus a matter of conscience. As we have seen, it has been argued that approval of same-sex relationships is a matter of equality, not morality.[86] But what is equality if not also a matter of morality, of right and wrong, of deeply held convictions about how human beings should or should not be treated? As we have seen, conscience is inherently concerned with action, whatever may be said about religion. The court's limitation of marriage commissioners' rights to matters of worship, not to matters of their right to live their beliefs, could not have been successful had freedom of conscience been before them. But, again, freedom of conscience was the forgotten right.

7. Conclusion

In this chapter, we have looked at rights of conscience. Although it is the first right named by the Charter, rarely has the jurisprudence considered the issues rights of conscience raise. All too often conscience is subsumed under the heading "religion" and its broader aspects are ignored. Provincial and Federal human rights legislation is generally silent about rights of conscience, leaving them to be protected, if at all, through defences to the imposition of penalties under those statutes based upon Charter rights.

Protection of conscience has, perhaps more than any other human right, the capacity to undermine the rights of others and produce apparent conflicts with them. Conscience is all-pervasive, unlike religion, and therefore protecting it may affect more situations and more people than protecting narrower religious rights.[87] Conscience is also undeniably concerned with action and cannot be confined to personal belief held discreetly private in the mind. For these reasons, we need to analyse more carefully the relationship of rights of conscience to other human rights, emphasizing their mutual dependence. We also need to keep our eyes firmly on the basis for rights of freedom of conscience under the Charter. What degree of protection of conscience best serves the preservation of a free and democratic society? This in turn should lead us to consider the effects of protecting conscience on the inclusion or exclusion of groups of people in our society, the openness of our public debate to contrary views, and our willingness to tolerate difference. At this point, the Canadian debate in the press and before the courts seems to have more to do with our personal beliefs and a wish to impose those beliefs on others than on the factors I have identified.

If, as I have argued throughout, freedom of conscience and religion is a key component in the maintenance of a democratic society, several recent court decisions raise red flags with respect to freedom of religion. In chapter 4, I analysed the *Hutterian Brethren* case in detail. It took a limited view of the scope of religious freedom and the need for government to pay attention to the beliefs of religious minorities. But cases like *Trinity Western University* and now the *Re Marriage Commissioners* reference also appear to be limiting freedom of religion to a personal, private commitment that can be lived only as long as it does not limit equality rights. This was a matter raised in chapter 2 and these latter cases confirm that it is a serious problem that courts have not confronted. Freedom of conscience has the potential to affirm the right to lived belief. While it needs to be carefully analysed and applied, it will need to be brought in from the shadows, it appears, if free exchange of ideas and recognition of difference are to survive.

As noted, protection of freedom of conscience is a worrisome activity. Undoubtedly, we need to recognize some limits on it. However, space can be made in our society for the exercise of conscientious belief. Of greatest importance is realizing that where the violation of conscience consists of compelling others to undertake an action against their conscience at peril of serious penalty or exclusion from important parts of our social life, only the strongest justifications can serve. Hurt feelings, personal distaste, or rhetorical claims should not be enough.

In the next chapter, we will conclude our examination of freedom of conscience and religion in Canada by drawing together some of the themes we have explored and making some recommendations for new avenues for judicial and legislative action.

Chapter Eight

Can We Change? (And Why We Should)

1. Introduction

We only need to pick up a paper today and we will see some issue of religion or conscience in public debate. Belief systems underlie every choice we make, both publicly and privately. Political theorists, in the past, have seemed to speak as if human beings could grow a common skin over the bones of their diverse beliefs. As the world has become smaller through communication and immigration, this becomes harder to believe. We are confronted with difference, not as a remote and interesting phenomenon, but as a part of our daily lives. The differences in our beliefs lead to different preferences about the way our lives are lived and governed. They are often irreconcilable. This is the reality Canadian society must acknowledge and with which it must cope.

The prevalence of belief in decision making seems to be affirmed by psychological research.[1] While our political theorists have emphasized rational argument, the roots of those arguments appear very likely to lie in the functions of the human mind that need to construct consistent stories that fit with previous experiences. People are affected by a wide variety of modes of seeing the world that are not and cannot be wholly rational. Rational argument is always structured upon ways of seeing the world, interpreting information, and making associations with our personal and cultural past. It is time that our courts and our legislatures acknowledged these realities and began to determine how we can live with them.

Some common commitment, of course, is essential for our survival. The question is: How much is necessary? The answer I have indirectly proposed throughout this book is: Not much. That no doubt will surprise many readers, as we have only recently emerged from a society in which many values were held in common. But the fundamental commitment required is a commitment to live together in peace. This is the commitment that the law must enforce. Indeed, it is the commitment that the law is capable of enforcing. The common law with which we are familiar began, after all, simply as a way to keep order in the land. With our supposedly sophisticated views of the regulatory society, we have often lost sight of this basic function.

A decision to live in peace and to use the mechanisms of law to enforce that decision does implicate other choices. It seems probable that it requires a democratic system of government. Given our diverse beliefs, a totalitarian state will only be able to maintain itself by repressing some sets of belief. Of course, all states must repress beliefs of those who would violently overthrow them; that is a given. But a totalitarian regime must also foreclose the possibility of change within the moral, religious, and political choices made in consequence of the governing elite's beliefs. This requires widespread repression of all contrary opinions, lest they become challenges to the group in power. Only in a democracy is there the possibility of convincing others to change and then effecting that change. Perhaps that possibility is small in most of our modern democratic states; but it is there. And because it is there, other belief systems, other views, and advocacy for other choices can be permitted.

But if a democracy is not to become a de facto totalitarian state, it must be a restrained democracy. Choices about political results will be made when a group holding a particular belief secures enough political power to make them. Those choices can never be allowed to be choices that undermine the possibility of change. To the extent that they are, the democracy has failed and peace will fail too. The courts must therefore act as a brake upon the legislative power of the majority to protect the minority views from unnecessary limitation. That, as I have suggested, is not the only limitation that is needed. It is also necessary for the courts to foster and promote the divergent beliefs that do not undermine the civil order and preserve their role in the democratic discussions essential to the formation of good public policy. While the legislature may reasonably adopt limited policies that do not unnecessarily repress contrary beliefs, the courts must also exercise restraint in their imposition of one belief over another.

In the first chapter, I told the reader that we would not begin with a commitment to a particular substantive view of democracy. We started with a minimalist approach, adopting only a procedural idea of citizen participation. Nonetheless, as we have developed the themes of the book, questions about the balance of majority rule and principled limits have emerged. Again, because this is not a work of political theory, no doubt many questions on this topic remain unanswered, or answered only in broad outline. However, the reader might consider whether the place at which we have arrived does not echo some of the ideas of C. Edwin Baker, who suggested modifications to Rawls's theory of democracy by stipulating three crucial principles as follows:

> First is a "political participation principle." The legal order should recognize the fundamental nature of people's right to participate in a fair "choice democracy" that seeks to advance or implement conceptions of the good society. Second is a "no subordinating or denigrating purpose principle." The state in advancing conceptions of the good must not engage in practices, and the political process must not choose policies that purposefully subordinate or denigrate the inherent worth of any category of citizens or their reasonable conception of the good. Third is a "just wants principle." The state must seek of guarantee to each member the availability of those resources and opportunities that the existing society treats as necessary for full life and participation in that society.[2]

I appreciate that these ideas are only sketched in this book, and the third principle proposed extends considerably beyond the reach of where we have gone, although in his emphasis on participation Baker might also be wary of the exclusion of citizens from parts of our society that is the logical outcome of some of the judicial decisions we have reviewed. However, my focus is on freedom of conscience and religion and its particular role and treatment in a democratic society; other avenues and broader issues can only be acknowledged and left for the reader's future thought.

In this chapter, we will reflect upon the opportunity that Canada has in its system of governance and its Charter to achieve this open, democratic, and peaceful state. Based on what we have learned so far about the interpretation of freedom of conscience and religion in Canada, I will suggest several reforms that need to be adopted to adjust the development of the jurisprudence to that end. I will then review some current trends that seem to threaten our ability to achieve these purposes. These trends can be changed. We can redirect our present course to preserve freedom and peace because we have the tools at hand. However, this redirection, if it comes, will be the result of a conscious choice to lay down our attempts to adopt repressive strategies to achieve dominance of our own beliefs. If we cannot make these choices, then Canada will have wasted what is perhaps one of the greatest opportunities a country has ever had.

2. The Charter and the Human Rights Codes

We have spent much of the preceding seven chapters discussing case law and legislation related to freedom of conscience and religion. The Charter names freedom of conscience and religion as the first of the fundamental human rights. I have suggested why this is so and, even more, that this is an accurate statement of what is essential in a free and democratic society. Courts have tended to treat freedom of conscience and religion as of less importance than freedom of expression and equality.[3] Where both freedom of religion and freedom of expression are at issue, the court has tended to rely on freedom of expression arguments. Freedom of conscience is almost never raised or discussed in the Charter jurisprudence.[4] Freedom of religion has been most frequently defended when a court is able to see it as connected to equality arguments – in particular, minority rights.[5]

Although the Charter recognizes the need for limits to all rights and freedoms, the courts have paid little regard to the Charter's own words defining these limits. In interpreting "justifiable in a free and democratic society,"[6] the courts have devised a complex test requiring the law to be passed for a purpose of sufficient importance to justify overriding a Charter right and to be tailored in a way that does the least harm to the right possible.[7] But courts have given little content to what is required to justify overriding a Charter right. They have paid more attention to the government's stated purposes than to whether those purposes and their legislative expression have anything to do with the preservation of freedom and democracy.[8] Indeed, these concepts appear to be missing from the judicial decisions. As a result, the application of the elaborate *Oakes*[9] test frequently seems a disguised application of judicial preferences in the contest before the court.

Beginning with the early jurisprudence, Canadian courts have come perilously close to using freedom of conscience and religion as a means of protecting the sensibilities of particular groups.[10] I have several times pointed out the impossibility of a democratic state attempting to guard its citizens (or some of its citizens) from offensive behaviour of others. If offensive behaviour can lead to violence between groups, the solution is for the law to tackle the violence, not try to remove the offensive conduct. Because of the highly subjective nature of what is offensive and the proclivity of some groups more than others to react aggressively to offence, efforts to control the behaviour that offends are bound to require repressive laws that are applied unequally to different cases. In many cases, the offensive behaviour is highly unlikely to lead to violence; where it does, the law should confine itself to what it does best and what it can do with the least intrusion into freedom and democratic debate.

We often believe that problems of violence are best attacked by looking at the causes of the violence and attempting to remedy them. This no doubt explains in part the motivation for those who believe in protecting citizens from offence. In many cases, trying to eliminate the causes of violence – such as poverty or drug abuse, for example – is a useful strategy. But what if the elimination requires repression? What if the repression is of differences that we need for our society to flourish? In this case, eliminating the cause of potential violence should be directed at restraining the violence and rejecting the extreme feeling of offence that leads to it. To be a part of Canadian society, it should not be necessary to give up one's religion, conscience, or culture. But it should be necessary to give up any idea that one's religion, conscience, or culture should be defended violently from the ideas of others.

It is not up to the courts to decide intractable moral questions. Doing so short-cuts the democratic process and represses contrary views before the society has had the opportunity to arrive at a majority opinion. Rarely are courts in a position where they need to make these decisions. They can, instead, aim to hold an even hand between competing views.[11] And "an even hand" does not mean adoption of a definition of tolerance that requires the elimination of difference or commitment to the pluralistic belief that all beliefs are equally true (and, therefore, untrue). If that is the only way to peace, then our Charter rights mean very little. As we have seen, the courts have reflexively tended to that position instead of considering what true neutrality might look like.

Where the legislature has spoken, the role of the courts is to ensure that democratic debate stays alive by tempering the legislative will to the extent that minority opinions can still be expressed and minority rights protected. Where the legislature has not yet spoken, the courts must strive to create neutral spaces where all views can be heard. In many cases, arguments over incommensurate values will never be resolved. Canadians do not need to have them resolved at the price of limiting debate. We can live with uncertainty and ambiguity in our public life; courts can help us to do just that.

The Charter, as I have noted, provides the tools for these principles to be implemented. In fact, in its commitment to multiculturalism, to fundamental freedom, and to limits only as justified in a free and democratic society, it has mandated many of these principles by implication. All the courts need to do is to recognize the possibilities and the pitfalls. Because our common law system progresses on a case-by-case basis, courts have thus far exercised inadequate foresight of how their decisions can undermine Charter values. In attempting to defend "Charter values," courts have more often ignored them.

Human rights codes do not fit easily with the Charter as defences of freedom of conscience and religion or as compatible with a free and democratic society. Because they apply not to the actions of the state but to personal interactions among private citizens, the codes have a role to play in ensuring participation in important social aspects of life for all. But confusion has developed over the use of these statutes. Human rights proponents seem to consider the so-called human rights codes an attempt to produce by legislation a discrimination-free society.[12] This has led to the inclusion in many of the codes of the infamous "discriminatory publication" provisions that go beyond ensuring participation in economic and social life to protection of some groups from offensive opinions. What I have already said about this tendency in Charter jurisprudence also applies here. Moreover, efforts to legislate equality over all social interactions are liable to destroy a democratic society. The degree of repression and intrusion into private life required by this goal leads directly to the totalitarianism that leads away from social peace. Preservation of a free, democratic, and peaceful society requires principally one thing: an understanding that my rights cannot be maintained unless I am also committed to maintain your rights. Human rights codes (really anti-discrimination legislation) have the potential to be applied to extinguish some rights in the name of equality.

Reforming human rights codes is a necessary step. Repeal of the discriminatory publication provisions is a simple measure.[13] More radically, the theory and philosophy behind provincial human rights statutes need to change to recognize that these statutes play only a limited part in constructing a just world. Human rights to be free from discriminatory treatment must recognize that they coexist with human rights to believe and act upon beliefs that of necessity discriminate in some situations and about some things. As long as these expressions do not restrict the participation of others in democratic and social life, human rights legislation should not be interpreted to interfere with them.

The interaction between the Charter and human rights codes should logically lead to this result. I have earlier referred to the Supreme Court of Canada extending equality right under the Charter to include sexual orientation and mandating the inclusion of sexual orientation in human rights statutes.[14] Human rights codes, like all other government activities, must comply with the Charter. The fundamental freedom of conscience, which is not recognized under provincial human rights legislation, will need to find its place in the interpretation and limitation of anti-discrimination codes. While this has not yet become a major issue, it is likely to do so in the future, particularly if the courts continue to narrow the scope of freedom of religion. This can provide an opportunity for the courts to return some balance to anti-discrimination legislation and to express an understanding of the interdependency of human rights, including both rights to be free from discrimination that has harmful social effects and rights to follow one's conscience.

Much of this summarizes the ground we have covered in earlier chapters. Nothing really seems to prevent courts from recognizing these principles. But several incidents that have been in the news as I write this concluding chapter illustrate tendencies in Canadian society that could lead away from an open, democratic society. The reader will probably be able to think of other illustrations that would serve just as well. These are current and therefore also illustrate the immediacy of the threat these tendencies pose.

3. Be Afraid. Be Very Afraid

The American public is regularly inundated with messages of fear about those who believe differently from whatever segment is being propagandized. The "right" is led to believe that President Obama is the anti-Christ while the "left" is led to believe that the Republican Party is dominated by those who want to establish a theocracy. It may be said that this is the sign of a deeply divided society. Canadians have tended to consider that the divisions lie less deeply here than they do in our southern neighbour's territory. Canadians think of themselves as "moderate" and less extreme.

There may be some truth in this. The United States is deeply divided on religious, philosophical, and, ultimately, political lines. But it seems quite likely that many Canadians in fact are no less divided. The same religious organizations compete for membership in Canada as they do in the United States. Jews, Evangelical Protestants, Muslims, and Roman Catholics, to say nothing of those who do not precisely match up with any particular religious demographic but who are passionately devoted to environmentalism or feminism or whatever, exist with the same differences in Canada as they do in the United States. While America is divided into "red" and "blue" states, in Canada much of the West federally votes Conservative and the East, Liberal or NDP, with urban centres and rural areas similarly divided. A major difference may not be so much the lack of division as the fact that we have not, until now, been so worried about it.

There are two strands to the fears I am naming here. One raises a concern that needs to be acted upon; the other does not. The strand on which we should resist acting is the fear that my side of a particular policy debate will lose. Like everyone else, you and I no doubt have strong beliefs about what is right and good. Perhaps at this time, our government and legislation generally reflect what you think is right and good; perhaps they reflect what I think. In either case, one element in being afraid of those who disagree with me about what is right and good and what should be enacted in government legislation is that if you can persuade enough people that your beliefs are better than mine, my views will be excluded from public policy and yours will be adopted. Therefore, fear may persuade me that I should try very hard and by all possible rhetorical means to ensure that you do not have the opportunity to have even a hearing for your opinions. One way I can do that is to convince others that they should be afraid of you and your opinions. If people can be made sufficiently afraid, they may outlaw your opinions in legislation, and courts may refuse to defend your rights to express and live your beliefs.

This fear seems to have invaded Canada, as witnessed by comments of the Bloc Québécois party leader, M. Giles Duceppe, in Parliament on May 27, 2010. He raised as a matter of national concern an allegation that some Conservative MPs formed a "pro-life" block in the Conservative caucus.[15] As well, some were apparently Roman Catholics and members of the Opus Dei organization. M. Duceppe did not indicate why this should concern him, although since the Bloc is pro-choice in its views it undoubtedly disagrees with any possible legal limits that might be placed on abortion. But his calling attention to the fact that there are MPs who differ from his and his party's belief hardly seems worth the trouble. The implication is that there is something to be afraid of in the debate. It is not a long step from there to an argument that Roman Catholics (or other identifiable groups opposed to a particular policy) should be ineligible for public office.

This impulse is a profoundly anti-democratic one. The function of democracy, as I said in the first chapter, is to promote debate, to be open to change, and to accept, with limitations, the will of the legislators elected by the public vote. If my side loses a public policy debate, I should be able to carry on the argument and perhaps I will win another day. I should also be entitled to the protection of the law for my conscience, insofar as the law can accommodate me without destroying the policy chosen by the democratic government. Other than these accommodations, the law should have no tolerance for protecting either of us against being outvoted in public opinion.

The second strand is a legitimate ground for taking action, insofar as it is a real concern. This second element to the fear is that not only will my side lose but, if I do lose on a particular issue, your side will revoke the democratic machinery by which I may still carry on and argue the point another day. How realistic this fear may be in any given case is unclear. Certainly few groups advocate abolishing the constitution, the courts, or the democratic system. Of course, with power comes a certain degree of entrenchment that is inevitable. It is always easier to defend the settled opinion than to promote new ideas. But this is true for all power-seeking groups and belief systems and does not generally constitute a real threat to the possibility of change.

The problem with this second strand of fear is that it is often used to justify fear and hence repression of contrary opinion on particular matters of public policy. This seems to cast doubt on the proponents' honesty in raising the fear of totalitarianism. If the fear really is that a particular group, upon gaining the support of public opinion for its policy platform, might attempt to eliminate its opposition through repressive means, the solution is not to stifle the expression of belief on matters that do not call for the dismantling of the democratic machinery, but to ensure that the democratic process cannot easily be derailed. This calls for more, not less, open public debate. It also calls for stronger protection for conscience and minority viewpoints, not a weakening of their rights to be heard.

Canada has remained relatively free until recently of public expression of this fear. However, recently Marci McDonald has published a book warning of the rising of the Christian Right in Canada. As reported in the *National Post*, in an interview about her book, *The Armageddon Factor*,[16] Ms McDonald apparently suggested that influences in the Harper government were contrary to Canadian "values" because they expressed the views of social conservatives. No doubt Ms McDonald does not like those views and does not believe them to be morally right. However, in expressing the fear that elected members of Parliament might disagree with her opinions, and that this is something we should fear, she is leading us down the path of intolerance. If the voters do not like the beliefs of their representatives, they do not have to elect them in the next election. Nothing in the disagreement suggests that these MPs are not committed to free and open elections and debate. Hints at totalitarian ambitions seem principally to be included to widen divisions on policy matters and increase suspicion of those who disagree.

As long as the democratic structures are in place with safeguards employed by the courts to protect minority voices, there is no legitimate excuse for fear of diverse public opinions or of their expressions. In Canada, these fears may be increasing. If so, we need to remind ourselves that the stronger the democratic process, the more diverse opinions we will hear; and the more diverse opinions we can hear without being afraid, the stronger the democratic process will be.

4. Rhetoric, Relativism, and Multiculturalism

No one needs to believe that others' beliefs are just as good as his. Indeed, it would be amazing to find anyone who did. One of the most annoying pronouncements that our culture is prone to is that of excluding wide swathes of our populace from the moral high ground because their beliefs exclude others. As is obvious, this pronouncement is self-contradictory. We no longer live in a society unified by the bonds of similar religion, culture, and ways of thinking. The day of moral, ethical, and spiritual homogeneity is over.

No one needs to reject her belief that there are ideas that are better than others or worse than others; that some modes of life are better than others; that some belief systems are truer (or even "true" in an absolute sense) and produce better results than others; that some family structures, religions, philosophies, and commitments are preferable to others and that they produce a better society and better citizens. But the day when we agreed on which of these ideas, beliefs, family structures, religions, philosophies, and commitments are better is also over.

A mature democratic state is able to cope with these facts. It does so, not by requiring its citizens to pretend that "better," "true," and "preferable" do not exist, but by requiring its citizens to commit to the proposition that the only legitimate way to achieve victory for our vision of "better," "true," and "preferable" is by persuasion. Persuasion is, as I suggested in chapter 1, carried on through our democratic processes and our social conversations. Even when it formulates itself in legislation, it must exercise restraint towards those who have not yet been persuaded, particularly a restraint that does not exclude that minority from ongoing debate.

The methods by which we carry on these conversations need a rethink.[17] Postmodernists accept that most seemingly logical arguments are in fact riddled with unstated premises and unacknowledged assumptions. Therefore, it is sometimes said that all argument is, in fact, rhetoric or, in other words, just an effort to persuade others on emotional grounds. This idea has influenced our public discourse profoundly. Alongside this idea also flourishes the theory that our private beliefs have no place in public discourse; only reasons generally available to all, whatever their beliefs, should be the basis on which public policy is argued.

When both these assumptions are made and acted upon together, I suggest that we get something very like the level of public debate that we have in Canada. Reasoned argument is believed to be both essential and naïve. The discourse that is put forward as reason is then often just an effort to manipulate emotions, dressed in reason's clothes. Language is used to create both effects simultaneously. A report of a conflict in the paper refers to one side as "genocidal" and to the other as "oppressed"; one group is misogynist while the other is progressive. Name-calling that evokes fear and distrust or compassion and sympathy is endemic. One party's "freedom fighters" are the other party's terrorists. And this is all aided by appropriate visual images. It has often been said that if baby seals looked like cows, no one would have cared about the Newfoundland seal hunt. Few people are satisfied with this state of affairs.

I have taken the position earlier in this book that, indeed, our belief systems are the key to our arguments and to how we hear and respond to the arguments of others. Therefore, I suggested, the idea that belief systems can be kept out of public discourse is unrealistic. But the solution to the problem this presents is not to proceed cynically to appeal to underlying beliefs while pretending to reason objectively. The solution is to try to reveal the beliefs we have that motivate our arguments and to try to understand the often unacknowledged assumptions that guide our reasoning and our choices and the reasoning and choices of others. This cannot happen without robustly defended freedom of conscience and religion. Public debate is what it is today primarily because we are not prepared to express our beliefs honestly or to hear without fear the contrary beliefs of others. Canadians and their institutions must begin to rethink their attitudes to freedom of religion and conscience; to what it means for our public debate and to what it can add to our society.

The solutions to cases of freedom of conscience and religion are not easy ones. For this reason, I have suggested in this book not so much a solution to those issues as a methodology by which we can approach them and think about them. Our goal is to judge the consistency of our possible solutions with democratic principles and the likelihood that those solutions will support an inclusive, peaceful, and democratic society. That methodology can still leave choices of what is the best solution to the problem before us. Ideally, the major choices will be made through democratic processes.

5. Conclusion

Canada tends to be smug about its cultural and religious tolerance. Compared with many nations in the world, it has done a better job than they. However, as we become more diverse, we may become more afraid; as we become more afraid, the temptations to betray what are our fundamental Canadian values – our commitment to democracy and peace without which no human rights are possible – also grow. Our courts have not yet developed a theoretical approach to freedom of conscience and religion that supports our democratic commitments. That may not be surprising because the degree of diversity in belief systems that we now experience has come upon us unawares. Not only are we more multicultural than we might have predicted in 1980, when the Charter became law, but divisions in belief among us have also become more obvious.

We must learn to adapt to this reality. If we are to do so, then our first step should be to rethink the meaning of the fundamental freedom of conscience and religion. The alternative is to drift down roads that may lead us where we do not wish to go. It has been suggested that there are two approaches to a pluralist society: one (convergence pluralism) assumes we will all gradually adopt common values; the other (accommodation pluralism) accepts that this is not a likely outcome.[18] The vision of a united planetary federation with common humanitarian values as television portrayed it in the "Star Trek" series is, our experience with immigration and diversity seems to suggest, a far-fetched vision. In any event, it seems probable that it could not be achieved without first passing through a stage of accommodation pluralism. Perhaps in some far-distant future values will then again coincide; perhaps not. But attempting to enforce convergence pluralism is unlikely to result in anything other than divisiveness and social unrest.

The course on which our courts have so far taken us is more reflective, I suggest, of adherence to the vision of social harmony produced by uniformity than to that produced by genuine accommodation and acceptance of difference. This could change and, as Professor Lauwers says, "with the appropriate level of humility on the part of politicians and judges, there may yet be success in accommodating diversity and achieving peace, order and good government."[19] That level of humility, I suggest, requires an acceptance of a different role for courts, for human rights codes, and for public institutions, and a different understanding of the role and interaction of human rights and human dignity from what we have yet achieved. It is time to rethink these vital issues. It is time that we acknowledge in our courts and in our legislatures that we want to live in a society where we are all, as the constitution assures us we are, free to believe.

Notes

1. Introduction: How Freedom of Conscience and Religion Are Protected and Why It Matters

1 *National Post*, August 5, 2011. The B.C. Supreme Court determined that a "right to die" did exist under the Charter, distinguishing the *Rodriguez* decision (*infra*, note 2). The decision is being appealed. See *Carter v. Canada (Attorney General)* 2012 BCSC 886 (CanLII) The plaintiff has since died.

2 [1993] SCR 517.

3 The question of a Charter "right to die" has been widely discussed in the legal literature. For one review, see Fran Carnerie, "Euthanasia and Self-Determinism: Is There a Charter Right to Die in Canada?" 32 McGill L.J. 299 (1986–7).

4 Stephen L. Carter, *The Culture of Disbelief: How American Law and Politics Trivialize Religious Devotion* (Basic Books, 1993) at p. 51.

5 Timothy Macklem, "Faith as a Secular Value," 45 McGill L.J. 1 (2000), at p. 51.

6 Other writers have acknowledged the role of faith and religious belief in supporting the democratic processes, although to a lesser degree than I will argue. See Janet Epp Buckingham, "The Fundamentals of Religious Freedom: The Case for Recognizing Collective Aspects of Religion," 36 Sup. Ct. L. Rev. (2nd) 251 (2007).

7 The Constitution Act, 1982, being Schedule B to the Canada Act 1982 (U.K.), 1982, c. 11, Part I. Hereafter, the Canadian Charter will be cited without further reference.

8 The Charter, s. 2(b), (c), and (d).

9 Section 2 of the Charter sets out the freedoms; sections 3–23 set out a variety of rights, including equality rights, legal rights, and language rights.

10 The Charter, s. 1.

11 *Multani v. Commission scolaire Marguerite-Bourgeoys*, [2006] 1 SCR 256.

12 For example, see *Schreiber v. Canada (Attorney-General)*, [1998] 1 SCR 824.

13 Considerable debate has taken place over whether a variety of economic rights should be recognized in Canada.

14 See the concluding chapter for additional comments.

15 For example, see the well-known work by Edward S. Herman and Noam Chomsky, *Manufacturing Consent* (Pantheon, 2002).

16 A similar idea is put forward by Margaret Somerville in *The Ethical Imagination* (House of Anansi, 2006) in describing the process of finding a shared ethic in biomedical technology. It is suggested here that this is simply an example of how, on the broader scale, democracies should and must function.

17 An Act to Confer the Electoral Franchise upon Women, S.C. 1918, c. 20.

18 *Syndicat Northcrest v. Amselem*, [2004] 2 SCR 551; 2004 SCC 47 (CanLII) at para. 39 (CanLII).

19 See the discussion in Iain T. Benson, "Notes towards a (Re) Definition of the Secular," 33 U.B.C. L. Rev. 519 (2000). In the paper, Dr Benson quotes Aldous Huxley as saying, "It is impossible to live without a metaphysic" (p. 532). See also, in the same journal, David M. Brown, "Freedom From or Freedom For: Religion as a Case Study in Defining the Content of Charter Rights," 33 U.B.C. L. Rev. 551 (1999–2000).

20 Although some religions certainly would not consider transcendence a requirement – for example, some forms of Confucianism or even some liberal interpretations of Christianity.

21 [1985] 1 SCR 295; 1985 SCC 69 (CanLII).

22 Ibid., para. 122 (CanLII).

23 Perhaps the best-known example would be John Rawls, *Political Liberalism* (Columbia University Press, 1995). For critiques of this view, see Michael W. McConnell, "Secular Reason and the Misguided Attempt to Exclude Religious Argument from Democratic Deliberation," 1 Journal of Law, Philosophy and Culture 159 (2007) or Jonathan Chaplin, "Beyond Liberal Restraints: Defending Religiously-Based Arguments in Law and Public Policy," 33 U.B.C. L. Rev. 617 (2000).

24 In fact, it has been argued that every state has an "established" belief system, even when it is not an established religion. See Rex Ahdar and Ian Leigh, "Is Establishment Consistent with Religious Freedom?" 49 McGill L.J. 635 (2003–4).

25 The well-known story of the struggle against slavery in Britain is told, for example, in Eric Metaxas, *William Wilberforce and the Heroic Campaign to End Slavery* (HarperCollins Canada, 2007).

26 The Charter, s. 32. Of course, that control can significantly affect private rights as well, but I will address this at a later point.
27 But if the curtailment was considered "a reasonable limit prescribed by law" that could be justified in a "free and democratic society," such proscription could be upheld by the courts. Alternatively, s. 33(1) of the Charter allows the Federal parliament or provincial legislature to declare a law to be effective "notwithstanding" many of the rights or freedoms conferred by the Charter, including freedom of conscience and religion.
28 The Charter, s. 15.
29 The Charter, s. 1.
30 *R. v. Oakes*, [1986] 1 SCR 103.
31 For example, in British Columbia, the Human Rights Code, RSBC 1996, c. 210; in Alberta, the Human Rights, Citizenship and Multiculturalism Act, R.S.A. 2000, c. H-14; in Saskatchewan, the Saskatchewan Human Rights Code, S.S. 1979, c. S-24.1; in Manitoba, the Human Rights Code, C.C.S.M., c. H175; in Ontario, the Human Rights Code, R.S.O. 1990, c. H-19; in Nova Scotia, the Human Rights Act, R.S.N.S. 1989, c. 214; in Quebec, the Charter of Human Rights and Freedoms, R.S.Q., c. C012.
32 Canadian Human Rights Act, R.S.C. 1985, c. H-6.
33 For example, the B.C. statute contains these transactions; the Nova Scotia statute includes volunteer public service; Ontario adds the right to contract on equal terms.
34 For example, such provisions, with variations, are found in the statutes of B.C., Ontario, and Nova Scotia.
35 B.C. uses this term exclusively.
36 Manitoba, Saskatchewan, Nova Scotia, and Ontario all refer to "creed" with or without the term "religion."
37 Alberta uses "religious belief."
38 Saskatchewan defines "creed" as "religious creed."
39 *Supra*, note 32, s. 3(1).
40 For example, Manitoba's statute includes in its definition of discrimination "differential treatment on the basis of the individual's actual or presumed membership in or association with some class or group of persons rather than on the basis of personal merit."
41 Both characteristics would seem irrelevant to renting accommodation. This is one of the indicia that legislators seem to use in determining which characteristics should be prohibited grounds of discrimination for which transactions; it does not seem to be the only indicator, however, as noted below.
42 British Columbia had such a provision until January, 2008. Most provinces have eliminated the exception.

246 Notes to pages 17–23

43 One of the leading cases was *McKinney v. University of Guelph*, [1990] 3 SCR 229.
44 See the decision of Prowse J.A. in *Greater Vancouver Regional District Employees' Union v. Greater Vancouver Regional District* (2001), 206 D.L.R. (4th) 220 (BCCA).
45 *Hydro-Québec v. Syndicat des employés de techniques professionelles* (2008), 294 D.L.R. (4th) 407 (SCC).
46 See the Ontario statute for an example.
47 The "undue hardship" test is not provided for in B.C.'s legislation, but see *British Columbia (Public Service Employee Relations Committee) v. BCGSEU*, [1994] 3 SCR 3.
48 *Supra*, note 11.
49 See the discussion in chapter 3.
50 An example is found in *Smith and Chymyshyn v. Knights of Columbus and Others*, 2005 BCHRT 544.
51 See *National Post*, Wednesday, March 18, 2009, discussing "Israel Apartheid Week."
52 See *National Post*, Wednesday, February 18, 2009, "Bountiful Leaders in Court on Polygamy Charges."
53 *Globe and Mail*, Monday, September 10, 2007, "PM Assails Election Veil Decision."
54 "New atheists" such as Richard Dawkins or Christopher Hitchens may fall within this category.
55 *National Post*, Thursday, December 18, 2008, "Quebec Religion Course Causing Strife." See also the discussion of legal challenges to this curriculum in chapter 6, below.
56 John Milbank, "Hume versus Kant: Faith, Reason and Feeling," 27 Modern Theology 276 (April 2011).

2. Early Cases: Getting Off on the Wrong Foot

1 *R. v. Big M Drug Mart*, [1985] 1 SCR 295; 1985 Can LII 69 (S.C.C.). Generally, I will cite the case in this chapter simply as "*Big M Drug Mart*." All paragraph references are to the CanLII version.
2 The court in *Big M Drug Mart* put the emphasis on freedom from coercion (see para. 95). However, later cases, such as *Amselem* (discussed in chapter 3), have emphasized the positive side of the freedom.
3 For example, special days of religious observance such as Ramadan.
4 Often some broad moral precepts, such as honesty.

5 The moral claims of most belief systems, such as the Ten Commandments in Judaism and Christianity, are believed to be universally binding, even if not all persons would recognize them as such.

6 Many faiths (and non-religious belief systems) proselytize out of the belief that the highest human good is achieved by accepting their belief system.

7 I am not suggesting that because the exercise of one's freedom of religion and conscience interferes with the rights of someone else, that is necessarily sufficient cause to curtail the exercise of rights of conscience and religion in all cases. But if the exercise of conscience and religion is to be curtailed, interference with a right of someone else is a necessary basis. Indeed, if the interference is permitted by a court, it becomes axiomatic that there is now a right to interfere. Cases in which legally recognized rights of both parties appear in conflict such that courts need to choose between them will be discussed specifically in a later chapter.

8 An interesting illustration is the fate of the Occupiers' movement in the courts. The general conclusion appears to have been that while the Occupiers had the right to use the public space to demonstrate, when their demonstration substantially excluded other citizens from the public space, their rights were curtailed. See *Vancouver (City) v. O'Flynn-Magee*, 2011 BCSC 1647 (CanLII).

9 I note here that readers may be more familiar with the U.S. system, in which government aid to religion is prohibited by their constitution in most cases. This is not the Canadian situation. The American position will be discussed later in this chapter.

10 In fact, the courts do not characterize the cases discussed in this chapter as presenting a conflict of rights at all. Rather, they classify them only as a case of citizens' rights against the state. It is my contention that this is inaccurate.

11 Lord's Day Act, R.S.C. 1970, c. L-13.

12 *Supra*, note 1.

13 See for example *Principal Investment Ltd. v. Thiele Estate* (1987), 37 D.L.R. (4th) 398 (B.C.C.A.); 1987 CanLII 2740 (B.C.C.A.), in which McLaughlin J.A. cites a number of the cases in para. 37–9.

14 *Supra*, note 11. Sections 4, 6, and 7 contained exemptions if provided by provincial law or municipal charter. Section 4 contained the basic prohibition against selling goods or real estate, carrying on one's calling, or for gain to work or employ anyone to work.

15 Ontario Law Reform Commission, *Report on Sunday Observance Legislation*, Toronto, Department of Justice, 1970.

16 Canadian constitutional law textbooks discuss the division of powers question. See Peter W. Hogg, *Constitutional Law of Canada* (Thompson Carswell, 2006).

17 Lord's Day (Ontario) Act, R.S.O. 1897, c. 246.

18 *Attorney-General for Ontario v. Hamilton Street Railway Co.*, [1903] A.C. 524 (P.C.).

19 In *Big M Drug Mart*, the court traced Sunday observance laws back to a statute passed in the reign of Henry VI, The Sunday Fairs Act, 27 Hen. 6, c. 5.

20 When the provincial statute was declared invalid, the Federal government stepped in and the original Federal Lord's Day Act was enacted.

21 *R. v. Big M Drug Mart*, [1983] 4 W.W.R. 54 (Alta. Prov. Ct.).

22 *Big M Drug Mart*, para. 146.

23 Ibid., para. 90.

24 *Andrews v. Law Society of B.C.*, [1989] 1 SCR 143; 1989 CanLII 2 (S.C.C.).

25 *Egan v. Canada*, [1995] 2 SCR 513; 1995 CanLII 98 (S.C.C.).

26 Homosexual relations were not decriminalized in Canada until 1969.

27 *Big M Drug Mart*, para. 91.

28 I say "semantic" because, as I shall argue, the distinction between "purpose" and "effect" that the court drew cannot be as clear as it implies.

29 [1963] SCR 145.

30 Canadian Bill of Rights, R.S.C. 1970, App. III.

31 *Robertson and Rosetanni v. R.*, [1963] SCR 651, quoted in *Big M Drug Mart* at para. 69.

32 *Big M Drug Mart*, para. 86.

33 Ibid., para. 88.

34 Ibid., para. 89.

35 This occurred during the English Reformation, in which, of course, political issues were involved. See the court's discussion in *Big M Drug Mart*, para. 51–3.

36 Sir William Blackstone, *Commentaries on the Laws of England in Four Volumes* (Callaghan, 1872) .

37 *Big M Drug Mart*, para. 93, 99, and 136, to select three examples.

38 Ibid., para. 98.

39 Ibid., para. 133.

40 To follow the argument that "rights" are a normative state of affairs brought about in one's own life, see Nicolas Wolterstorff, *Justice: Rights and Wrongs* (Princeton University Press, 2008).

41 There is a question, of course, as to whether the legislation violates any other right to which you are entitled. It certainly diminishes your property

rights (which, as in the earlier example of burning down my house, you would be entitled to maintain against other private citizens), but these rights are not constitutionally protected against government action and are regularly limited by bylaw or statute.

42 Part of the problem here may be the fact that we do not regard "religion" as simply one of a broader category of "belief systems." Yet, as I argued in chapter 1, the First Nation's beliefs in its history and culture are every bit as much an "organizing belief system" as Islam or Judaism.

43 *Big M Drug Mart*, para. 97.

44 [1986] 2 SCR 713; 1986 CanLII 12 (S.C.C.).

45 The Constitution of the United States of America, First Amendment, ratified December 15, 1791.

46 For an extensive discussion of the various theories of the relationship between the two clauses, see Michael W. McConnell, John H. Garvey, and Thomas C. Berg, *Religion and the Constitution* (Aspen Law and Business, 2002).

47 Four cases on this topic were decided at once. They were *McGowan v. Maryland, infra,* note 48; *Braunfeld v. Brown,* 366 U.S. 599 (1961); *Two Guys from Harrison-Allentown Inc. v. McGinley,* 366 U.S. 582 (1961); and *Gallagher v. Crown Kosher Supermarket of Massachusetts Inc.,* 366 U.S. 617 (1961). Reference here will be made only to *McGowan.*

48 366 U.S. 420 (1961).

49 Ibid.

50 In his dissent, Justice Douglas moves between the establishment clause and the free exercise clause as reflections of each other. He finds that the state imposition of a law designed originally to favour the religious exercise of Christians imposed burdens upon other faiths, limiting their free exercise. He also makes a number of statements suggesting that he sees the laws as imposition of Christian religious practice, but apart from the prohibition on the state's adoption of such imposition in the establishment clause, seems to provide no separate justification for why this violates free exercise.

51 *Big M Drug Mart*, para 109.

52 Ibid., para 109.

53 R.S.O. 1980, c. 453.

54 *R. v. Edwards Books and Art Ltd.*, cited, *supra,* at note 44. All specific references will be to paragraph numbers in the CanLII citation.

55 *Edwards Books,* para. 99.

56 Professor Petter, in his article "Not 'Never on a Sunday' – *R. v. Videoflicks Ltd. et al.,*" 49 Sask. L. Rev. 98 (1984–5), made the argument that it was not

the legislation that imposed the burden, but the religious faith itself. This argument was rejected by Beetz and McIntyre JJ. With respect to Professor Petter, I find the majority view more persuasive as the legislation did make the practice of faiths other than Sunday-observant faiths more costly.

57 *Edwards Books*, para. 122.

58 There was disagreement among the majority and minority on this point. Wilson J. argued that the limitation of the exemption to small businesses could not be justified under s. 1 of the Charter, as the result was to protect freedom of religion for some who observed Saturday as a Sabbath, but not all.

59 *Supra*, note 15.

60 Ibid., p. 267, quoted by the court in *Edwards Books*, para. 125.

61 *Edwards Books*, para. 126.

62 Wilson J. (dissenting in part) suggested that the fact the Act was confined to retail workers and did not include other occupations meant that the government "has put its own value on the common pause day" (para. 231).

63 The argument in *Edwards Books*, as has been pointed out, might have been made on the basis of an equality right (see Monahan and Petter, "Developments in Constitutional Law: The 1986–87 Term," Sup. Ct. L. Rev. 61 (1988) at pp. 81–2). The basis for *Big M Drug Mart* may also reflect concerns for equality. These connections will be discussed briefly below and further explored in later chapters.

64 See *Big M Drug Mart*, para. 97 and following, in which the court expresses concern for the minority and the insensitivity of the majority who may not realize the negative effects upon minority groups of exposure to the dominant culture.

65 *Big M Drug Mart*, para. 96 and following.

66 Membership in a group suffering from historical disadvantage is one of the factors on which a claim to violation of s. 15(1) equality rights can be based. See *Law v. Canada (Minister of Employment and Immigration)*, [1999] 1 SCR 497; 1999 CanLII 675 (S.C.C.).

67 *Big M Drug Mart*, para. 96.

68 Ibid., para. 97.

69 CanLII provides over 800 cited references.

70 For example, see *B.C. and Yukon Territory Building and Construction Trades Council v. British Columbia (Attorney-General)* (1985), 22 D.L.R. (4th) 450 (B.C.S.C.), which was a case under s. 15(1) of the Charter.

71 The Constitution Act does provide for and protect publicly funded denominational schools in some provinces. As well, other provinces, such

as British Columbia, allow limited public funding for any religious school that meets provincial curriculum requirements.

72 See the *Huffington Post*, July 25, 2011: "Several faith-based groups plan to protest outside the Toronto District School Board's headquarters today over allowing Muslim prayers in a school." See also *HolyPost*, November 21, 2011, an article by Tristin Hopper entitled "Tempers Flare at Meeting on Toronto School's Muslim Prayer Sessions."

73 (1988), 65 O.R. (2d) 641 (C.A.); 1988 CanLII 189 (ON C.A.). Further references will be to paragraph numbers in the CanLII citation.

74 R.S.O. 1980, c. 129; O. Reg. 262/80.

75 S. 28(10), (11), and (12).

76 55 O.R. (2d) 749 (Div. Ct.).

77 This case is often seen as the first in a trilogy of Ontario Court of Appeal cases that limited religious instruction in schools and refused public funding to parents who wanted religious education for their children. See also *Civil Liberties Association v. Ontario (Minister of Education)* (1990), 71 O.R. (2d) 341 (C.A.) and *Adler v. Ontario* (1994), 19 O.R. (3d) 1 (C.A.), affirmed [1996] S.C.R. 609.

78 *Zylberberg*, p. 23.

79 *Abington School District v. Schempp*, 374 U.S. 203 (1963).

80 This characterization of *Zylberberg* has been accepted by some commentators without question. See Elizabeth J. Shilton, "Religion and Public Education in Canada after the Charter," in *Religious Conscience, the State and the Law*, ed. John McLaren and Harold Coward (State University of New York Press, 1999), at p. 213.

81 *Zylberberg*, p. 1 (dissenting opinion).

82 Based upon the finding of *Big M Drug Mart* that a religious motivation would, itself, make legislation bad, whatever its effects, Lacourcière J.A. had to make a finding that the purpose of the law was not purely religious in nature. Whether you can legitimately divide moral beliefs from religious beliefs in all cases, or whether the fact that moral beliefs, held independently from religious beliefs, are themselves a belief system to which the freedom of conscience and religion protection applies, is another story.

83 *Zylberberg*, p. 8.

84 Ibid., p. 40. I have already briefly alluded to the role of equality rights in *Edwards Books* and in *Big M Drug Mart*. At this point, I will not attempt to analyse whether the opinion of Lacourcière J.A. on this issue would have been a reasonable way of disposing of the case. The difficulty in using equality rights to limit public expression of belief is that the equality right is rarely analysed in any rigorous way. Rather, it usually consists

of a vague sense that someone is not being treated equally; this would not be adequate to found a claim for violation of s. 15 rights, nor, I will suggest, ought it to be sufficient to limit fundamental freedoms through court action.

85 Ibid., p. 8. In this respect, the reasoning of Lacourcière J.A. is reflective of the argument in this chapter.

86 See Richard Bauman and David Schneiderman, "The Constitutional Context of Religious Practices in Saskatchewan Public Schools," 60 Sask. L. Rev. 265 (1996) for another example of writers who argue that the display of Christian faith "creates an educational environment hostile to students not of the dominant faith" (p. 284).

87 See the discussion, *infra*, chapter 6.

88 The legislature's role in deciding conflicts over belief systems will be addressed in chapter 3.

89 (1999), 47 O.R. (3d) 301 (C.A.); 1999 CanLII 3786 (ON C.A.). References below are to the CanLII citation.

90 Ibid., at para. 18.

91 (2004), 69 O.R. (3d) 742; 2004 CanLII 13978 (ON S.C.).

92 It did find that the purpose was to impose a "moral" tone (ibid., para. 18). Given that a moral system of beliefs is a matter of conscience as well, it is still not defensible to argue that this is a distinguishing feature from the *Freitag* decision.

93 This, I suggest, is the case even if the expression is that of the majoritarian religious position.

94 Richard Moon, "Government Support for Religious Practice," in *Law and Religious Pluralism in Canada*, ed. Richard Moon (UBC Press, 2008), p. 217.

95 Ibid., at p. 229.

96 My approach may be contrasted with that of Professor Ben Berger in his article "The Limits of Belief: Freedom of Religion, Secularism and the Liberal State," 1 Can. J. of Law and Society 39 (2002), in which he postulates denying Charter protection to those acts which are inimical to Charter "values." This point will be more fully addressed when we consider limits to freedom of conscience and religion in the next chapters.

97 In "Freedom From or Freedom For? Religion as a Case Study in Defining the Context of Charter Rights," 33 U.B.C. L. Rev. 551 (1999–2000), David M. Brown suggests in discussing these cases that the health of public institutions is "threatened by the absence of religious voices which serve as a restraint on the inherent tendency of democracy to unravel any checks on the passions and thus prompt its own destruction" (p. 613). I would agree,

although perhaps not for quite the same reasons, that suppressing the expression of belief is inimical to democracy.

3. Culture Wars: Majority versus Minority Values

1 *Globe and Mail*, Monday, January 29, 2007.
2 Ibid.
3 *Building for the Future: A Time for Reconciliation*, Abridged Report, Commission de consultation sur les pratiques d'accommodement reliées aux differénces culturelles, 2008, Gouvernement du Québec, p. 13. The Report will be cited in this chapter as the Bouchard/Taylor Report, without further endnotes.
4 Ibid., p. 74.
5 The Bouchard/Taylor Report made the point that Quebecers of French origin appeared more concerned about accommodations than other Quebecers. However, the survey in *Maclean's* magazine, while it found higher rates of disapproval of accommodation in Quebec, reported majority disapproval across the country.
6 An example is found in the Commercial Arbitration Act RSBC 1996, c. 55. All provinces have similar acts. In light of the discussion, *infra*, it may be noted that the B.C. act renders arbitration agreements that exclude the jurisdiction of the courts under the Divorce Act (Can.) or the Family Relations Act of the province ineffective.
7 Marion Boyd, *Dispute Resolution in Family Law: Protecting Choice, Promoting Inclusion*, Government of Ontario, December 2004.
8 Criminal Code RSC 1985, c. C-46, s. 293(1) prohibits "polygamy" and "any kind of conjugal union with more than one person at the same time." The charges were later dismissed on the basis that the attorney-general had improperly refused to take a prosecutorial recommendation as final. This will be discussed in more detail later in the chapter.
9 See Andrew Mayeda, "Ottawa Girds for Polygamy Challenge," Canwest News Service, *National Post*, March 25, 2009.
10 For an example, see letter of Dr Gail Robinson, director, Women's Mental Health Clinic, University Health Network, Toronto, published in the *National Post*, March 27, 2009.
11 *Reference re: Section 293 of the Criminal Code of Canada*, 2011 BCSC 1588 (CanLII). The decision is discussed in more detail later in the chapter.
12 Bouchard/Taylor Report, pp. 18–21, pp. 61–2.
13 Ibid., pp. 23–6.

14 The charges were dismissed on the grounds that the attorney-general, having appointed a special prosecutor who recommended against laying criminal charges, then refused to take that prosecutor's advice, but appointed a second prosecutor who recommended charges be laid. The court held this to be in violation of the purposes for which special prosecutors were provided in legislation, which was to avoid political interference. See *Blackmore v. British Columbia (Attorney-General)*, 2009 BCSC 1299.

15 *Supra*, note 11.

16 *Begum (by her litigation friend Rahman) v. Governors of Denbigh High School*, [2006] UKHL 15.

17 See discussion, chapter 1, *supra*, pp. 16–18.

18 *Supra*, note 12.

19 See *British Columbia (Public Service Employee Relations Commission) v. BCG-SEU*, [1999] 3 SCR 3; 1999 Can LII 652 (SCC).

20 This is an employment case, of course. However, similar considerations apply in cases of discrimination in services commonly available to the public. See *B.C. Superintendant of Motor Vehicles v. B.C. Council of Human Rights*, [1999] 3 SCR 868; 1999 CanLII 646 (SCC).

21 [2004] 2 SCR 551; 2004 SCC 47 (CanLII). Paragraph references are to the CanLII citation.

22 R.S.Q., c. C-12.

23 Manitoba has a similar Charter. See chapter 1.

24 RSBC 1995, c. 210, s.9.

25 *Amselem*, para. 37.

26 [1998] R.J.Q. 1892 (C.S.).

27 *Amselem*, para. 48–50.

28 Ibid., para. 135. The judges concurring on this point were Bastarache, Le Bel, and Deschamps JJ.

29 *Supra*, note 22, s.3.

30 Ibid., s. 6.

31 Ibid., s. 1.

32 *Amselem*, para. 84.

33 Ibid., para. 148.

34 See, however, other views in Kathryn Bromley Chan, "The Duelling Narratives of Religious Freedom: A Comment on *Syndicat Northwest v. Amselem*," 43 Alta. L. Rev. 451 (2005–6).

35 [2006] 1 SCR 256; 2006 SCC 6 (CanLII). References are to paragraphs from the CanLII version.

36 Ibid., para. 24–31.

37 It has been noted that *Multani* was a "prime example of substantive equality" in its approach. See Lana K.L. Li, "Cultural Factors in the Law," 44 U.B.C. L. Rev. 111 (2011), at p. 146.
38 *Supra*, note 35, para. 52–6.
39 (1994), [1995] 1 F.C. 158; 1994 CanLII 350 (F.C.).
40 [2005] R.J.Q. 470 (C.S.); 2005 CanLII 746 (QC CS).
41 [2007] 3 SCR 607; 2007 SCC 54 (CanLII). References are to paragraph numbers in the CanLII version.
42 *Bruker*, para. 68.
43 Ibid., para. 63–4.
44 Ibid., para. 79.
45 Ibid., para. 2.
46 Ibid.
47 Ibid., para. 82.
48 Ibid.
49 Ibid., para. 92.
50 Ibid.
51 R. Jukier and S. Van Praagh, writing in "Civil Law and Religion in the Supreme Court of Canada: What Should We *Get* out of *Bruker v. Marcovitz*?" 43 Sup. Ct. L. Rev. 382 (2008), noted, "It is possible to read *Bruker* v. *Marcovitz* as an affirmation of the subjugation of religious doctrine and practice to the state's commitment to gender equality" (at p. 402).
52 S. 33 of the Charter permits a legislature expressly to provide that a statute may operate "notwithstanding" certain Charter provisions, including s. 2 and s. 15.
53 The question of "activist judges" and their shaping of Canadian society is, of course, a much broader debate. For a strong presentation of the view that such actions are anti-democratic, see F.L. Morton and Rainer Knopf, *The Charter Revolution and the Court Party* (University of Toronto Press, 2000). Contrary views are often expressed by the legal profession and the judiciary. See The Honourable Beverley McLachlin C.J.C., "Charter Myths," 33 U.B.C. L. Rev. 23 (1999–2000). While not wanting to distract from the analysis of primary sources, I suggest that analysis of the cases makes clear that despite their protests, judges have often used personal values to shape Canadian civil life. We will see this more directly in the next chapter.
54 F.C. DeCoste, writing in "Caesar's Faith: Limited Government and Freedom of Religions in *Bruker v. Marcovitz*," 32 Dal. L.J. 153 (2009), commented, "we may, I think, expect no relief from the Court's relentless march toward the subordination of private life, its values, practices and

traditions, to the sovereignty of judicially-manufactured state values" (at p. 178).

55 See, for example, Janice Gross Stein, "Searching for Equality" in *Uneasy Partners* (Wilfrid Laurier University Press, 2007).

56 Cited *supra*, note 3.

57 Ibid., pp. 17–21.

58 Of particular concern was the decision in *Multani*, discussed above.

59 *Supra*, note 3, pp. 38–9.

60 Ibid., pp. 23–6.

61 As noted, the Quebec Charter contains both general rights and freedoms and anti-discrimination provisions.

62 See *Amselem* and *Multani, supra.*

63 Bouchard/Taylor Report, *supra*, note 5, pp. 56–7.

64 Consider, for example, the writings of Reginald W. Bibby in such books as *The Emerging Millennials: How Canada's Newest Generation Is Responding to Change and Choice* (Project Canada Books, 2009).

65 I would argue for all the population as, the reader will recall, I take the position that a system of belief is a fundamental part of our consciousness.

66 See Heather M. MacNaughton and Jessie Connell, "A Delicate Balance: The Challenges Faced by Our Democratic Institutions in Reconciling the Competing Rights and Interests of a Diverse Population," 44 U.B.C. L. Rev. 149 (2011), noting at p. 150 that Canada has over two hundred ethnic groups which are also highly religiously diverse.

67 *Supra*, note 3, p. 59.

68 Ibid.

69 Ibid., p. 57. The Canadian Charter has a similar provision.

70 Ibid., p. 46.

71 Ibid., p. 48.

72 Ibid., p. 60. It should be noted, however, that for cultural reasons the Legislative Assembly declined to remove the crucifix. This also points out the complex interaction of culture with religion, a topic that is beyond the scope of what we are trying to do here.

73 *Supra*, note 39.

74 *Supra*, note 16.

75 Of the panel of five, three judges found no violation; two dissented on this point.

76 *Ahmad v. United Kingdom* (1981), 4 EHRR 126.

77 *Karaduman v. Turkey* (1993), 74 DR 93.

78 I have suggested that Canada's approach is preferable, requiring limits to religious freedom to be found only in an analysis of s. 1 of the Charter.

However, M.H. Ogilvie in "Freedom of Religion in Canada and the United Kingdom: A Hopeful Beginning for a Fruitful Dialogue?" 48 Sup. Ct. L. Rev. (2nd) 409 (2009) noted in discussing the House of Lords' adoption of internal limits that "one strength ... is that the choices can be seen to be made as such, whereas the Oakes test obfuscates the personal values chosen by the courts by dressing them up as the logical outcome of a convoluted legal test ... a cloak of legality ... to a value or moral choice" (p. 425).

79 *Begum*, para. 92 and following.

80 Article 9 of the European Convention on Human Rights.

81 *Begum*, para. 97.

82 Several high-profile cases have confronted this issue. See, for example, *B. (S.J.) (Litigation guardian of) v. B.C.* (2005), 42 B.C.L.R. (4th) 321; *Director of Child and Family Services v. A.C.* (2007), 276 D.L.R. (4th) 41 (Man. C.A.).

83 For example, The Child and Family Services Act, SM 1985–6, c.8 – Cap. C80. All provinces have comparable legislation.

84 Mature minors, as well as adults, may be allowed to make their own decisions in such cases. However, courts have been reluctant to give effect to this potential right. See *A.C. v. Manitoba (Director of Child and Family Services)*, 2009 SCC 30 (CanLII).

85 A good summary of the debate on autonomy can be found in Anne Phillips, *Multiculturalism without Culture* (Oxford University Press, 2007), pp. 101–6.

86 Lori G. Beaman, *Defining Harm: Religious Freedom and the Limits of the Law* (UBC Press, 2008).

87 *Bruker*, judgment of Deschamps J., para. 101 and following.

88 There is a question as to the degree to which private institutions, such as religious bodies, should be made to comply with equality provisions of Canadian law. I will say more on this in a later chapter. It is, however, my opinion that at least in circumstances in which one has chosen adherence to a particular group, and when exit from that group is available, one has no right to compel the group to change its character or beliefs. The choice is, rather, to continue in the group under the terms of the group or to leave. Groups have a greater or lesser tolerance for internal dissent.

89 Commentators have raised problems with the idea that preserving an exit is a sufficient answer to cultural practices that Canadian society would consider oppressive. See Anne Phillips, *supra*, note 85, especially chapter 4, "Autonomy, Coercion and Constraint." While I do not deny the problems with providing a genuine ability to exit a culture (or a belief system), it is difficult to construct legally workable alternatives. At least, the legal system must preserve the "exit" option; to improve that option as a realistic

one, a number of strategies are available both legally and socially. One, I suggest, is the presentation of realistic alternatives.

90 While the Criminal Code provisions (*supra*, note 8) speak of polygamy, the issue really centres around polygyny or the marriage of one man to more than one woman. Polygamy also includes polyandry, the marriage of one woman to more than one man.

91 Criminal Code, *supra*, note 8.

92 Boyd Report, *supra*, note 7, p. 3, citing Judy Van Rhijn, "First Steps Taken for Islamic Arbitration Board," Law Times, November 24, 2003.

93 See CTV.ca report, Monday, September 12, 2005, "McGuinty Rules Out Use of Sharia Law in Ontario."

94 Boyd Report, section 4, "Summary of Consultations."

95 See www.nosharia.com, "International Campaign against Shari'a Court in Canada."

96 Boyd Report, section 2, "The Law and Practice of Arbitration."

97 Ibid., section 3, "Family Law and Inheritance Law."

98 Ibid., section 8, "Recommendations."

99 SO 1991, c. 17.

100 Boyd Report, section 4 and section 5, "Constitutional Considerations."

101 Ibid., section 5, p. 72.

102 This approach is consistent with that suggested by Ayelet Shachar in "Religion, State and the Problem of Gender: New Modes of Citizenship and Governance in Diverse Societies," 50 McGill L. J. 49 (2005). The author comments that the "desire to rely on change from within the minority group as the preferred method of achieving gender equality ... avoid[s] the trap of the either-or dilemma, and in the process free[s] women from the excruciating plight of being caught between competing group, state, religious and gender loyalties" (p. 77).

103 The presumption of undue influence in contract law could be applied in some cases. See the classic case, *Allcard v. Skinner* (1887), 36 Ch.D. 145 (C.A.)

104 Boyd Report, section 4, pp. 29–30.

105 Ibid., section 3.

106 *Supra*, note 11.

107 Given the overwhelmingly Judeo-Christian nature of Canadian society at the time, this seems an optimistic conclusion about the sophistication of the motives of parliamentarians.

108 *Supra*, note 11, para. 752.

109 Ibid., para. 1343.

110 Ibid.

111 Ibid., para. 1350.

112 Ibid., para. 555.

113 Ibid., para. 546.

114 Benjamin L. Berger, "Moral Judgment, Criminal Law and the Constitutional Protection of Religion," 40 Sup. Ct. L. Rev. (2nd) 515 (2008), at p. 580.

115 It is in situations such as Bountiful, however, that the question of whether the availability of an exit is a sufficient protection is most forceful. Limits to education and rights to property in the community make exit more costly and less practical. However, see the "Fifth Estate" program, "Bust Up in Bountiful," aired January 25, 2006, in which ex-members Jane Blackmore and Debbie Palmer were interviewed.

116 He did find the provision overly broad in criminalizing behaviour of minors between the age of twelve and seventeen.

117 See Anne Phillips, *supra*, note 85, pp. 119–23 for a discussion of these measures.

118 At the time of writing, the appeal period has passed without an appeal being launched. However, when the matter comes up again, it will likely be in the context of a criminal prosecution, in which case, an appeal judgment is almost certain.

119 Boyd Report, section 4.

120 I will discuss this in the next chapter. A good summary of the difficulty with the presumption that religion be kept out of the public debate can be found in Benjamin Berger, "Law's Religion: Rendering Culture," 45 Osgoode Hall L.J. 277 (2007).

4. When Religion and Politics Intertwine

1 Gerard Bouchard and Charles Taylor, *Building the Future: A Time for Reconciliation* (Gouvernement du Québec, 2008).

2 *Maclean's* magazine, April 28, 2009, "What Canadians Think of Sikhs, Jews, Christians, Muslims ..." by John Geddes. Currently available at http://www2.macleans.ca/2009/04/28/what-canadians-think-of-sikhs-jews-christians-muslims/.

3 See discussion in the Bouchard/Taylor Report, *supra*, note 1, pp. 23–6.

4 See discussion, chapter 3, at pp. 71–7.

5 John Rawls, *Political Liberalism* (Columbia University Press, 2005), pp. 440–90.

6 Benjamin Berger, "Law's Religion: Rendering Culture," 45 Osgoode Hall L.J. 277 (2007).

7 *Supra*, note 5, pp. 22–8. I have already warned the reader that I am not writing a book of political philosophy. Rawls's analysis is far more sophisticated than I am able to convey here briefly. However, simplified versions of his arguments are often used – perhaps misused – to suggest

that religion and conscience belong solely to the sector of the private. My aim is to look at how decisions are actually made by citizens.

8 See Jonathan Chaplin, "Beyond Liberal Restraint: Defending Religiously-Based Arguments in Law and Public Policy," 33 U.B.C. L. Rev. 617 (2000) at p. 640.

9 The difficulty which Rawls and other theorists face has been discussed in the article by Robert P. Kraynak, "Justice without Foundations," 32 The New Atlantic 103 (Summer, 2011), p. 103. He notes the difficulties in preserving ideas of justice and human dignity once reliance on religious belief is ruled out. Of course, his conclusions are highly controversial.

10 See Margaret Somerville, *The Ethical Imagination* (House of Anansi, 2006), pp. 6–7, in which she talks of identifying a shared ethics where belief systems overlap. Even without an overlap of belief, however, I suggest that political decisions will often be made on a shared preferred outcome.

11 R.S.C. 1985, c. C-46, s. 46(2)(a) makes it a crime to use force or violence to overthrow the government of Canada.

12 Although it is sometimes said that equality is the foundation of human rights. For example, Lori G. Beaman, "A Cross National Comparison of Approaches to Religious Diversity" in *Religion and Diversity in Canada*, ed. Lori G. Beaman and Peter Beyer (Brill, 2008), at p. 211: "The beginning place of human rights legislation is equality."

13 *Chamberlain v. Surrey School District No. 36*, [2002] 4 S.C.R. 710; 2002 SCC 86 (CanLII). Further references to the *Chamberlain* decision in the Supreme Court of Canada will be made to *Chamberlain* (SCC); paragraph references are to the CanLII version.

14 See W. Barnett Pearce and Stephen W. Littlejohn, *Moral Conflict: When Social Worlds Collide* (Sage Publications, 1997), pp. 15–18.

15 Ibid., at pp. 75–6.

16 Ibid., at pp. 3–5 where a typical example of moral conflict is described.

17 *Chamberlain v. Surrey School District No. 36*, [2000] 10 W.W.R. 393 (B.C.C.A.); 2000 BCCA 519 (CanLII). See para. 63.

18 *Supra*, note 13. *Chamberlain*, SCC.

19 RSBC 1996, c. 412.

20 Ibid., s. 76.

21 *Supra*, note 17.

22 *Chamberlain v. School District #36 (Surrey)* (1998), 60 BCLR (3d) 311; 1998 CanLII 6723 (BCSC).

23 *Chamberlain* (SCC), para. 19.

24 Ibid., at para. 25.

25 See McLachlin C.J. in *Chamberlain*, para. 4–16. The leading decision on this matter is *New Brunswick Board of Management v. Dunsmuir*, 2008 SCC 9 (CanLII), where the Supreme Court simplified the standard somewhat.

26 *Chamberlain* (SCC), para. 14.

27 See particularly the decision of the trial judge, *supra*, note 22, at para. 94, in which she relied in part on evidence that one of the trustees had "campaigned for several years to promote a greater role for religion in governance of the community."

28 See the decision at trial, *supra*, note 22, para. 86.

29 *Chamberlain* (SCC), para. 55.

30 Ibid., para. 25.

31 Ibid., para. 64–6.

32 Ibid., para 175.

33 The dissenting judgment of Gonthier J. recognizes the disagreement over the word "tolerance," for example.

34 *Zylberberg v. Sudbury Board of Education* (1988), 65 O.R. (2d) 641 (C.A.); 1988 CanLII 189 (ONCA).

35 See chapter 2, p. 48.

36 *Chamberlain* (SCC), para 20.

37 One can think of numerous examples, ranging from attitudes and behaviour around the environment to multiple-partnered families.

38 See the dissenting judgment of Gonthier J. at para. 102–18.

39 [2007] 3 SCR 607; 2007 SCC 54 (CanLII).

40 [2006] 1 SCR 256; 2006 SCC 6 (CanLII).

41 See Bruce MacDougall, "A Respectful Distance: Appellate Courts Consider Religious Motivation of Public Figures in Homosexual Equality Discourse," 35 U.B.C. L. Rev. 511 (2001–2), and in a similar vein, his "Silence in the Classroom: Limits on Homosexual Expression and Visibility in Education and the Privileging of Homophobic Religious Ideology," 61 Sask. L. Rev. 41 (1998).

42 *Trinity Western University v. British Columbia College of Teachers*, [2001] 1 S.C.R. 772; 2001 SCC 31 (CanLII). Citations are to paragraphs in the CanLII version.

43 Ibid., para. 4.

44 Although none of the court discussed this implication. As noted earlier, the majority judgment in *Chamberlain* made little reference to freedom of religion and conscience. In *Trinity Western University*, the application of s. 2(a) of the Charter was central.

45 *Trinity Western University*, para. 36. The interesting question might be whether signing the pledge of conduct was not taking action on their

beliefs (L'Heureux-Dubé J. held that it was) and also whether or how one would "take action" on the pledge other than by refraining oneself from the prohibited behaviour – surely not discriminatory conduct. These issues were unexplored by the majority. The judgment, however, is often cited for the proposition that the freedom to believe something is broader than the freedom to act upon that belief.

46 Ibid., para 38.
47 As Janet Epp Buckingham has said in "Caesar and God: Limits to Religious Freedom in Canada and South Africa," 15 Sup. Ct. L. Rev. (2nd) 462 (2000) at p. 487, the dissent was "not so much a 'balancing' as a dismissal of the claims of TWU and its students."
48 Ibid., para 80.
49 Ibid., para 69.
50 For another perspective, see Patricia Hughes, "The Intersection of Public and Private under the Charter," 52 U.N.B. L.J. 201 (2003), in which she criticized the majority, arguing for public control of "private decisions" with "public consequences."
51 *Ross v. New Brunswick School District No. 15* (1991), 121 N.B.R. (2d) 361 (Q.B.); (1993), 142 N.B.R. (2d) 1 (C.A.); [1996] 1 S.C.R. 825; 1996 CanLII 237 (SCC). References to the decision of the Supreme Court of Canada are to paragraph numbers in the CanLII version.
52 Ibid., para. 45.
53 Ibid., para 39.
54 Ibid., para. 46, quoting from *Fraser v. Public Service Staff Relations Board*, [1985] 2 S.C.R. 455.
55 Ibid., para. 71.
56 For a contrary view, see Stuart Ryan, "Malcolm Ross and Free Speech," 41 U.N.B. L.J. 311 (1992). The difficulty with requiring Mr Ross to be fired if he continued anti-Semitic publications, which the author does not acknowledge, is that unless these publications cross the border of hate speech, they are not necessarily illegal, however objectionable they may be.
57 *Supra*, note 51, para. 107.
58 Ibid., para. 89–93.
59 Ibid., para. 94.
60 Ibid., para. 44.
61 Ibid., para. 45.
62 (2005), 255 D.L.R. (4th) 169 (B.C.C.A.); 2005 BCCA 327 (CanLII). References are to paragraph numbers in the CanLII verson.
63 Ibid., at para. 50.
64 Ibid., at para. 33.

65 Ibid., at para. 34–5.
66 Ibid., at para. 44–5.
67 Ibid., at para. 76.
68 *Supra*, note 62.
69 (2006), 267 D.L.R. (4th) 733 (Sask. C.A.); 2006 SKCA 41 (CanLII). Paragraph references are to the CanLII version.
70 Ibid., at para. 6. The references were Romans 1:26, Leviticus 18:22, Leviticus 20:13, and 1 Corinthians 6:9–10.
71 S.S. 1979, c. S-24.1.
72 Ibid., s. 14(1)(b).
73 *Owens*, para. 1.
74 (2002), 228 Sask. R. 148 (Q.B.).
75 [1990] 3 SCR 892.
76 Following its own decision, as well, in *Saskatchewan (Human Rights Commission) v. Bell*, [1994] 5 W.W.R. 460 (Sask. C.A.).
77 *Owens*, at para. 75–81.
78 Ibid., at para. 66.
79 (2008), 289 D.L.R. (4th) 506 (Sask. C.A.). Leave to appeal to the Supreme Court of Canada was refused; Docket # 32524, 2008-05-29.
80 The recent S.C.C. decision in *Saskatchewan v. Whatcott*, 2013 SCC 11 (CanLII) was released just as this manuscript was going to press. It affirmed the approach of *Taylor*, but rendered inoperative the words of the section prohibiting speech that did not promote hatred.
81 (1996), 139 D.L.R. (4th) 480 (B.C.S.C.).
82 Access to Abortion Services Act, R.S.B.C. 1996, c.1.
83 (2008), 298 D.L.R. (4th) 317; 2008 BCCA 340 (CanLII). References are to paragraphs in the CanLII version.
84 Ibid., at para. 82.
85 *Supra*, note 34. See earlier discussion, chapter 2.
86 *R. v. Big M Drug Mart*, [1985] 1 S.C.R. 295. See chapter 2.
87 [1986] 2 S.C.R. 713.
88 2009 SCC 37 (CanLII). References are to paragraphs in the CanLII version.
89 Seven judges sat on the case. The split was 4–3.
90 (2006), 57 Alta. L.R. (4th) 300 (Q.B.)
91 (2007), 77 Alta. L.R. (4th) 281 (C.A.). If you count all the judges who heard the case – one Q.B. judge and three on the Court of Appeal (one of whom dissented) – six out of the eleven would have found in favour of the Colony.
92 The issue of an infringement was conceded by the government. McLachlin C.J. pointed out that no real inquiry had been held into whether the infringement was more than trivial or insubstantial and the point did not

seem to have been conceded. But she proceeded as if the point had been established. This may suggest a new and more stringent approach to what constitutes an infringement sufficient to engage the Charter protection.

93 *Hutterian Brethren* (SCC), at para. 41–7.

94 Ibid., at para. 48–52.

95 Aharon Barak, "Proportional Effect: The Israeli Experience," 57 U.T.L.R. 369 (2007).

96 *Hutterian Brethren* (SCC), at para. 55.

97 McLachlin C.J. used the phrase twenty-one times in her judgment. See para. 56.

98 Ibid., at para. 60.

99 Ibid., at para. 56.

100 See the dissenting judgment of Abella J. at para. 158.

101 *Supra*, note 91, at para. 41.

102 Ibid., at para. 44.

103 The court's acceptance of the government's stated objectives has been widely criticized. For example, Howard Kilowicz, Richard Haigh, and Adrienne Ng in "Calculations of Conscience: The Costs and Benefits of Religious and Conscientious Freedom," 48 Alta L. Rev. 679 (2011), note that the Court appeared "enamored" with government data (at p. 698). Marshall Haughey, in "The Camera and the Colony: A Comment on *Alberta v. Hutterian Brethren of Wilson Colony*," 74 Sask. L. Rev. 59 (2011), wrote that the "majority seemed to prefer theoretical reasoning over established evidence" (at p. 60).

104 *Supra*, note 40.

105 *Hutterian Brethren* (S.C.C.), at para. 69. Professor Benjamin Berger, in "Section 1, Constitutional Reasoning and Cultural Difference: Assessing the Impacts of *Alberta v. Hutterian Brethren of Wilson Colony*," 51 Sup. Ct. L. Rev. (2nd) 25 (2010), suggested difficulty in foreseeing the "sheer scope of possible conflict between religious and government objectives" (at p. 28). With respect to Professor Berger, I suggest the problem is less extensive and less unpredictable than he or the court suggests.

106 Ibid., at para. 90.

107 Richard Moon, "Accommodation without Compromise: Comment on *Alberta v. Hutterian Brethren of Wilson Colony*," 51 Sup. Ct. L. Rev. (2nd) 95 (2010), at p. 115.

108 *Supra*, note 87, 1986 CanLII 12 (S.C.C.).

109 Ibid., at para. 148.

110 See chapter 1 and chapter 3 for more detailed discussion of the test.

111 *Hutterian Brethren* (SCC), at para. 76.

112 This aspect of the case has been widely criticized. Professor Moon, *supra*, note 107, at p. 95 stated that the court "understate[d] the impact of the requirement." Professors Kilowicz, Haigh, and Ng, *supra*, note 103 noted at p. 700 that the court downplayed the effect of the denial of the exemption and concluded, "They have been wronged" (p. 714). Professor Haughey, *supra*, note 103, states that the court "does not fully consider … the practical realities of the Hutterites' rural way of life" (p. 79).

113 *Supra*, note 88, at para. 98.

114 *Supra*, note 40, at para. 40.

115 *Supra*, note 40.

116 *Syndicat Northcrest v. Amselem*, [2003] 2 S.C.R. 551.

117 *Grant v. Canada (Attorney-General)* (1994), [1995] 1 F.C. 158.

5. Human Rights: A Zero Sum Game?

1 The Constitution Act, 1982, being Schedule B to the Canada Act 1982 (U.K.), 1982, c. 11, Part I.

2 For example, *Syndicat Northcrest v. Amselem*, [2004] 2 SCR 551 was a decision about private rights under the Quebec Charter. However, the Supreme Court noted that its reasoning would have been applicable to a case under the Canadian Charter.

3 Canadian Human Rights Act, R.S.C. 1985, c. H-6.

4 The Human Rights Code, C.C.S.M., c. H175, s. 9 (2).

5 Saskatchewan Human Rights Code, S.S. 1979, c. S-24.1, s. 13(1) and s. 16(1).

6 Human Rights Code, R.S.B.C. 1996, c. 210, s. 13(4).

7 *Supra*, note 5, s. 16(7).

8 *Supra*, note 6, s. 41.

9 For example, the Saskatchewan act, *supra*, note 5.

10 Human Rights Code, R.S.O. 1990, c. H.19, s. 11(2) and (3).

11 The point was established in *Andrews v. Law Society of British Columbia*, [1989] 1 SCR 143 and has been repeated in numerous cases.

12 *Law v. Canada (Minister of Employment and Immigration)*, [1999] 1 SCR 497; 1999 CanLII 675 (SCC). Paragraph references are to the CanLII version.

13 Ibid., para. 51.

14 Ibid., para. 62 and following.

15 For a review of the various positions, see Donna Greschner, "Does *Law* Advance the Cause of Equality?," 27 Queen's L.J. 299 (2001).

16 [2008] 2 S.C.R. 483; 2008 SCC 41 (CanLII); paragraph references are to the CanLII version.
17 Ibid., at para. 21–4.
18 Alberta Human Rights Act, R.S.A. 2000, c. A-25.5, s. 7(1)(a) and (b).
19 *Supra*, note 6, s. 1.
20 See *Nixon v. Vancouver Rape Relief*, [2006] 4 W.W.R. 213 (B.C.C.A.).
21 *McGill University Health Centre (Montreal General Hospital) v. Syndicat des employés de l'Hôpital général de Montréal*, [2007] 1 SCR 161.
22 [2009] 1 W.W.R. 274 (B.C.C.A.).
23 [2009] 2 SCR 567; 2009 SCC 37 (CanLII); paragraph references are to the CanLII version.
24 Ibid., at para. 105–8.
25 Ibid., at para. 108.
26 In 1841, the act unifying Upper and Lower Canada made allowances for religious diversity.
27 Some commentators have, however, supported the importance of human dignity as a foundational concept. See Lorne Sossin, "The 'Supremacy of God,' Human Dignity and the Charter of Rights and Freedoms," 52 U.N.B. L.J. 227 (2003), in which he states, "The concept of human dignity represents a key normative aspiration of Charter jurisprudence" (p. 228).
28 See Robert P. Kraynak, "Justice without Foundations," 32 The New Atlantic 103 (Summer, 2011).
29 Professor Sossin, *supra*, note 27, agrees that the concept is "inherently subjective" (at p. 230).
30 *Supra*, note 12, at para. 53, Iacobucci J. stated, "Human dignity means that an individual or group *feels* self-respect and self-worth" (emphasis mine).
31 See Greschner, *supra* note 15.
32 For a similar approach, see Christopher L. Eisgruber and Lawrence G. Sager, *Religious Freedom and the Constitution* (Harvard University Press, 2007). They employ a concept of "equal liberty" which, they note "does not ask whether and when religion is good or bad. Equal liberty seeks to set fair terms of co-operation for a religiously diverse people who accept the obligation to treat one another with respect as equal members of our political community" (at p. 158).
33 [1985] 2 SCR 536; 1985 CanLII 18 (SCC). Paragraph references are to the CanLII version.
34 Ibid., discussed at para. 6–8.
35 Ibid., discussed at para. 8–9.
36 This issue was later resolved with the court deciding that the two types of discrimination should be treated in the same way.

37 *Supra*, note 33, at para. 20–9.
38 [1992] 2 SCR 970.
39 Ibid. The union as well as the employer had a duty to accommodate and neither could contract out of human rights legislation.
40 [1994] 2 S.C.R. 525.
41 (2000), 50 O.R. (3d) 560 (C.A.).
42 *Supra*, note 12.
43 *Supra*, note 16.
44 *Van Der Smit v. Alberta* (2009), 4 Alta. L.R. (5th) 372 (Q.B.); 2009 ABQB 121 (CanLII). Paragraph references are to the CanLII version.
45 Ibid., at para. 70–2.
46 *Supra*, note 23.
47 *Supra*, note 44, at para. 81–7.
48 In May, 2008, the CFS passed a motion supporting student societies who wished to deny support to pro-life campus clubs. See *The Martlet*, November 5, 2008, "Students Can Deny Clubs Status: Court."
49 See, for example, the University Act, R.S.B.C. 1996, c. 468, s. 27.1.
50 *Bartram v. Okanagan University College Students' Association – Kelowna*, 2005 BCHRT 174.
51 *Macapagal and Others v. Capilano College Students' Union (No. 2)*, 2008 BCHRT 13.
52 *Gray and Others v. University of British Columbia Students' Union – Okanagan (No. 2)*, 2008 BCHRT 16.
53 *Gray v. UBC Students' Union*, 2008 BCSC 1530 (CanLII).
54 Ibid., at para. 13.
55 *University of British Columbia v. Berg*, [1993] 2 SCR 353.
56 The court applied a relationship test. The university supplied a service to its students and the incidents at issue were part of that public relationship.
57 Mark Steyn, *America Alone: The End of the World As We Know It* (Regnery Press, 2006).
58 Numerous editorials can be cited here. The controversy is ongoing. See, for example, George Jonas, "Freedom's Panhandlers," *National Post*, March 3, 2010.
59 Richard Moon, "Report to the Canadian Human Rights Commission Concerning Section 13 of the Canadian Human Rights Act and the Regulation of Hate Speech on the Internet" (2008), posted on the website of the Canadian Human Rights Commission, www.chrc-ccdp.gc.ca. The recommendation for repeal is found in section 6 of the report.
60 *Supra*, note 10, s. 13.
61 April 9, 2008. Posted on the website of the Ontario Human Rights Commission, www.ohrc.on.ca.

62 *Supra*, note 3. Bill C-304 was passed by the House of Commons in the summer of 2012 and will, if passed by the Senate, repeal s. 13 of the Human Rights Act. At time of writing, the bill had passed first reading in the Senate.
63 *Owens v. Human Rights Tribunal of Saskatchewan* (2006), 267 D.L.R. (4th) 733 (SKCA).
64 *Canada (Human Rights Commission) v. Taylor*, [1990] 3 S.C.R. 892.
65 The constitutionality of these sections was again under attack in a case heard by the Supreme Court of Canada in late 2011. See p. 263, note 80.
66 *Canadian Islamic Congress v. Rogers Media Inc.*, CHRC 20071008.
67 *Supra*, note 6.
68 *Elmasry and Habib v. Roger's Publishing and MacQueen (No. 4)*, 2008 BCHRT 378.
69 Ezra Levant, *Shakedown: How Our Government Is Undermining Democracy in the Name of Human Rights* (McClelland and Stewart 2009).
70 *Supra*, note 59.
71 See also his paper, "The Attack on Human Rights Commissions and the Corruption of Public Discourse," 73 Sask. L. Rev. 93 (2010), in which he also suggested that claims by Steyn and Levant were overstated.
72 *Supra*, note 59, "Introduction, b) Summary of Recommendations."
73 Ibid., section 5, "The Role of Non-State Actors in the Prevention of Hate Speech."
74 (1988), 65 O.R. (2d) 641 (C.A.); 1988 CanLII 189 (ON CA). Page references are to the CanLII version.
75 Ibid., p. 40–1.
76 Ibid.; the dissenting judgment begins after p. 41 and is numbered separately.
77 Ibid., p. 44.
78 Ibid., p. 44–5. He would have granted an order of prohibition against the practice of the Sudbury Board, although he noted that this was not what the parents were requesting.
79 Those of us who recall such opening exercises, however, may be permitted to doubt that much religious purpose was served by them.
80 *Supra*, note 23.
81 And I have argued in the last chapter that this result may occur as an unintended consequence of the *Wilson Colony* decision where the court is considering legislative or regulatory actions under s. 15.
82 2010 QCCS 2631 (CanLII).
83 Ibid., para. 25.
84 Ibid., para. 54.

85 *S.L. and D.J. v. Commission scholaire des Chênes and Attorney General of Quebec,* 2012 SCC 7 (CanLII).
86 Ibid., para. 35.
87 1985 CanLII 69 (SCC).
88 *Freitag v. Penetanguishene,* 1999 CanLII 3786 (ON SC).
89 Although, as I noted in chapter 2, there was a perfectly good argument in *Big M Drug Mart* that the provision imposed a burden on those practising other faiths, this was not key to the decision.
90 In fact, this would be to import a "non-establishment" clause into Canadian law, something our Charter did not do.
91 *Supra,* note 85, para. 32.
92 Ibid., para. 30.
93 Ibid., para. 32.
94 *Quebec v. Loyola High School,* 2012 QCCA 2139 (CanLII).

6. Conflicting Rights: A Balancing Act?

1 *Dagenais v. Canadian Broadcasting Corporation,* [1994] 3 SCR 835 at p. 877. This is only one of the many times the Supreme Court of Canada has made this point. See also *Reference Re Same-Sex Marriage,* [2004] 3 SCR 698, 2004 SCC 79 (CanLII).
2 Later in this chapter, we will look at cases in which the court is said to have "balanced" the right. I should also note at this point that the court of course does sometimes limit the remedy requested, as when it awards a lesser amount of damages or narrows the scope of the remedy. However, it remains in essence a "win/lose" proposition.
3 *Balancing Conflicting Rights: Towards and Analytical Framework,* www.ohr. on.ca/en/resources/discussion_consultation/balancingrights. The author of the paper is not listed. The commission notes that the views in the paper are not necessarily its own views.
4 [2001] 1 SCR 772, 2001 SCC 31 (CanLII). Paragraph citations are from the CanLII version.
5 Ibid., at para 36.
6 Ibid., at para. 38.
7 The court suggested that specific files of graduates and opinions of principals might have been solicited. However, the evidentiary problems would have been substantial.
8 The dissent in the case by L'Heureux-Dubé suggests something of this sort. See chapter 3.

9 See for example Benjamin Berger, "The Limits of Belief: Freedom of Religion, Secularism and the Liberal State," 1 Can. J. of Law and Society 39 (2002), at p. 60.
10 See comment by Iain Benson, director of the Centre for Cultural Renewal, "Pluralism and the Respect for Religious Freedom," LexView 46.0.
11 See *Balancing Conflicting Rights*, *supra*, note 3.
12 See discussion in chapter 7 on conscience and medical ethics.
13 [1984] 2 SCR 603, 1984 CanLII 128 (SCC). Page references are to the CanLII verson.
14 R.S.B.C. 1979, c. 186.
15 Ibid., s. 8.
16 Human Rights Code, R.S.B.C. 1996, c. 210, s. 13.
17 Now found in s. 13(4).
18 Then s. 22; now found in s. 41.
19 *Supra*, note 13, at p. 624–5.
20 Ibid., at p. 628.
21 Ibid., at p. 626.
22 An exception to this may be found in the statutes of Quebec, Saskatchewan, and Manitoba, which also contain sections conferring rights upon citizens in terms similar to the Charter of Rights. As we will see in the next chapter, only Quebec appears to recognize this feature as broadening the application of the human rights legislation.
23 2008 HRTO 22 (CanLII).
24 *Ontario Human Rights Commission v. Christian Horizons*, 2010 ONSC 2105 (CanLII).
25 R.S.O. 1990, c. H. 19.
26 Ibid., s. 24(1)(b).
27 Ibid., s. 24(1)(a).
28 *Supra*, note 23, para. 117.
29 Ibid., para. 132–55.
30 *Supra*, note 24, para. 57–66.
31 Ibid., para. 73.
32 *Supra*, note 23, para. 161–202.
33 *Supra*, note 24, para. 79–106.
34 Ibid., at para. 93.
35 Ibid., at para. 64–5.
36 It would appear that supervisors or managers who set policy for the organization could be required to share the precepts of the evangelical belief. See ibid., at para. 66 and 93.
37 *Supra*, note 23, para. 203–40.

38 *Supra*, note 24, para. 107–12.
39 *Supra*, note 23, para. 158–9.
40 An excellent review of the problems of religious organizations and employment discrimination in Canada can be found in Professor Alvin Esau's paper "Islands of Exclusivity: Religious Organizations and Employment Discrimination," 33 U.B.C. L. Rev. 719 (1999–2000). The author comments on p 719 that some of the greatest difficulties arise with respect to lifestyle issues.
41 See the comments of the court, *supra*, note 24, at para. 70–2.
42 The court seemed to recognize this at para. 104. Interestingly, other parts of the lifestyle statement, such as smoking and drinking alcohol, expressly referred to conduct within the observation of the residents and did not seem to require total abstention, provided it was not done in a setting that undermined the organization's principles.
43 The court commented that Ms Heintz remained a Christian and participated in prayer and Bible readings at work. *Supra*, note 24, at para. 101.
44 U.S. Supreme Court, No. 10-553, January 11, 2012.
45 For example, see the Ontario Human Rights Code, *supra*, note 25, s. 14.
46 For a comment on the Board of Inquiry decision, see Bradley Miller, "Case Comment *Brillinger* v. *Brockie*," 33 U.B.C. L. Rev. 825 (1999–2000). Mr Miller suggests that the so-called "balancing of rights" "suggests a quantitative and value-free analysis and tends to obscure the controversial and necessarily moral nature of the judgment" (p. 832).
47 *Brockie v. Ontario Human Rights Commission* (2002), 222 D.L.R. (4th) 174, [2002] O.J. No. 2375 (Ont. D.C.) (Q.L.).
48 Ibid., para. 33–5.
49 Ibid., para. 51.
50 *Owens v. Saskatchewan (Human Rights Commission)*.
51 *Supra*, note 47, para. 42.
52 Ibid., para. 57–8.
53 [2005] B.C. H.R.T. D. No. 544.
54 Ibid., para. 24–6.
55 *Supra*, note 15, s. 8.
56 See *Multani v. Commission scholaire Marguerite-Bourgeoys*, [2006] 1 SCR 256.
57 *Supra*, note 53, para. 53–91.
58 Ibid., at para. 106–28.
59 *Hall (Litigation Guardian of) v. Powers* (2002), 59 O.R. (3d) 423 (S.C.), [2002] CanLII 49475 (ON SC). Paragraph references are to the CanLII version.
60 *RJR-McDonald Inc. v. Canada (Attorney General)*, [1994] 1 SCR 311 sets out the test and is cited by the court in *Hall* at para. 11.

61 *Hall v. Durham Catholic District School Board* (2005), 80 O.R. (3d) 462 (S.C.).
62 *Supra*, note 59, at para. 30.
63 Ibid., para. 31.
64 Ibid., para. 49.
65 See the discussion of *Loyola High School* in the preceding chapter.
66 *Supra*, note 61.
67 Zoe Oxaal, "Second-Guessing the Bishop: Section 93, the Charter, and the 'Religious Government Actor' in the Gay Prom Date Case," 66 Sask. L. Rev. 455 (2003), at p. 481.
68 Bruce MacDougall, "The Separation of Church and Date: Destabilizing Traditional Religion-Based Legal Norms on Sexuality," 36 U.B.C. L. Rev. 1 (2003), at p. 7.
69 Alberta Human Rights Tribunal, Complaint No. S. 2002/08-0137.
70 *Boissoin v. Lund*, 2009 ABQB 592 (CanLII).
71 *Canada v. Taylor*, [1990] 3 S.C.R. 892.
72 *Supra*, note 70, at para. 149. See also p. 263, note 80.
73 Ibid., at para. 31–8.
74 *Lund v. Boissoin*, 2012 ABCA 300 (CanLII).
75 Ibid., para. 42.
76 *Supra*, note 14, s. 3(a).
77 Ibid., s. 3(c), (d), and (e).
78 *Supra*, note 25, Preamble.
79 Ibid.

7. Freedom of Conscience: The Forgotten Human Right

1 See *supra*, chapter 3.
2 *Catechism of the Catholic Church* (Doubleday, 1997) paragraph 1777.
3 Charter s. 27 recognizes Canada's multicultural heritage.
4 *Egan v. Canada*, [1995] 2 S.C.R. 513.
5 *Vriend v. Alberta*, [1998] 1 S.C. 493.
6 In *Egan*, the government conceded that sexual orientation was protected by s. 15. However, the court commented that it agreed with the concession because sexual orientation was a "deeply personal characteristic that is either unchangeable or changeable only at unacceptable personal costs."
7 Chapter 7.
8 *Hutterian Brethren of Wilson Colony v. Alberta*, *supra*, chapter 4.
9 See *Holy Post*, December 16, 2011.
10 See Christopher Tollefsen, "Conscience, Religion and the State," Am. J. Juris 54 (2009).

11 *R. v. Latimer*, 1995 CanLII 3993 (SK CA). This point was not appealed to the Supreme Court of Canada, which ordered a new trial on the basis that the Crown had improperly questioned jurors ([1997] 1 SCR 217).
12 [1993] 3 SCR 519.
13 [1988] 1 SCR 30.
14 *The Guardian*, http://www.guardian.co.uk/, March 31, 2010.
15 BBC News, http://www.bbc.co.uk/, May 19, 2010.
16 See the *Montreal Gazette*, montrealgazette.com, March 27, 2010.
17 Macleans.ca, About Face, April 7, 2010.
18 Ibid.
19 CBC News, December 12, 2011. The minister noted that the veil was not a religious requirement but a cultural tradition. Available at http://www.cbc.ca/news/canada/story/2011/12/12/pol-kenny-citizenship-rules.html.
20 Macleans.ca, "Tempest in a Niqab," March 24, 2010.
21 Ottawacitizen.com.
22 [2009] 2 S.C.R. 567.
23 There is a substantial literature detailing this debate. See, for example, A. Gold, "Physicians' 'Right of Conscience' – Beyond Politics," 38 Journal of Law, Medicine and Ethics 1 (2010); Suzanne Davis and Paul Lansing, "When Two Fundamental Rights Collide at the Pharmacy: The Struggle to Balance the Consumer's Right to Access Contraception and the Pharmacist's Right of Conscience," 12 DePaul Journal of Health Care Law 67 (2009); Kimberly A. Parr, "Beyond Politics: A Social and Cultural History of Federal Health Care Conscience Protections, 35 American Journal of Law and Medicine 4 (2009) at p. 620; Tollefson, *supra*, note 10.
24 *C v. Dr. A, Dr. B and Dr. C*, 2002 BCHRT 23. See also the earlier decision in *Moore v. British Columbia (Ministry of Social Services)*, 1992 B.C.C.H.R.D. No. 15.
25 *Ontario Human Rights Commission v. Christian Horizons*, 2010 ONSC 2105 (CanLII).
26 We will later discuss whether the failure to protect conscience in human rights statutes might, in itself, violate the Charter.
27 *McFarlane v. Relate Avon Limited*, [2010] EWCA Civ. B1 (April 29, 2010).
28 Paragraph 3(1)(a) and (b).
29 [2009] EWCA Civ 1357.
30 Human Rights Code, R.S.B.C. 1996, c. 210, s. 13(4).
31 *British Columbia (Public Service Employee Relations Commission) v. BCGSEU*, [1999] 3 SCR 3. The test laid out by the Supreme Court required that it is "impossible" to accommodate individuals sharing the characteristic without imposing undue hardship on the employer.

32 *Supra*, note 25.

33 Human Rights Code, R.S.O. 1990, c. H.19.

34 *Supra*, note 24.

35 See http://www.ohrc.on.ca/en/submission-ontario-human-rights-commission-college-physicians-and-surgeons-ontario-regarding-draft-0.

36 See ibid., in section entitled "Moral or Religious Beliefs."

37 The *National Post* reported this at LifeSiteNews.com, Monday, September 15, 2008.

38 *Physicians and the Ontario Human Rights Code*, Policy Statement 5 – 08, College of Physicians and Surgeons of Ontario.

39 The point has been repeated many times. But see *Reference Re Same Sex Marriage*, [2004] 3 S.C.R. 698; 2004 SCC 79 (CanLII).

40 See Tollefson, *supra*, note 10; See also Iain Benson, *Physicians, Patients, Human Rights and Referrals: A Principled Approach to Respecting the Rights of Patients and Physicians in Ontario*, Submission to the College of Physicians and Surgeons in Ontario, September 12, 2008.

41 See discussion in chapter 6.

42 See, for example, *Barbeau v. British Columbia (Attorney-General)*, 2003 BCCA 51 (CanLII); *Halpern v. Canada (Attorney General)*, 2002 CanLII 42749 (ON. S.C.D.C.).

43 The decisions were not without their critics. See F.C. DeCoste, "The Halpern Transformation: Same-Sex Marriage, Civil Society and the Limits of Liberal Law," 41 Alta. L. Rev. 619 (2003–4).

44 *Supra*, note 39. Paragraph references are to the CanLII version.

45 The use of the reference procedure, which we see here and will consider again later in the chapter, has been seriously criticized as being "used by one branch to obtain a quasi-legal result outside of ordinary and available legal processes." See Carissima Mathen, "Mutability and Method in the Marriage Reference," 43 U.N.B. L.J. (2005), at p. 61. The reader will recall that technically reference decisions are not legally binding.

46 *Supra,* note 39, para. 2. A fourth question was also raised specific to Quebec, but the court declined to answer it for reasons that are not relevant to our discussion.

47 It has been suggested that the court was clear in stating that "religious freedom is in no way threatened by the Federal government's proposed Act." See Bruce Ryder, "State Neutrality and Freedom of Conscience and Religion," 29 Sup. Ct. L. Rev. (2nd) 169 (2005), at p. 198. The comment appears ironic in light of the decision of the Saskatchewan Court of Appeal noted *infra*, note 79.

48 *Supra*, note 39, para. 1.

49 Ibid., para. 55.
50 Ibid., para. 58.
51 Ibid., para. 59.
52 *M.J. v. Nichols* (2008), 63 C.H.R.R. D/145 (Sask. H.R.T.).
53 *Orville Nichols v. M.J.*, 2009 SKQB 299 (CanLII).
54 Ibid., para. 29.
55 The Marriage Act, 1995, S.S. 1995, c. M-41.
56 *Supra*, note 53, para. 16.
57 The Saskatchewan Human Rights Code, S.S. 1979, c. S-24.1.
58 *Supra*, note 53, at para. 30–3.
59 Ibid., at para. 39 and 57.
60 Ibid., para. 41–57.
61 Ibid., para. 67.
62 The citation, of course, is from *Trinity Western University v. B.C.C.T.*, [2001] 1 S.C.R. 772 at para. 36. The discussion in *Nichols* took place at para. 72.
63 *Nichols*, ibid., at para. 73.
64 In support of this conclusion, see Bruce MacDougall, "Refusing to Offici-ate at Same-Sex Civil Marriages," 69 Sask. L. Rev. 351 (2006), in which he argues that by tolerating officials "who refuse to accord a benefit to same-sex couples, the government would effectively be accepting for itself such views." Why accommodation of divergent beliefs implies acceptance of those beliefs he does not explain. See *contra*, Trotter, *infra*, note 67.
65 *Supra*, note 53, at para. 53. Section 30 of the Marriage Act, *supra*, note 55, al-lows the commission to be limited by religion or nationality.
66 *Supra*, note 57.
67 It has also been noted that "Rights-bearing citizens do not lose their human rights when they enter public employment." See Geoffry Trotter, "The Right to Decline Performance of Same-Sex Civil Marriages: The Duty to Accommodate Public Servants. A Response to Prof. Bruce MacDougall," 70 Sask. L. Rev. 365 (2007), at p. 385.
68 *Mulluni v. Commission Scholaire Marguerite-Bourgeoys*, [2006] 1 S.C.R. 256.
69 *Supra*, note 57.
70 See *Syndicat Northcrest v. Amselem*, [2004] 2 S.C.R. 551, where Mr Amselem successfully asserted his right to freedom of religion against his condomin-ium board. See our discussion in chapter 3.
71 See *Nichols*, *supra*, note 53, at para. 16.
72 See *Gordy v. Painter's Lodge (Oak Bay Marina Ltd.)*, 2000 BCHRT 16, reversed on other grounds 2002 BCCA 495.
73 Ibid. See also *Nixon v. Vancouver Rape Relief Society*, 2002 BCHRT 1. For a general discussion of the issue, see Stephanie D. James and Carolyn M.

MacEachern, "The Scope of Section 13," Continuing Legal Education Society of B.C., Human Rights Conference, 2008.
74 See *Nichols*, para. 8.
75 Charles Lewis, "Gay Marriage Refusal Case Tests Rights," *National Post*, May 10, 2010, quoting Abby Deshman, a lawyer for the Canadian Civil Liberties Association.
76 See F.C. DeCoste, *supra*, note 43 at p. 631.
77 See also F.C. DeCoste, "Courting Leviathan: Limited Government and Social Freedom in *Reference Re Same-Sex Marriage*," 42 Alta. L. Rev. 1099 (2004–5).
78 *Supra*, note 55.
79 See *Hutterian Brethren of Wilson Colony*, [2009] 2 S.C.R. 567.
80 *Re Marriage Commissioners Appointed under the Marriage Act*, 2011 SKCA 3 (Can LII).
81 Ibid., para. 41.
82 Ibid., para. 50.
83 S.C. 2005, c. 33.
84 *Supra*, note 80, para. 93.
85 Ibid., para. 95–6.
86 See MacDougall, *supra*, note 64, at p. 365.
87 For a discussion on the potentially broad scope of freedom of conscience, see David M. Brown, "Neutrality or Privilege? A Comment on Religious Freedom," 29 Sup. Ct. L. Rev. (2nd) 221 (2005).

8. Can We Change? (And Why We Should)

1 See the work by Nobel Prize winner Daniel Kahneman, popularized in his recent book, *Thinking Fast and Slow* (Doubleday Canada, 2011).
2 C. Edwin Baker, "Rawls, Equality and Democracy," 34 Philosophy and Social Criticism 203 (2008) at p. 222. Of course, as in all formulations of democracy and its limits, the various general words such as "purposefully," "reasonable," and "necessary" can be the subject of endless debate.
3 See the discussion in chapter 4, under "A Tale of Two Teachers" and in the same chapter, "The Protest Cases."
4 See chapter 7.
5 See chapter 3, under "The Accommodation Cases."
6 The Charter, s. 1.
7 For a discussion of this test, see particularly chapter 2, under "Preferential Religious Treatment and the Canadian Charter." See also chapter 4, under "When the Legislature Has Spoken."

8 See discussion in chapter 4 relating to *Alberta v. Hutterian Brethren of Wilson Colony*, 2009 SCC 37 (CanLII).

9 *R. v. Oakes*, [1986] 1 S.C.R. 103.

10 See chapter 2, under "The Seminal Case," discussion of *R. v. Big M Drug Mart*, [1985], 1 S.C.R. 285, and later in that same chapter, under "The Consequences of *Big M Drug Mart*."

11 See discussion in chapter 3.

12 See discussion of the Ontario Human Rights Commission, for example, cited in chapter 5, the Commission's *Statement concerning Issues Raised by Complaints against Maclean's Magazine*.

13 A discussion of this repeal is reviewed in chapter 5. It also may be the case that the provisions, under challenge in the S.C.C., may be struck down as unconstitutional.

14 *Vriend v. Alberta*, [1998] 1 S.C.R. 493, discussed in chapter 7.

15 Reported, *inter alia*, in the *National Post*, Friday, June 4, 2010.

16 Marci McDonald, *The Armageddon Factor: The Rise of Christian Nationalism in Canada* (Random House Canada, 2010).

17 See W. Barnett Pearce and Stephen W. Littlejohn, *Moral Conflict: When Social Worlds Collide* (Sage Publications, 1997), discussed in chapter 4.

18 Peter D. Lauwers, "Religion and the Ambiguities of Liberal Pluralism: A Canadian Perspective," 37 Sup. Ct. L. Rev. (2nd) 1 (2007).

19 Ibid., at p. 45.

Bibliography

Books

Beaman, Lori G. *Defining Harm: Religious Freedom and the Limits of the Law.* UBC Press, 2008.

Beaman, Lori G., and Peter Beyer, eds. *Religion and Diversity in Canada.* Brill, 2008.

Blackstone, Sir William. *Commentaries on the Laws of England in Four Volumes.* Callaghan, 1872.

Bibby, Reginald W. *The Boomer Factor: What Canada's Most Famous Generation Is Leaving Behind.* Project Canada Books, 2006.

Bibby, Reginald W. *The Emerging Millennials: How Canada's Newest Generation Is Responding to Change and Choice.* Project Canada Books, 2009.

Carter, Stephen L. *The Culture of Disbelief: How American Law and Politics Trivialize Religious Devotion.* Basic Books, 1993.

Catechism of the Catholic Church. Doubleday, 1997.

Eisenberg, Avigail, ed. *Diversity and Equality: The Changing Framework of Freedom in Canada.* UBC Press, 2006.

Eisgruber, Christopher L., and Lawrence G. Sager. *Religious Freedom and the Constitution.* Harvard University Press, 2007.

Herman, Edward S., and Noam Chomsky. *Manufacturing Consent.* Pantheon, 2002.

Hogg, Peter W. *Constitutional Law of Canada.* Thompson Carswell, 2006.

Kahneman, Daniel. *Thinking Fast and Slow.* Doubleday Canada, 2011.

Levant, Ezra. *Shakedown: How Our Government Is Undermining Democracy in the Name of Human Rights.* McClelland & Stewart, 2009.

McConnell, Michael W., John H. Garvey, and Thomas C. Berg. *Religion and the Constitution.* Aspen Law and Business, 2002.

McDonald, Marci. *The Armageddon Factor: The Rise of Christian Nationalism in Canada*. Random House Canada, 2010.

McLaren, John, and Harold Coward, eds. *Religious Conscience, the State and the Law*. State University of New York Press, 1999.

Metaxas, Eric. *William Wilberforce and the Heroic Campaign to End Slavery*. HarperCollins Canada, 2007.

Morton, F.L., and Rainer Knopf. *The Charter Revolution and the Court Party*. University of Toronto Press, 2000.

Moon, Richard, ed. *Law and Religious Pluralism in Canada*. UBC Press, 2008.

Neuhaus, Richard John. *The Naked Public Square*. 2nd ed. Wm. B. Eerdmans, 1984.

Novak, David. *In Defense of Religious Liberty*. ISI Books, 2009.

Pearce, W. Barnett, and Stephen W. Littlejohn. *Moral Conflict: When Social Worlds Collide*. Sage Publications, 1997.

Phillips, Anne. *Multiculturalism without Culture*. Oxford University Press, 2007.

Rawls, John. *Political Liberalism*. Columbia University Press, 2005.

Somerville, Margaret. *The Ethical Imagination*. House of Anansi, 2006.

Stein, Janice Gross, et al., eds. *Uneasy Partners*. Wilfrid Laurier University Press, 2007.

Steyn, Mark. *America Alone: The End of the World As We Know It*. Regnery Press, 2006.

Taylor, Charles. *A Secular Age*. Harvard University Press, 2007.

Wolterstorff, Nicholas. *Justice: Rights and Wrongs*. Princeton University Press, 2008.

Articles and Reports

Ahdar, Rex, and Ian Leigh. "Is Establishment Consistent with Religious Freedom?" 49 McGill L.J. 635 (2003–4).

Baker, C. Edwin. "Rawls, Equality and Democracy." 34 Philosophy and Social Criticism 203 (2008).

Barak, Aharon. "Proportional Effect: The Israeli Experience." 57 U.T.L.R. 369 (2007).

Bauman, Richard, and David Schneiderman. "The Constitutional Context of Religious Practices in Saskatchewan Public Schools: God Was in the Details." 60 Sask. L. Rev. 265 (1996).

Beaman, Lori G. "A Cross National Comparison of Approaches to Religious Diversity." In *Religion and Diversity in Canada*, ed. Lori G. Beaman and Peter Beyer. Brill, 2008.

Benson, Iain T. "Notes towards a (Re) Definition of the Secular." 33 U.B.C. L. Rev. 519 (2000).

Benson, Iain. *Physicians, Patients, Human Rights and Referrals: A Principled Approach to Respecting the Rights of Patients and Physicians in Ontario.* A Submission to the College of Physicians and Surgeons in Ontario, September 12, 2008.

Benson, Iain. "Pluralism and the Respect for Religious Freedom." LexView 46.0.

Berger, Benjamin. "The Limits of Belief: Freedom of Religion, Secularism and the Liberal State." 1 Can. J. of Law and Society 39 (2002).

Berger, Benjamin. "Law's Religion: Rendering Culture." 45 Osgoode Hall L.J. 277 (2007).

Berger, Benjamin L. "Moral Judgment, Criminal Law and the Constitutional Protection of Religion." 40 Sup. Ct. L. Rev. (2nd) 515 (2008).

Berger, Benjamin. "Section 1, Constitutional Reasoning and Cultural Difference: Assessing the Impacts of *Alberta v. Hutterian Brethren of Wilson Colony.*" 51 Sup. Ct. L. Rev. (2nd) 25 (2010).

Bouchard, Gerard, and Charles Taylor. *Building for the Future: A Time for Reconciliation.* Abridged Report, Commission de consultation sur les pratiques d'accommodement reliées aux différences culturelles. Gouvernement du Québec, 2008.

Boyd, Marion. *Dispute Resolution in Family Law: Protecting Choice, Promoting Inclusion,* Government of Ontario, December, 2004.

Brake, Deborah L. "When Equality Leaves Everyone Worse Off." 46 William and Mary L. Rev. 513 (2004).

Brown, David M. "Freedom From or Freedom For: Religion as a Case Study in Defining the Content of Charter Rights." 33 U.B.C. L. Rev. 551 (1999–2000).

Brown, David M. "Neutrality or Privilege? A Comment on Religious Freedom." 29 Sup. Ct. L. Rev. (2nd) 221 (2005).

Buckingham, Janet Epp. "Caesar and God: Limits to Religious Freedom in Canada and South Africa." 15 Sup. Ct. L. Rev. (2nd) 462 (2000).

Buckingham, Janet Epp. "The Fundamentals of Religious Freedom: The Case for Recognizing Collective Aspects of Religion." 36 Sup. Ct. L. Rev. (2nd) 251 (2007).

Carnerie, Fran. "Euthanasia and Self-Determinism: Is There a Charter Right to Die in Canada?" 32 McGill L.J. 299 (1986–7).

Chan, Kathryn Bromley. "The Duelling Narratives of Religious Freedom: A Comment on *Syndicat Northwest v. Amselem.*" 43 Alta. L. Rev. 451 (2005–6).

Chaplin, Jonathan. "Beyond Liberal Restraints: Defending Religiously-Based Arguments in Law and Public Policy." 33 U.B.C. L. Rev. 617 (2000).

Charney, Robert E. "How Can There Be Any Sin in Sincere? State Inquiries into Sincerity of Religious Belief." 51 Sup. Ct. L. Rev. (2nd) 47 (2010).

College of Physicians and Surgeons of Ontario. *Physicians and the Ontario Human Rights Code*. Policy Statement 5 – 08.

Davis, Suzanne, and Paul Lansing. "When Two Fundamental Rights Collide at the Pharmacy: The Struggle to Balance the Consumer's Right to Access Contraception and the Pharmacist's Right of Conscience." 12 DePaul Journal of Health Care Law 67 (2009).

DeCoste, F.C. "The Halpern Transformation: Same-Sex Marriage, Civil Society and the Limits of Liberal Law." 41 Alta. L. Rev. 619 (2003–4).

DeCoste, F.C. "Courting Leviathan: Limited Government and Social Freedom in *Reference Re Same-Sex Marriage*." 42 Alta. L. Rev. 1099 (2004–5).

DeCoste, F.C. "Caesar's Faith: Limited Government and Freedom of Religions in *Bruker* v. *Marcovitz*." 32 Dal. L.J. 153 (2009).

Esau, Alvin. "Islands of Exclusivity: Religious Organizations and Employment Discrimination." 33 U.B.C. L. Rev. 719 (1999–2000).

Gold, A. "Physicians' 'Right of Conscience' – beyond Politics." 38 Journal of Law, Medicine & Ethics 1 (Spring 2010): 134–42. http://dx.doi.org/10.1111/j.1748-720X.2010.00473.x. Medline:20446991.

Greschner, Donna. "Does *Law* Advance the Cause of Equality?" 27 Queen's L.J. 299 (2001).

Haughey, Marshall. "The Camera and the Colony: A Comment on *Alberta v. Hutterian Brethren of Wilson Colony*." 74 Sask. L. Rev. 59 (2011).

Hughes, Patricia. "The Intersection of Public and Private under the Charter." 52 U.N.B. L.J. 201 (2003).

James, Stephanie D., and Carolyn M. MacEachern. "The Scope of Section 13." Continuing Legal Education Society of B.C., Human Rights Conference, 2008.

Jukier, R., and S. Van Praagh. "Civil Law and Religion in the Supreme Court of Canada: What Should We *Get* out of *Bruker v. Marcovitz*?" 43 Sup. Ct. L. Rev. 382 (2008).

Kilowicz, Howard, Richard Haigh, and Adrienne Ng, "Calculations of Conscience: The Costs and Benefits of Religious and Conscientious Freedom." 48 Alta L. Rev. 679 (2011).

Kraynak, Robert P. "Justice without Foundations." 32 The New Atlantic 103 (Summer, 2011).

Lauwers, Peter D. "Religion and the Ambiguities of Liberal Pluralism: A Canadian Perspective." 37 Sup. Ct. L. Rev. (2nd) 1 (2007).

Li, Lana K.L. "Cultural Factors in the Law." 44 U.B.C. L. Rev. 111 (2011).

MacDougall, Bruce. "Silence in the Classroom: Limits on Homosexual Expression and Visibility in Education and the Privileging of Homophobic Religious Ideology." 61 Sask. L. Rev. 41 (1998).

MacDougall, Bruce. "A Respectful Distance: Appellate Courts Consider Religious Motivation of Public Figures in Homosexual Equality Discourse." 35 U.B.C. L. Rev. 511 (2001–2).

MacDougall, Bruce. "The Separation of Church and Date: Destabilizing Traditional Religion-Based Legal Norms on Sexuality." 36 U.B.C. L. Rev. 1 (2003).

MacDougall, Bruce. "Refusing to Officiate at Same-Sex Civil Marriages." 69 Sask. L. Rev. 351 (2006).

Macklem, Timothy. "Faith as a Secular Value." 45 McGill L.J. 1 (2000).

MacNaughton, Heather M., and Jessie Connell. "A Delicate Balance: The Challenges Faced by Our Democratic Institutions in Reconciling the Competing Rights and Interests of a Diverse Population." 44 U.B.C. L. Rev. 149 (2011).

McConnell, Michael W. "Secular Reason and the Misguided Attempt to Exclude Religious Argument from Democratic Deliberation." 1 Journal of Law, Philosophy and Culture 159 (2007).

McLachlin, The Honourable Beverley, C.J.C. "Charter Myths." 33 U.B.C. L. Rev. 23 (1999–2000).

Mathen, Carissima. "Mutability and Method in the Marriage Reference." 43 U.N.B. L.J. (2005).

Milbank, John. "Hume versus Kant: Faith, Reason and Feeling." 27 Modern Theology 276 (April 2011).

Miller, Bradley. "Case Comment Brillinger v. Brockie." 33 U.B.C. L. Rev. 825 (1999–2000).

Monahan, P., and A. Petter. "Developments in Constitutional Law: The 1986–87 Term." 10 Sup. Ct. L. Rev. 61 (1988).

Moon, Richard. "Government Support for Religious Practice." In Law and Religious Pluralism in Canada, ed. Richard Moon. UBC Press, 2008.

Moon, Richard. "Report to the Canadian Human Rights Commission Concerning Section 13 of the Canadian Human Rights Act and the Regulation of Hate Speech on the Internet" (2008). Posted on the website of the Canadian Human Rights Commission, www.chrc-ccdp.gc.ca.

Moon, Richard. "Accommodation without Compromise: Comment on Alberta v. Hutterian Brethren of Wilson Colony." 51 Sup. Ct. L. Rev. (2nd) 95 (2010).

Moon, Richard. "The Attack on Human Rights Commissions and the Corruption of Public Discourse." 73 Sask. L. Rev. 93 (2010).

Ogilvie, M.H. "Freedom of Religion in Canada and the United Kingdom: A Hopeful Beginning for a Fruitful Dialogue?" 48 Sup. Ct. L. Rev (2009).

Ontario Human Rights Commission. Document 2008-04-09. Posted on the website of the Ontario Human Rights Commission, www.ohrc.on.ca.

Ontario Human Rights Commission. *Balancing Conflicting Rights: Towards an Analytical Framework.* www.ohr.on.ca/en/resources/ discussion_consultation/balancingrights.

Oxaal, Zoe. "Second-Guessing the Bishop: Section 93, the Charter, and the 'Religious Government Actor' in the Gay Prom Date Case." 66 Sask. L. Rev. 455 (2003).

Parr, Kimberly A. "Beyond Politics: A Social and Cultural History of Federal Healthcare Conscience Protections." 35 American Journal of Law & Medicine 4 (2009): 620–46. Medline:20196285.

Petter, Andrew. "Not 'Never on a Sunday' – *R. v. Videoflicks Ltd. et al.*" 49 Sask. L. Rev. 98 (1984–5).

Ryan, Stuart. "Malcolm Ross and Free Speech." 41 U.N.B. L.J. 311 (1992).

Ryder, Bruce. "State Neutrality and Freedom of Conscience and Religion." 29 Sup. Ct. L. Rev. (2nd) 169 (2005).

Shachar, Ayelet. "Religion, State and the Problem of Gender: New Modes of Citizenship and Governance in Diverse Societies." 50 McGill L.J. 49 (2005).

Sossin, Lorne. "The 'Supremacy of God,' Human Dignity and the Charter of Rights and Freedoms." 52 U.N.B. L.J. 227 (2003).

Stein, Janice Gross. "Searching for Equality." In *Uneasy Partners*, ed. Janice Gross Stein et al. Wilfrid Laurier University Press, 2007.

Tollefsen, Christopher. "Conscience, Religion and the State." Am. J. Juris 54 (2009).

Trotter, Geoffry. "The Right to Decline Performance of Same-Sex Civil Marriages: The Duty to Accommodate Public Servants. A Response to Prof. Bruce MacDougall." 70 Sask. L. Rev. 365 (2007).

Urbinati, Nadia. "Unpolitical Democracy." 38 Political Theory 1 (2010): 65–92. http://dx.doi.org/10.1177/0090591709348188.

General Index

abortion, 5; and conscience, 198, 201–2, 209, 210–13. *See also* employment; medical services; pro-life block; pro-life student clubs; protests: and abortion

accommodation, 57, 58–9; changing approach to, 126–7; complaints about, 55, 56, 71; and criminal law, 91, 200; crisis in perception, 54, 71; duty of government, 127; in Europe, 78; in gay prom date, 188–9; laws of general application and, 123–5; Moon, Richard: on accommodation by state, 124; of refusal to perform same-sex marriages, 215–16, 218, 224–5; for religious practice in schools, 157–8; for religious practices, 5, 141–5; in rental of hall, 184–6, 189; requirement for in employment, 141–3, 209; in right to carry kirpan, 66; in right to personal succah, 64; taking husband's surname as, 67; as threat to equality, 95; in uniform for Mounties, 66. *See also* equality, substantive; undue hardship;

Bouchard/Taylor Commission: accommodation of minority belief; human rights legislation; Sunday closing laws: and reasonable accommodation

administrative law. *See* judicial review

America Alone, 150. *See under* discriminatory publication

American Medical Association, and physicians' rights to protection of conscience, 210

arbitration: process of, 54–5, 83–5; application of Charter to, 86. *See under* Boyd Report

Arbitration Act (Ont.): amendments to for family law arbitrations, 85; potential Charter challenge to amendments, 88–9

Armageddon Factor, The, 238

assisted suicide, 3–5, 201

atheism, 16, 156, 162

Atwood, Margaret, 83

Baker, C. Edwin, and theory of democracy, 231

equality rights; freedom of expression; fundamental freedoms; *Law* test; *Oakes* test; Quebec Charter of Rights and Freedoms; U.S. constitution; *and specific cases of application*: Ethics and Religious Culture course; kirpan; photo-licences; polygamy; prayer in schools; protests; public prayer; Sunday closing laws

Christian, 23, 55, 67, 129, 181; Christian Right, 237–8; and religious holidays, 142; and polygamy, 85, 89; and social service, 174–8; and teacher education program (Trinity Western University), 107–14, 168–71. *See also* prayer in schools; public prayer; religious symbols; Sunday closing laws

Civil Marriage Act (Can.), 226

coercion of belief: discussed, 51–2; and Lord's Day Act, 33–5; and Retail Business Holidays Act, 38; and school prayer, 46–8; and theistic prayer, 50; thought experiment in, 34, 52. *See also* compulsion of belief

compulsion of belief, as core issue in protection of freedom of conscience and religion, 23–5. *See also* coercion of belief

conscience: analogous to sexual orientation as fundamental to person, 197; bans of veiling of face, 202–6; and belief systems, 11, 195–6; and Charter (s. 15), 197, 213; and criminal law, 200–2; defined, 196; distinguished from religion, 65, 195–6, 227; employees' rights to exercise, 207–9, 219–20; freedom

of, 195–228; and human dignity, 144; interference with by state, 198–200, 221–4, 228; problems with protecting, 221–2; protection of government agents for, 218–19; providing services available to public and, 209–13; relevant questions to ask when state interferes with, 221–2; religious officials and, 214, 226; sliding scale of justification for interference with, 199–200; thought experiments in, 197, 198–9. *See also* abortion; assisted suicide; contraception; human rights legislation: conflicts with conscience, protection for conscience; marriage commissioners; medical services; mercy killing

Constitution Act (1867), 27, 28, 186

constitutional reference, effect of, 92–3. *See also under* Marriage Act (Sask.); same-sex marriage; polygamy

contraception, and conscience (US), 206. *See also* discrimination; medical services

creed, 16, 137; narrow interpretation of, 210–11; preference in employment on basis of, 177; in School Act (B.C.), 101. *See also* human rights legislation: creed as protected by; religion; religious beliefs

Criminal Code, 3, 97, 200, 201; and polygamy, 55, 83, 89, 90

democracy: as Charter value, 15, 166–7, 232; conceptions of, 230–1; equality rights in, 82, 97–8; limiting freedom of conscience and religion and, 19–20, 53; participation

protection of in human rights
legislation, 16–18, 58, 129, 135; and
rights of conscience, 207–9; rights
of religious organizations (B.C.),
171–4; rights of religious organizations (Ont.), 174–9; rights of
religious organizations (U.S.), 179.
See also under service commonly
available to the public
equality: as risk to democratic
society, 97, 234; as justification
for freedom of conscience and
religion, 71–5, 95; as a moral issue,
226. *See also* equality rights; equality, substantive
equality rights: and arbitration
under Sharia law, 85–8; and belief,
95–6; in Bouchard/Taylor report,
56–8, 71–2, 75–6, 93; in Charter (s.
15), 15, 59, 131–7, 225–6; forced retirement and, 17; and fundamental
freedoms, 43–4, 72–6, 95, 114, 232,
234–5; in gay couple excluded
from prom, 180; and human
dignity, 114; as limiting freedom
of conscience and religion, 227;
and majority/minority rights, 43;
and polygamy, 55–6; and prayer
in schools, 47–8, 156–8; problems
with, 95–8; protection of non-Ca-
nadians by, 30; public interest in,
69; and public prayer, 50–2; role
in society, 82; sexual orientation
protected by, 30; and Sharia law,
56, 86; and Sunday closing laws,
43; and wearing burqa, 205. *See
also* faith-based test for professions
equality, substantive: defined, 58; logical problems with, 136–7, 139; and
purposes of s. 15 of Charter, 133;

reaffirmed by court, 132–3
"establishment" clause. *See* U.S.
constitution
Ethics and Religious Culture course
(ERC): in Catholic schools, 159–60,
163–4; in public schools, 160–3
European Convention on Human
Rights, limits in compared to
Charter, 78–9
European Union, and protection of
religious freedom, 18, 78–9
Evangelical Fellowship of Canada,
4, 5

faith-based test: for marriage commissioners, 216, 222–3; for medical
profession, 211; for professions,
109; for public office (U.S.), 46; for
teachers, 169
Faleh, Hoda, 203–4
Farrow, Douglas, 159
free consent: to application of Sharia
law, 86; to discriminatory treatment, 80–1; to medical treatment,
80–2; to polygamy, 92
freedom of expression, 9, 232; as
core to democracy, 112–16; in
discipline of teachers, 109–16;
offensive portrayal of beliefs and,
154; for protests, 116–20, 126. *See
also* discriminatory publication;
fundamental freedoms
fundamental freedoms: compared,
232; described, 6–7; and human
rights legislation, 17–18, 128, 235;
and rights, 8–9; in Quebec Charter,
62; role in democracy, 9, 11–12, 14,
19, 20, 70–1, 73–4. *See also* conscience; democracy: role of freedom of conscience and religion

in; equality rights; freedom of
expression

Gay and Lesbian Educators, 99
get, agreement to provide, 67–71
Gibbons, Linda, and civil disobedience, 198
Globe and Mail, 54
government aid to religious expression, 26, 35, 50, 52
Gurney, Matt, 3, 4, 5

Habermas, Jurgen, 9
Hérouxville, 54–5
hierarchy of rights, 75, 165, 211
Hitchens, Christopher, and ban of
burqa, 204
human dignity, 98; and discrimination on basis of religion, 143–5;
exclusion from social goods as
violating, 139, 154; as foundation
of human rights, 114, 131, 133,
153; importance of concept, 134,
137–41; in *Law*, 134; and negative portrayal of beliefs, 153–5;
objective conception of, 138, 140,
155; reciprocal nature of, 140, 154,
190–1; requiring freedom and
equality, 114, 117; subjective conception of, 138–9, 155, 190–1; as
tool in solving moral conflict, 115;
and stereotyping, 139, 144–5
Human Rights Act (Can.), 16, 129,
151, 152
Human Rights Act (N.B.), 111
human rights adjudication, complaints about, 150–1
Human Rights Code (B.C.), 61, 135,
146, 151, 172, 174, 181, 183, 185
Human Rights Code (Ont.), 174, 181,
186, 210

Human Rights Code (Sask.), 117,
215, 217, 218
human rights legislation: and accommodation, 58–9, 124, 130, 157;
as anti-discrimination laws, 55–9,
173–4, 234–5; conflicts with conscience, 210–13; creed as protected
by, 16, 129; defences and exemptions under, 129–30, 134, 171–80;
described, 16–18, 128–32; differences from Charter, 17, 59, 67, 128;
differences in statutes, 16, 174;
federal human rights legislation,
129; fit with Charter, 124, 180–6,
234–5; freedom of association protected by, 173; and *Law* test, 134–6;
protection for conscience, 197, 207,
212–13, 227; protection of political
belief, 16, 129, 146; protection of
religious belief, 141–50; purposes
of, 166, 193; role of, 128–9, 194;
reform needed of, 234–5; risk of
extinguishing other rights, 234;
transactions protected by, 129. *See
also* accommodation; discrimination; discriminatory publication;
equality rights; Human Rights
Act (Can.), (N.B.); Human Rights
Code (B.C.), (Ont.), (Sask.); service
commonly available to the public
Hutterites, 121–6, 135–6, 198

incommensurate value systems,
98; differing use of language in,
103–4; lack of resolution for, 233–4;
nature of conflict, 99–100
injunction: as "Catch-22" in gay
prom date case, 187; jurisdiction of
courts, 186–7; requirements for, 187
Islam, 23, 44, 78, 82. *See also* Muslim;
Sharia law

historical origins and purpose of legislation prohibiting, 89; and personal autonomy, 91–2; social harms caused by, 89–90; social science evidence about, 90, 91; unavailability of accommodation for, 91. See also under names of specific religions
polygyny, 83. See also polygamy
prayer in schools, 23, 44–9; and legislative purposes, 46; as discrimination, 47–8, 155–8
pro-life block in Parliament, 236–7
Pro-Life Society of British Columbia, 4
pro-life student clubs: complaints of discrimination against student societies, 146–50; nexus to religion of, 147; offensive material distributed by, 148–9; as political belief, 146; student societies as offering service commonly available to public, 149–50
protests: and abortion, 116; carrying defamatory signs, 119; condemning homosexual conduct using scripture, 117–18; as expression of belief, 116; protection for, 116–20, 126; violating "bubble zone" of abortion clinic, 119–20
public expression of belief, 13, 22–6, 158. See also organizing belief systems; prayer in schools; public prayer
public prayer, 48–52, 76. See also organizing belief systems; prayer in schools; public expression of belief

Quebec Charter of Rights and Freedoms, 72; and Ethics and Religious

Culture course, 160; application to private contract (to provide get), 67–71, 80; application to private property, 60–1; compared to Canadian Charter, 60–1, 62–3, 69–70; interpretive clause recommended for, 75; limits in, 62–5, 68–9; no "hierarchy of rights" in, 75; right to personal succah protected by, 60–5

Rawls, John, 9, 96, 231
reasonable limits as prescribed by law. See Oakes test
religion, definition of, 11, 62. See also religious beliefs
religious beliefs: attitudes towards, 3–7, 54, 71–4, 95; ceremonies part of core of, 214; commercial activities and, 182–3; living belief as core of, 181–2; objective basis required to engage Charter protection for, 161–2; opposition to same-sex marriages as core to, 184; and organizing belief systems, 11–12; role in political decisions, 94, 101; subjective test only required to engage Charter protection for, 61–2, 64–5, 161–2; worship only as core of, 226. See also belief; Charter of Rights and Freedoms: specific cases of application; democracy: limiting freedom of conscience and religion and; discrimination: on basis of religion; employment: accommodation for religious belief
religious organizations: employment of non-adherents, 177–9; as intervenors, 4–5; preference in employment for members, 130,

171–9, 209; purposes of, 179–80; protection from requirement to use premises for same-sex marriage, 214; rights to exclude others, 177–8; and same-sex marriage, 183–6; and social service, 177; U.S. protections for, 179. *See also* denominational schools
religious symbols: removal of crucifix recommended, 76; wearing, 75–7. *See also* burqa; kirpan; jilbab; niqab; turban
Retail Business Holidays Act (Ont.), constitutionality of, 38–42
right not to be offended, 190, 232–3; difficulties with, 154–5; and Ethics and Religious Culture course, 161–2; personal hurt as, 225; and public prayer, 49–53; and Sunday closing laws, 35–6, 42
Right to Die Society of Canada, 5

same-sex marriage, 5; constitutional reference on, 213–15; and equality rights, 225; marriage commissioners and, 214–26; and racial discrimination, 220, 221, 223. *See also under* religious organizations
same-sex parents, 98–107
School Act (B.C): requirement for secular system, 101–2; tolerance required by, 106
secular: belief systems, 4, 195; common day of pause as, 28, 37, 38; French society as, 203; Quebec society as, 73; in School Act (B.C.), 101
secularism: as comprehensive world-view, 11; conflicts about,

5; as not neutral, 158–9; parental objections to teaching, 19, 158–9; views of sexual conduct as moral issue in society, 107
service commonly available to the public: hall rental, 183, 185; in human rights legislation, 18, 129; meaning of, 49–50; provision of medical services, 210–12; printing services, 181; serving as marriage commissioner, 219; student unions as, 149–51
Seventh Day Adventist, 141, 142
Sharia law, 54–6; in family law arbitrations, 82–9, 121; in private agreements to divorce, 87–8; and equality rights, 85–6
Sikh, 56, 65, 76. *See also* kirpan
social change, factors in, 10–11, 13–14
stare decisis, 29, 166
stereotyping. *See under* discrimination; human dignity
Steyn, Mark, 150, 152
St Pierre, Christine, 203
succah, 60–5
Succot, 60
suicide, assisted, 3–5, 12, 201
Sunday closing laws, 120; burden on practice of religion, 39–42; constitutionality of, 26–36, 38–42; duty of government in accommodation, 124–5; history of, 27–8, 32–3; jurisdiction over, 28–9; the Lord's Day Act, 26–36; Ontario Law Reform Commission report on, 27, 41; and reasonable accommodation, 40; shifting purpose of, 29–35; U.S. constitutionality, 36–8, 39. *See also under* equality rights

Taylor, Gloria, 1
tolerance, 5, 77; in Canada, 137; differing meanings of, 103–5, 106–8,
115; and an "even hand," 107, 159,
233; and polygamy, 91; required in
schools (B.C.), 102–3; and secularism, 158–9
turban, wearing, 66, 76–7

U.N. Declaration of Human Rights,
137
undue hardship, 17–18; and accommodation, 58–9, 142–4; and
administrative practices, 157;

hall rental for lesbian wedding
reception, 183–5; in human rights
legislation, 130; and marriage
commissioners, 219–20; pro-life
employees and, 207; and religious
practice in schools, 158; reschedu-
ling Sunday milk pickup as,
144–5
U.S. constitution: and Canadian law,
42; differences from Charter, 37–8;
on religion, 36
U.S. ministerial exception, 179

Wicca, 89

Index to Cases Discussed